IN HER
OWN WORDS

IN HER OWN WORDS

Oral Histories of Women Physicians

Edited by Regina Markell Morantz,
Cynthia Stodola Pomerleau,
and Carol Hansen Fenichel

YALE UNIVERSITY PRESS
NEW HAVEN AND LONDON

Printed in the United States of America by Vail-Ballou
Press, Binghamton, New York.

Library of Congress Cataloging in Publication Data
Main entry under title:

In her own words.

    Interviews with women physicians.
    Bibliography: p.
    Includes index.
    1. Women physicians—United States—Interviews.
2. Physicians—United States—Interviews.
I. Morantz, Regina Markell. II. Pomerleau,
Cynthia S. III. Fenichel, Carol. IV. Series.
[DNLM: 1. Physicians, Women—History—United States.
2. Physicians, Women—Biography—United States.
W1   C0778NH no. 8/WZ 112 135]
R692.I5   610'.92'2   [B]   81-13349
ISBN 0-300-03352-4 (lib bdg.)   AACR2

The paper in this book meets the guidelines for permanence
and durability of the Committee on Production Guidelines
for Book Longevity of the Council on Library Resources.

10   9   8   7   6   5   4   3   2   1

To our children—Alison Morantz, Jessica Morantz, Julie Pomerleau, Aimee Pomerleau, and David Fenichel—*and to all future women physicians, with the hope that this book will help to clear the stones from their path.*

It is not the custom to realize the positive fact, that methods and conclusions formed by one-half of the race only, must necessarily require revision as the other half of humanity rises into conscious responsibility.

—Elizabeth Blackwell, 1889

Contents

Illustrations

Preface

This book grew out of a two-year Oral History Project on Women in Medicine which was initiated in September 1976 at the Medical College at Pennsylvania. Our goal was to explore, through the eyes of those most vitally affected, the profound changes that have occurred over the past few decades in the nature of women's participation in the top ranks of the health-care field.

After soliciting names from hundreds of individuals, organizations, and institutions, we selected a group of approximately forty American women physicians with whom we conducted a series of in-depth interviews. The group was not representative in a statistical sense—that would have been impossible even if it were desirable. It was as diverse as we could make it with respect to age, specialty, practice pattern, life choices, and geographical distribution. We deliberately sought out women who pursued quiet careers as well as those who rose to prominence or led unusual lives. The common thread throughout their lives is their commitment to medicine, a commitment that links the generations together.

Similar considerations governed the selections for inclusion in this book. These nine interviews are neither the flashiest nor the most "typical." Taken as a whole, they convey a feeling for the heterogeneity and breadth of experience that have characterized women's participation in medicine during the twentieth century.

The interviews could have been arranged according to specialty, marital status, or any of a number of equally interesting factors. We have adopted a generational approach, believing that in the historical setting within which each woman forged her career lie the clues to what might be called the evolution of the female experience in medicine. A detailed and scholarly introduction attempts to place these individuals in their social and historical context. At the end of each section, we have tried to draw together some of the threads that connect the women within each group.

The original interviews ranged in length from three to seven hours and in some instances took place over a period of days. Consequently, all the interviews in this volume had to be cut. They were conducted by Dr. Regina Morantz, the principal interviewer for the oral history project, and were based on a questionnaire developed by Dr. Morantz. This questionnaire was designed to elicit not only extensive autobiographical data but also the interviewees' perceptions of current trends in medicine, particularly as they relate to issues of female health and women's increasing representation within the profession. Although the interviewer's questions have been deleted in the interest of concision and fluency, each interview should be viewed as a joint enterprise and as the creation of not one person but two (or, to be accurate, three, as the editor's contribution must also be acknowledged).

The dialogic character of these interviews—indeed, of all oral history—is both a virtue and a defect. The reader must bear in mind that these accounts are not necessarily what the interviewees would have produced had they been writing their autobiographies. Distortion is inherent in the process. Issues and incidents that the interviewee might have relegated to a footnote or passed over altogether may be pursued at length by the interviewer. Furthermore, the give-and-take of spoken conversation lacks the tightly constructed literary quality of a written work. On the other hand, oral history can provide unique insights into the thoughts and feelings underlying decisions made and actions taken. It can convey the flavor of a living, breathing personality as the written record never could. It can evoke memories and observations that otherwise might have been lost forever. A properly conducted interview offers a picture of life as it is lived on a day-to-day basis at a particular point in history and allows us to assess large historical movements from the point of view of the individual. As such, it is a valuable supplement to conventional historical research.

Nine individuals are represented in this volume, each giving her own version of how she came to be what she is. Yet, in the aggregate these accounts add up to something more, for each one is enhanced by being read in conjunction with the others. We have tried to capture the essence of individual experience without losing sight of either the evolution of medicine or the place of women in the profession. If the general reader finds inspiration herein and the researcher a rich body of source material, we shall have accomplished what we set out to do.

Acknowledgments

Given the scope of the oral history project on which this book is based, it would be impossible to list everyone who was involved in its formulation and execution. If we single out some below, it is not to minimize the roles of others but rather to accord recognition to those whose contributions were particularly substantial.

Much of the work for the project was carried out in the Florence A. Moore Library of Medicine at the Medical College of Pennsylvania. Several staff members, particularly Martha Kirby, were extremely helpful. Drs. Ira Gabrielson and Judith Mausner of the Department of Community and Preventive Medicine, the sponsor of the project, were unfailingly supportive. Drs. Doris Bartuska, June Klinghoffer, and Susan McLeer served on the project's Medical Advisory Board and gave willingly of their time and knowledge.

Drs. Alice Hoffman, Judith Leavitt, Peter Olch, and Barbara Sicherman, in their capacity as members of the project's Oral History Advisory Board, offered helpful criticism of the interview schedule and some of the interviews.

The historical introduction was read by Martin Pernick, Rosalind Rosenberg, Joyce Antler, William Chafe, Edna Manzer, Steven Stowe, John Burnham, Janet Sharistanian, and James Reed, all of whom offered constructive suggestions. Sue Zschoche loyally provided skillful research assistance.

We are especially grateful to Sandra Chaff, Director of the Archives and Special Collections on Women in Medicine at the Medical College of Pennsylvania, who furnished advice and encouragement far beyond the call of duty. She and her assistant, Margaret Jerrido, made innumerable contributions to our efforts. A large debt is also owed to Sarah Burke, who served as research assistant and general factotum for the project and helped with the preparation of this manuscript in its early stages. Later, Joyce Owens also provided invaluable help with the manuscript.

A project of this magnitude could not have been carried out without considerable support. Funding for the oral history project was provided by a grant from Roche Laboratories, Inc.

Finally, we extend our heartfelt thanks to all the women physicians interviewed. Their patience and generosity have made this book possible.

IN HER
OWN WORDS

Introduction

FROM ART TO SCIENCE: WOMEN PHYSICIANS IN AMERICAN MEDICINE, 1600–1980

REGINA MARKELL MORANTZ

When the young audience attending the fall session of Geneva Medical College in upstate New York listened to the Dean of the Faculty one morning in 1847, they probably only dimly comprehended the historical significance of the gentleman's words. In quavering tones, he spoke to them of a letter from a prominent physician in Philadelphia and sought their response to the writer's unconventional request.

For several months the physician had been preceptor to a lady student who had already attended a course of medical lectures in Cincinnati. He wished her to have the opportunity to graduate from an Eastern medical college, but his efforts in securing her acceptance had thus far ended in failure. A country college like Geneva, he hoped, would prove more open-minded. If not, the young woman's only other recourse would be to seek training in Europe. As the Dean spoke, a silence fell upon the room. For several moments the students sat transfixed as he concluded his remarks with the comment that the Faculty would accede to the request only if the students favored acceptance unanimously.

The students themselves did not realize that the Faculty was emphatically opposed to the admission of a woman. Not wanting to assume the sole responsibility for denying the request, they had thought that the students would reject the proposal, and they planned to use the actions of a united student body to justify their own response.

Steven Smith, then a bright young member of the class and later a prominent New York physician and public-health advocate, witnessed the ensuing events. Over half a century later, at a memorial service for his longtime friend and colleague, Elizabeth Blackwell, he recalled:

But the Faculty did not understand the tone and temper of the class. For a minute or two, after the departure of the Dean, there was a pause, then the ludicrousness of the situation seemed to seize the entire class, and a perfect Babel of talk, laughter, and cat-calls followed. Congratulations upon the new source of excitement were everywhere heard, and a demand was made for a class meeting to take action on the faculty's communication. . . . At length the question was put to vote, and the whole class arose and voted "Aye" with waving of handkerchiefs, throwing up of hats, and all manner of vocal demonstrations.

A fortnight or more had passed, and the incident . . . had ceased to interest any one, when one morning the Dean came into the class-room, evidently in a state of unusual agitation. The class took alarm, fearing some great calamity was about to befall the College, possibly its closure under the decree of the court that it was a public nuisance. He stated, with trembling voice, that . . . the female student . . . had arrived.

With this introduction . . . a lady . . . entered, whom he formally introduced as Miss Elizabeth Blackwell. . . . A hush fell upon the class as if each member had been stricken with paralysis. A death-like stillness prevailed during the lecture, and only the newly arrived student took notes. She retired with the Professor, and thereafter came in with him and sat on the platform during the lecture.[1]

Such was the inauspicious start of the formal movement to train women as physicians.

Colonial Healing and the Beginnings of Medical Professionalization

Of course, women had practiced healing in the past. So formidable was the custom of using midwives in the management of childbirth in the colonies that a man, Francis Rayns, was prosecuted and fined in 1646 by a Maine court for acting as a midwife.[2] Until the middle of the eighteenth century, colonial American women faced the perils of childbirth with the support of a community of other females who provided both companionship and medical assistance. The science of obstetrics as it is now known was still in its infancy. Midwifery in these years was a folk art that remained unquestionably women's work.[3] Moreover, many midwives earned the respect and high regard of their communities. Some even practiced folk medicine with the support and approval of the general public. Cotton Mather, for example, defended woman's natural affinity for healing and taught medicine to his own daughter.[4]

Unfortunately, public tolerance for female "doctresses" proved only temporary, perhaps because it was engendered primarily by two peculiarities of the seventeenth-century American environment. The first was the anomalous position of the medical profession itself. The English distinctions among physicians, surgeons, and apothecaries had no practical use in the colonies. Physicians, who in the mother country had been members of one of the "learned professions" and were drawn from the social elite, quickly lost that professional status in America, where most were trained, not at a university, but by apprenticeship. As jacks of all trades, they performed surgery, practiced dentistry, and sold drugs. Such blurring of professional distinctions created a fluid situation that, until the middle of the eighteenth century, allowed for quacks and even an occasional lady doctress. One estimate suggests that on the eve of the American Revolution there were approximately 3,500 medical practitioners in the colonies, only 400 of whom had received formal training.[5]

The relative flexibility of seventeenth-century sex roles may also account for the occasional presence of a successful female medical practitioner. In the primarily agricultural and subsistence economy of the New World, where the labor of each member of the family provided a vital contribution to its survival, writers and thinkers paid little attention to sexual distinctions concerning character, work roles, inherent nature, and intellect. This is not to suggest that colonial America did not distinguish between men's and women's work, or male and female spheres. It was the marked shortage of women throughout the colonial period coupled with fluid social and economic conditions that allowed some women a surprising degree of freedom and flexibility. Although most women worked within their homes and in the context of the family economy, it was possible to find women in a wide variety of jobs. There were female butchers, silversmiths, and upholsterers; there were women who ran plantations, mills, shipyards, shops, and taverns. They pursued journalism, printing, teaching, and the healing arts. Most acquired their skills through apprenticeship training, often within their immediate families.[6]

The presence of doctresses reflected both this role flexibility and the shortage of healers in the seventeenth-century colonies. But, even in this period, women healers stood outside of what was considered the profession of medicine. Whatever the reality of colonial practice, a so-called professional physician, one possessing a university degree, was by definition a man. Although colonial licensing laws did not explicitly bar women from the healing art, in the realm of social ideology a woman physician was a contradiction in terms. Consequently, women's participation in general medical practice did not last long. As colonial society became more differentiated early in the next century, the number of female medical practitioners apparently declined, probably because of the increasing availability of formally trained men and the hardening belief in the sexual division of labor.

In the middle of the eighteenth century, growing numbers of formally trained American physicians took steps to professionalize their ranks along European lines. After 1730, more and more young men found the means to finance medical study abroad. They came home inspired not only by European advances in medical science but also by the Europeans' self-conscious professionalism. Americans studying in Europe were impressed by the guilds, societies, publications, and hospitals they found there. Before long American medical schools, hospitals, and professional societies were established.

Thus, after a period of uncertainty, the organization of the American medical profession began to move gradually toward the public realm, although the change was not completed until the twentieth century. The model of gentlemanly professionalism gained increasing acceptance and inevitably dictated that women, who were denied access to a university education and relegated more and more to the private sphere because of changes in the ordering of family life, found themselves excluded from legitimate medical practice.

The developments in midwifery well illustrate this process of professionalization and exclusion. Seventeenth-century ignorance of anatomy, physiology, and surgery put physicians, surgeons, and midwives on an equal plane in the management of parturition. As long as childbirth continued to be defined as a normal process and all practitioners remained equally ignorant of the physiological mechanisms involved, custom and superstition barred men from the lying-in room. By the middle of the eighteenth century, however, improvements in the use of the forceps provided a major breakthrough in obstetrical practice and threatened the dominance of midwives, especially in difficult cases. Skilled mechanical interference to shorten protracted labor often meant life instead of death for mother and child. Gradually, with the approval of either parturient women themselves or their anxious husbands, determined and occasionally self-righteous male accoucheurs defied custom. Yet, technical improvements tell only half the story, for advances in anatomical research, primarily on the pregnant human uterus, also occurred. Taken together, the skillful use of forceps and the improved anatomical familiarity with the birth process opened the door of the lying-in chamber to the male accoucheur.

American expatriates in the middle of the eighteenth century often studied with the founders of the ''new obstetrics.'' Naturally these young men became caught up in all that was fresh and innovative about English medical practice. Before long, the management of childbirth among the urban middle classes on both sides of the Atlantic passed from the hands of the midwife to those of the professional physician. Although tradition, modesty, and midwives themselves resoundingly denounced male midwifery, it gained increasing acceptance among men and women of influence because it stood for safety, progress, and science.

Although some early male obstetricians were willing to work with the midwife and allow her to retain control over ''normal'' cases, professional tolerance did not last long. Physicians came to believe that professional as well as scientific considerations necessitated their medical control over parturition. Thus, after a period of intense competition between male and female practitioners, male obstetricians finally gained the upper hand.[7]

The presence of male physicians in the lying-in chamber engendered and mirrored a transformation in the social and scientific definition of childbirth. As Catherine Scholten has demonstrated, parturition evolved from an event in the female life cycle that was managed by a community of women to a more private experience that was confined to the immediate family and shared almost exclusively by a woman and her doctor.[8] In time, childbirth ceased to be viewed as natural and became defined by doctors as a disease. Moreover, the medicalization of parturition in the nineteenth century set the stage for its transferal in the twentieth century from the privacy of the home to the hospital. At first, the shift remained confined to middle- and upper-class Americans, but today the change has become universal. Scholten is correct in viewing the shift as a result, in part, of a new social appreciation of women, but she carefully points out that the new obstetrics was tied to the determination of physicians to professionalize and as such, signaled the diminution and disparagement of woman's participation in medical practice.

Changes in the management of childbirth reflected even more profound shifts in society at large. Recent work in women's history suggests that between the Revolution and 1830 the ideological lines between the public and private spheres hardened in America. No one described these developments better than Alexis de Tocqueville. Commenting that democracy had not led Americans to those erroneous doctrines prevalent in some parts of Europe that "would give to both [sexes] the same functions, impose on both the same duties, and grant them both the same rights," Tocqueville explained:

> The Americans have applied to the sexes the great principle of political economy which governs the manufactures of our age, by carefully dividing the duties of man from those of woman, in order that the great work of society may be the better carried on.
>
> In no country has such constant care been taken as in America to trace two clearly distinct lines of action for the two sexes, and to make them keep pace one with the other, but in two pathways which are always different. American women never manage the outward concerns of the family, or conduct a business, or take a part in political life; nor are they, on the other hand, ever compelled to perform the rough labor of the fields, or to make any of those laborious exertions which demand the exertion of physical strength. No families are so poor as to form an exception to this rule. If, on the one hand, an American woman cannot escape from the quiet circle of domestic employments, she is never forced, on the other, to go beyond it. Hence it is, that the women of America, who often exhibit a masculine strength of understanding and a manly energy, generally preserve great delicacy of personal appearance, and always retain the manners of women, although they sometimes show that they have the hearts and minds of men.[9]

Using women's letters and diaries, Nancy Cott has carefully traced and documented the changes Tocqueville described. Exploring the ideological dimensions of the "cult of domesticity," Cott suggests that the decade of the 1830s presents a paradox. She calls this paradox a "Janus'faced" conception of woman's roles. The ideology of domesticity reaffirmed woman's traditional connection with the private sphere. It dictated a limited and sex-specific role for women in the home and reflected the real subordination in marriage and society that was still woman's lot in the early nineteenth century. Although colonial society had shared similar assumptions about a woman's place, it was the appearance of universal white manhood suffrage and the gradual disintegration of woman's productive work in the family economy that threw woman's political and economic subordination into even sharper focus in the half century after the American Revolution. Thus, women, primarily educated, middle-class women, began to feel restricted and confined in ways that they had never felt before.[10]

And yet, although the ideology of domesticity *implied* inequality of the sexes and subordination of women in the public sphere, it also appeared to give women a great deal more power in the private realm. At the same time, the 1830s also were a turning point in women's public participation and social visibility. In the ideology of domesticity, the emphasis on the *socially transforming* aspects of a woman's role in the home proved almost revolutionary. Middle-class women used their newly gained power over domestic life to establish a base for self-assertion in the public sphere. Making the home a model for social interaction, women played an unprecedented part in what became the reformist critique of industrial America. Cott's work demonstrates that the ideology of domesticity, though seemingly contradicted by the appearance of feminism, emerged historically from the same social and economic roots as women's rights. Nineteenth-century feminism depended on domesticity for its moral and ideological power.[11]

The decline in female midwifery in the middle class reflected at its most basic level the beginnings of the particularization and professionalization of the occupational structure between 1780 and 1835. In turn, these occupational changes, at least in part, account for the growing ideological militancy of the belief in separate spheres for men and women. Because of real advances in anatomical knowledge and medical technology, what had once been an event in the private sphere dominated by custom and folk art passed into the public and professional realm. But, the doctrine of separate spheres and the cult of domesticity also kindled a new appreciation of women. Although this growing respect occasionally masked more traditional male assumptions about female inferiority, male obstetricians frequently merely were demonstrating their high regard for women when they argued that their knowledge would reduce both the dangers and the pain of childbearing. Yet in the final analysis, it was the feminist possibilities inherent in a belief that emphasized women's transforming powers in the social realm that inspired some women to reassert their influence in matters of sickness and health far more comprehensively than they had previously—by training as professional physicians.

The Limitations and Potentialities of Female Superiority, the Rise of Medical Sects, and the Crisis in Nineteenth-Century Medical Professionalism

The apology for male midwifery published in 1820 by an anonymous Boston doctor, reputed to be John Ware, serves as a measure of just how far the previously described changes had progressed. One historian has suggested that Ware's pamphlet was prompted by a controversy surrounding the appointment of a Scottish midwife, Janet Alexander, by John C. Warren and James Jackson, two prominent early nineteenth-century Boston physicians who wanted her to handle their normal deliveries. Young general practitioners like Ware apparently depended on midwifery cases to win the confidence and patronage of middle-class families. Prestigious surgeons like Jackson and Warren, who already had fine reputations, did not. Yet, in opposing female midwifery, Ware's pamphlet moved well beyond a defense of his pocketbook. In the course of its twenty-two pages, the author managed to touch on most of the arguments that would be leveled against women physicians in the decades to come.[12]

Ware's confident assertion that probably in no other city in America were midwifery cases "so entirely confined to male practitioners" unwittingly reveals that the "new obstetrics" had not totally eradicated deep-seated, cultural objections to men in the lying-in room. For almost a century, the enemies of male midwifery had argued that the practice threatened the moral fabric of society by compromising female modesty. Cott has suggested that between the years 1780 and 1820, the belief in female delicacy became even more prevalent because of the nineteenth-century transformation of woman's image from innately sensual to naturally moral. This new emphasis on woman's intellectual and spiritual power disarmed the older Puritan notions of female carnality. It replaced the conviction that women were the inheritors of Eve's legacy with assertions of female purity and superiority. Ironically, women themselves embraced the shift as a means of enhancing their status, gaining control over indiscriminate male lust in the sexual arena, and depreciating the sexual characteristics that had served as a justification for their exclusion from public life. Eventually the change in emphasis from female physiology to female spirituality would transform itself into Victorian prudery and so exaggerate female delicacy that it would foster a dangerous ignorance of physiology among women. Both feminists and male physicians would question the negative aspects of this ideology of "passionlessness" once it became entrenched, but they did so in different ways and for different motives.[13]

Ware too noted female delicacy and spirituality when he recognized that "the circumstances, which would render females agreeable and most desirable as attendants . . . are obvious." But for him, as for most of his colleagues, the choice was one of delicacy of feeling versus safety, with "safety . . . the first circumstance to be regarded."[14]

In order to prove the physicians' claims of providing greater safety for women, Ware attempted to discredit the older notion of childbirth as a natural or "mechanical" event. Childbirth was complicated, he warned, and "no one can thoroughly understand the nature and treatment of labour, who does not understand thoroughly *the profession of medicine as a whole.*"

Of course this excluded midwives. Ware cautioned that ignorant of general physiology, midwives could not even detect, much less cope with, placenta previa, shock, convulsions, or puerperal fever. "Mere manual adroitness," according to him, was hopelessly inadequate. Thus, for Ware the choice clearly lay "between the true and legitimate practitioners of the profession, and ignorant and assuming pretenders."[15]

·The idea of teaching women medicine led Ware to the second part of his argument. Reflecting the nineteenth century's new respect for woman's intellect, Ware was quick to deny "any intellectual inferiority or incompetence in the sex." He admitted quite simply that his objections to women were "founded rather upon the nature of their moral qualities, than of the powers of their minds, and upon those very qualities, which render them, in their appropriate sphere, the pride, the ornament, and the blessing of mankind."[16] His objections well demonstrate the limitations of an ideology of female moral superiority in effecting female emancipation. In surrendering to an image that defined their sex in terms of innate purity and moral righteousness, women discovered that they had traded one congeries of exaggerated female characteristics for another. Although the ideology could allow women to gain social and familial power, the concept also could be used against them by conservatives like Ware. Female moral superiority gave credence to the idea of separate spheres and encouraged men like Ware to use Victorian sexual stereotyping to keep women out of medicine.

According to the Victorian stereotype, what distinguished women from men was their inability to restrain their "natural tendency to sympathy" as men could and as physicians must. "The profession of medicine," Ware observed, "does not afford a field for the display and indulgence of those finer feelings." It was "obvious" to him that "we cannot instruct women as we do men in the science of medicine; we cannot carry them into the dissecting room and the hospital." He admitted that medical training required men to subdue many of their "more delicate feelings" and their capacity for "refined sensibility" but went on to say that "in females they [such sensibilities] must be destroyed." He concluded by stating that "a female could scarce pass through the course of education requisite to prepare her, as she ought to be prepared, for the practice of midwifery, without destroying those moral qualities of character, which are essential to the office."[17]

Unfortunately for Ware and his colleagues, not all of his readers agreed with him. The transition from the midwife to the male accoucheur was not accomplished without severe protest, not just from midwives themselves, but from social conservatives who saw it as an outrage to female modesty. From the end of the eighteenth century on, both English and American critics railed against the moral depravity of the new obstetrics. Doctors were accused of taking advantage of innocent female patients. Horror stories about modest women who were so shocked by the presence of a strange man in the bedchamber that they ceased to labor appeared repeatedly in opposition literature.[18]

As the belief in female "passionlessness" gained ground in the nineteenth century, it often turned the virtues of innocence and purity into the less desirable traits of ignorance and prudery. Victorian delicacy threatened to make it difficult for physicians to treat their women patients at all. Doctors themselves often found it hard to balance the competing claims of professionalism and delicacy. Some of them, like Charles Meigs, Professor of Obstetrics and Diseases of Women and Children at Jefferson Medical College in Philadelphia, shared the culture's exaggerated conceptions of womanhood. Although Meigs worried constantly that female delicacy often prevented doctors from giving their women patients adequate treatment, his remarkable ambivalence became apparent when he observed:

It is perhaps best, upon the whole, that this great degree of modesty should exist, even to the extent of putting a bar to researches.... I confess I am proud to say that, in this country . . . there are women who prefer to suffer the extremity of danger and pain, rather than waive those scruples of delicacy which prevent their maladies from being fully explored. I say it is an evidence of the dominion of a fine morality in our society.[19]

Meigs's private conflict between professional concerns and emerging cultural norms was not uncommon. In the nineteenth century, portions of the medical establishment accepted the idea of female "passionlessness" so thoroughly that they moved the grounds for its conceptual application from the spiritual to the somatic. Only when the role of doctors in this transformation is thoroughly recognized can the import of Meigs's remarks be understood fully.[20]

It should be recognized that not all physicians found comfort in Meigs's remarks. In 1817, Dr. Thomas Ewell had proposed that the American government sponsor schools of midwifery modeled after those in Europe,[21] but his reasons for the proposal stemmed from his belief that male doctors treating parturient women engendered social depravity. Like William Shippen, Jr. and Samuel Bard before him, he hoped to upgrade the quality of midwifery practice in normal cases, while retaining for the physician control of difficult and dangerous deliveries. Although his program met with scant success, a generation later a lay health reformer by the name of Samuel Gregory repeated Ewell's arguments with a considerably more practical result. Gregory drew support not only from social conservatives but also from feminists, who joined him in an uneasy alliance to establish a medical school for women in Boston.[22]

Besides the emergence of Victorian prudery, other historical factors in the 1840s encouraged the movement to train women in medicine. The medical profession once more found itself in a situation of disillusionment and flux that threatened the professional and institutional progress made at the end of the eighteenth century. Advances in medical science aroused questions about the worth of traditional therapeutics. Between 1800 and 1840, extraordinary new research was conducted in Europe, most notably in France by the so-called Paris school. Investigators painstakingly correlated bedside symptoms with lesions observed during autopsies. For the first time, physicians began to distinguish clearly between various diseases. This "relatively cold-blooded" approach to human illness, as Richard Shryock has wryly pointed out, was "of little aid to the sick.''[23] Indeed, French clinicians became so skeptical of accepted therapeutics that they discredited the assumptions of heroic medicine, which relied on monistic approaches to disease and distinguished among symptoms rather than discrete illnesses. Unfortunately, in taking the first hesitant steps toward a concept of specific etiology, the clinicians undermined public and professional confidence in older therapies before they were able to put anything in their place. The eventual result was occasional therapeutic nihilism among physicians and public revulsion against the harshness of regular practice.

The discovery of anaesthesia at the end of the 1840s also called into question older concepts of professionalism. If professionalism is defined as involving not only licensing and standards but also a set of values and prescriptions for behavior that help people to balance conflicting occupational demands, we can see why this occurred. Nineteenth-century professional ideas were shaped by the social structure, values, and technical capabilities of the age.[24] As Martin Pernick has shown, before anaesthesia the possible necessity of inflicting physical pain on patients was a part of the daily reality of professional practice and constituted an integral feature of the self-image and ideology of physicians. Physicians and surgeons sought to balance empathy with cool detachment; the best surgeon knew that the physician's first responsibility was to cure, not to soothe. One author observed that the two professional prerequisites for a surgeon were a strong stomach and a willingness to ''cut like an executioner.''[25]

As we have seen, John Ware used this need for detachment as an argument against teaching women medicine. According to him, females could not achieve such emotional distance. Ware's views were so typical that women themselves occasionally shared them. ''The Past, with the lancet, and poison, and operative surgery,'' wrote Mary Gove Nichols, a hydropathic physician, feminist, and health reformer, ''did not insult woman by asking her to become a physician; and the Past has not asked her to become hangman, general, or jailer. We may well excuse all believers in allopathy if they judge women unfit for the profession.''[26] The use of ether and chloroform, however, quickly undermined a major objection to women practitioners while also ''feminizing'' medicine by calling into question the ''heroic'' image of the physician.[27]

These important changes in medical science and technology were accompanied by institutional growing pains. Efforts to raise standards floundered in the antebellum period. One factor contributing to the problem was the proliferation of proprietary medical schools, which were set up by private physicians to provide an educational program, not for its own sake, but for their profit. The ensuing intense competition for students lowered standards. Clinical facilities remained meagre or nonexistent. Eventually, even the university-affiliated colleges of medicine could not attract students without reducing their requirements. It became possible to turn oneself into a doctor in less than a year merely by attending two terms of didactic lectures. Scores of young men held a medical degree with little or no clinical experience and often without ever having witnessed a single childbirth. The degeneration of medical education in the first half of the nineteenth century made a mockery of physicians' claims to superior skill in the lying-in chamber.

Jacksonian anti-elitism added to the profession's difficulties, as hostility to all professional distinctions became a featured aspect of American political rhetoric. Beginning around 1830, most states responded by abolishing restrictive licensing legislation, which already had proved difficult to enforce. Although the American Medical Association and the New York Academy of Medicine were founded in 1846 to counter such trends, there was little progress in medical education until the end of the century.[28]

Probably none of the aforementioned problems bothered physicians as much as the rise of sectarianism and the proliferation of quackery. Although these two phenomena were different, regular physicians often defiantly lumped them together. Physicians looked on helplessly as the timeworn habit of self-dosing encouraged the small-scale patent medicine industry in the nineteenth century to adopt aggressive methods of advertising and thus emerge as a million dollar business at the end of the nineteenth century.

Sectarians presented a different challenge. Responding in part to the growing dissatisfaction with heroic medicine, the followers of several new medical systems began to compete with the regular profession for public patronage, legitimacy, and authority. Some of these sects opposed the physician's heroic methods and use of drugs and substituted for them the belief that only nature should do the healing. Hydropaths, for example, used only water, shunning surgery and drugs altogether. Others, like the Botanics, substituted so-called natural remedies for chemical and mineral ones. Homeopaths, although they used a variety of drugs, believed in such miniscule doses that their prescriptions had no effect. Like other sectarians, they too believed strongly in the healing powers of nature.[29]

In time, these sectarians formed their own professional institutions—schools, journals, and societies. Favoring the popular diffusion of professional knowledge, their schools often welcomed women students, and consequently middle-class women gravitated to sectarian medicine in large numbers. Many of the first generation of women doctors received their degrees from sectarian institutions. The challenge posed by sectarian medicine to older concepts of professionalism worked in favor of women. Paradoxically, in the mid-nineteenth century the abandonment of licensing legislation and the ease of access to a medical degree actually served to maintain a professional identity for all medical practitioners by conferring the title of doctor on a large proportion of them. This temporary fluidity allowed women who wished to achieve professional status to do so before definitions of professionalism crystallized once more.[30]

The health-reform movement provided still another alternative to a public tired of bloodletting and calomel. Beginning in the antebellum period, self-help in health matters, dietary reform, temperance, hydrotherapy, and physiological instruction merged in a comprehensive campaign to save the nation by combating ill health. Never before had the search for good health given rise to such wide-spread public activity. Health reformers played a critical role in transforming public attitudes toward sickness and death by promoting the assumption that men and women were responsible for their own health, the health of their families, and the health of society at large.

The popularity of both sectarian medicine and health reform reflected the nineteenth-century shift from the spiritual to the material, from theology to a religion of health, from a concern with the soul to a concern for the body. It was this fundamental change that helped to shape the character of the mid-nineteenth-century reformist consciousness.[31] No longer were sickness and death to be tolerated with a stoicism and resignation that contrasted the limited moral choices of man with the all-powerful inscrutability of God. "Many people," Mary Gove Nichols observed, "seem to think that all diseases are immediate visitations from the Almighty, arising from no cause but his *immediate* dispensation.... Many seem to have no idea that there are established laws with respect to life and health, and that the transgression of these laws is followed by disease." In other words, disease was man's doing, not God's. Human beings could affect the future by manipulating the environment according to nature's laws and by gaining conscious control of themselves.[32]

Although the health-reform movement attracted both men and women, it was the middle-class woman, by virtue of her new role in an increasingly complex society, that made up the health reformers' primary constituency. Her concern with health reform demonstrates not only the more general ideological transition from religion to health but also woman's central role in the transformation of values that prepared the reformist elements of the middle class to cope with the problems of industrialization and urbanization.[33]

The cult of domesticity gave women new power in the private sphere. The separation of home and work reduced the father's role in domestic life, while mothers and children found themselves alone in the household. At the same time, changes in religious ideas enhanced the importance of parental nurture over predestination. The harsh doctrine of infant depravity bowed to a new belief in the malleability of young minds. Children and childhood were romanticized. American mothers confronted new responsibilities as a reformed and reconstituted family served as the ideological model for social institutions and for society as a whole. Many of the new tasks fell under the rubrics of physiology, hygiene, and health. Because the changing structure of the nineteenth-century family increasingly dictated that women school their children in "modern" values, wives and mothers welcomed the practical solutions offered in health-reform journals and tracts.[34]

Sectarians ardently supported the health-reform movement, especially its emphasis on the woman's central role in domestic medicine. Botanics, particularly the followers of Samuel Thomson, rallied around the motto "Every man his own physician." Thomsonians stressed the responsibilities of the wife and mother in preventive family hygiene, and homeopaths and hydropaths followed suit.

For a number of brave, ambitious, and talented women health reform provided an outlet and an escape from a domesticity that they found increasingly narrow and confining. Although health reformers shared with conservative nineteenth-century Americans the belief that a woman's role was invested with cosmic moral significance, they subscribed to the widest possible definition of woman's sphere. They understood that to purify society some women might have to enter it.[35]

It is not surprising, therefore, that many health reformers became feminists. Equally significant, however, was the fact that the health reformers' emphasis on preventive hygiene and physiological science formed one of the central tenets of feminist ideology. William Leach has argued that some feminists viewed natural rights in wholly hygienic terms and relied heavily on ideological tools derived from science and hygiene rather than abstract principles of justice in their argument for female equality in the public and private spheres.[36]

Thus, the movement to teach women medicine developed logically from the confluence of several factors: the denigration of regular heroic practice, the structural growing pains of a profession in transition, the health reformers' assessment of woman's natural healing abilities, and the feminist belief in the centrality of scientific hygiene to female emancipation.

In addition to these developments, the doctrine of "passionlessness" gave rise to such elaborate exaggerations of female delicacy that social conservatives and even some feminists viewed the training of women physicians as a necessary solution to the problems arising from female reluctance to disclose symptoms to male practitioners. Elizabeth Blackwell admitted in her autobiography that her first encounter with the idea of studying medicine arose from the agonized suggestion of a friend, dying of what was probably uterine cancer, that her sufferings would have been considerably alleviated had she been "treated by a lady doctor."[37] Although many feminists remained ambivalent about the practical value of women doctors to women of extreme modesty, Blackwell herself always used the concern about the potential compromise of female delicacy generated by male treatment as an argument in favor of training women in medicine.[38] By 1848, Boston feminists joined the social conservative Samuel Gregory to establish a school of midwifery that would be incorporated in 1856 as the New England Female Medical College.

Women Enter the Medical Profession

By the middle of the nineteenth century, the crisis in medical professionalism was acute. Public denunciation of heroic therapeutics could not be ignored, and some outspoken reformers believed that teaching women medicine would offer a solution to the criticism. Ann Preston, the future Dean of the Woman's Medical College of Pennsylvania, announced in her 1851 graduate medical thesis entitled "General Diagnosis," "The time is passing when . . . the licensed graduate whose lancet is sprung for every head-ache and *heart-ache* that he may meet can obtain public confidence." Her classmate Angenette Hunt believed the current dissatisfaction with the medical profession was well deserved. "The merit of the Physician," she declared defiantly, "is not now estimated by the quantity of medicines he prescribes, but by the effect produced, and the public throat is rebelling against swallowing nauseous drugs for the pleasure and profit of the doctors." Hunt continued her thesis by stating, "there is a female side to *this subject,* as well as most others." She went on to observe that a woman's natural abilities fitted her for health care. With proper preparation she could exercise her talents in a new sphere. "One not bounded," Hunt added significantly, "by the kitchen and the nursery."[39]

Hunt's remarks attest to the fact that female physicians viewed their campaign to study and practice medicine as part of a larger effort to adapt traditional concepts of womanhood to the demands of an unstable, complex, and rapidly industrializing society. For many feminists, particularly women doctors, this redefinition explicitly called for a more intensive role within the family for all women and implicitly demanded a more comprehensive role for at least some women in society at large. Their particular brand of feminism rarely led these early generations of women physicians to challenge the cult of domesticity. Because they were genuinely comfortable with the concept of separate sexual spheres, they argued that women, by virtue of their special skills at nurturance, had a role in medicine that could compensate for and be complementary to the role and achievements of men.[40]

A few believed with Samuel Gregory that women physicians had a "repugnance to . . . the experimental and heroic . . ." and as "the handmaids of nature" would hasten the decline of heroic therapeutics by promoting "a milder and less energetic mode of practice." There is, in fact, scattered evidence to suggest that at least some women doctors preferred milder therapies.[41] But, whatever their attitudes toward heroic dosing, most women physicians agreed with Elizabeth Blackwell that the primary task of the "medical movement amongst women in America" was "for the purpose of occupying positions which men cannot fully occupy, and exercizing an influence which men cannot wield at all." Agreeing with Blackwell's approach, pioneer women doctors argued that their influence should be concentrated primarily on women and children and in the domestic sphere. "Ladies," Dean Ann Preston told the graduating class of the Woman's Medical College of Pennsylvania in 1857, "it is for the very purpose of making home enjoyments more complete that you have been delegated today to bear health and hope to the abodes you enter." Elizabeth and Emily Blackwell emphasized that women physicians must be the "connecting link" between the science of the medical profession and the everyday life of women. In 1860, they

complained bitterly that while the interest of men in pure science had "revolutionized" medicine it had had "little direct effect on domestic life."[42]

Because they believed that men had sorely neglected prevention, women
physicians embraced preventive medicine as their professional province. In the
1850s, Harriet Hunt, a pioneer feminist and woman doctor, had mapped out the
goals of the women's medical movement. "We should give to man cheerfully the
curative department, and woman the preventive," she announced to the audience
at the Second Woman's Rights Convention in Worcester, Massachusetts.
"The female physician must be preventive. She must look upon life through
sanitary channels." Dr. Amanda C. Price asked in her graduation thesis of
1871, "How many men do we find teaching the laws of health . . . ? It seems
to be their ambition to cure disease, and very seldom do any of them think it
worth their while to teach their patients how to prevent a return of their maladies." To Price's classmate Prudence Saur, being a physician meant more than
being able to "diagnose and treat Scarlatina." "How much more God-like,"
she observed, "to *prevent* as well as *cure*!"[43]

Armed with the conviction that medical science needed the "leaven of tender
humanity that women represent," hundreds of women sought medical training in
the decades following Elizabeth Blackwell's graduation from Geneva Medical
College.[44] By 1880, a handful of medical schools accepted women on a regular
basis, but still disatisfied with the progress of medical coeducation, female
pioneers founded five "regular" and several sectarian women's medical colleges. They built dispensaries and hospitals to provide clinical training for female
graduates. By the end of the nineteenth century, female physicians numbered
between 4 and 5 percent of the profession, a figure that remained relatively stable
until the 1960s.[45]

The majority of male medical professionals did not welcome their female
colleagues, whom they viewed as an economic threat in a profession already
burdened with an oversupply of practitioners. When the graduates of the orthodox female medical colleges sought admission to local and national medical
societies, they were rejected on the grounds that their training was either irregular
or of poor quality. Opponents held women's allegedly inferior training against
them, yet denied them access to the type of education that was acceptable and
often refused to consult with them or ostracized those male practitioners who did.
These insults were perpetrated despite the fact that a fair number of medical
women received excellent training in the nineteenth century. A comparative
study of curricula and clinical offerings in several nineteenth-century medical
schools suggests that those women who earned their diplomas at the orthodox
women's colleges endured a vigorous, demanding, and refreshingly progressive
course of study. Other women, self-conscious about their inadequacies and determined to procure proper preparation, sought postgraduate training in Europe.[46]

As Mary Roth Walsh's study of discrimination against women physicians has
shown, the regular medical profession objected on many levels to the entrance of

women into its ranks. In the first place, the vast majority of doctors were traditionalists who subscribed to the cult of domesticity with the same intense tenacity as their nonmedical brethren. Placing women on a pedestal and cementing them firmly within the confines of the home, they worried that women who sought professional training would avoid their responsibility to raise children and thus disrupt American family life. Believers in the cult of domesticity felt that because women kept men respectable through the "home influence," their venturing out into the world could demoralize both sexes. Woman's mission was not to pursue science but "to rear the offspring and ever fan the flame of piety, patriotism and love upon the sacred altar of her home."[47]

Other physicians cited woman's inferior intellect, her passivity of mind, her physical weakness, and her tendency toward hysteria. John Ware's conviction that medical education with its "ghastly" rituals and "blood and agony" in the dissecting room would harden women's hearts and leave them bereft of softness and empathy reappeared in elaborate guise. The *Boston Medical and Surgical Journal* continued to grumble about increasing economic competition.[48] More subtle and more insidious was the fear that the influx of women would alter the image of the profession by feminizing it in unacceptable ways. "The primary requisite for a good surgeon," insisted Edmund Andrews, "is *to be a man,*—a man of courage. . . ." Few physicians were prepared to surrender their masculinity gracefully. One Boston doctor taunted women physicians with the remark, "If they cannot stride a mustang or mend bullet holes, so much the better for an enterprizing and skillful practitioner of the sterner sex."[49]

Opponents of women physicians were neither scientific nor consistent. They praised women's abilities as nurses but rejected their competence in medicine; they offered their arguments for female inferiority, vulnerability, and dependence alongside their claims for women's moral superiority and domestic responsibility. There were even some medical men who successfully hid their prejudices in the cloak of science. In the 1870s and the 1880s, these physicians managed to transfer the grounds for the argument over female nature from the spiritual to the somatic.

Rallying around a book entitled *Sex in Education: A Fair Chance for Girls,* published in 1873, by E. H. Clarke, a Harvard professor, they based their case against women almost entirely on biological factors. Menstruation was depicted as mysteriously debilitating and higher education in any subject as sapping the energy needed for the normal development of the reproductive organs. The results, lamented Clarke with total seriousness, were "those grievous maladies which torture a woman's earthly existence: leuchorrhoea, [sic] amenorrhea, dysmenorrhea, chronic and acute ovaritis, prolapsus uteri, hysteria, neuralgia, and the like."[50] He concluded that higher education for women produced "monstrous brains and puny bodies; abnormally active cerebration and abnormally weak digestion; flowing thought and constipated bowels."[51]

The biological argument proved particularly vexing to feminists. M. Carey Thomas, the indomitable president of Bryn Mawr and a fierce supporter of women physicians, recalled years later that "we did not know when we began whether women's health could stand the strain of education. We were haunted in those days, by the clanging chains of that gloomy little specter, Dr. Edward H. Clarke's *Sex in Education*."[52]

When the feminist community launched a full-scale counterattack against the Clarke thesis, women physicians armed themselves with original research and statistics to lend scientific respectability to the campaign. Mary Putnam Jacobi, for example, won Harvard Medical School's esteemed Boylston Prize in 1876 for her essay "The Question of Rest for Women During Menstruation." Her study challenged conservative medical opinion with sophisticated statistical analyses and case studies. In 1881, Emily and Augusta Pope, graduates of the New England Female Medical College, and Emma Call, an early alumna of the University of Michigan Medical School, published a survey of women physicians sponsored by the American Social Science Association. While serving as staff physicians at the New England Hospital for Women and Children, they summarized the results of their findings on the health of 430 women doctors and concluded that "some unnecessary anxiety has been wasted on this point." They went on to say, "We do not think it would be easy to find a better record of health among an equal number of women, taken at random, from all over the country."[53] Women physicians who held resident positions at the various women's colleges painstakingly monitored the physiological effects of higher education on their charges. Several of these women published studies that added to the growing body of scientific literature seriously questioning Clarke's thesis. Indeed, one of the important contributions women physicians made to the feminist movement in the late nineteenth century arose from their willingness to challenge on scientific and empirical grounds the somatic definition of woman's nature and to push toward innovative and less biologically constricting approaches to female health and hygiene.[54]

Women physicians also made important contributions to feminism by their example. Medicine attracted larger numbers of women in the nineteenth century than any of the other so-called learned professions. Feminists concerned with women's professional advancement particularly wanted women to have equal access to medical training. M. Carey Thomas gave the woman physician a central role in the "furtherance of the intellectual life of women in general." So too did Mary Putnam Jacobi, who argued that there would "be no really higher education for women, until at least one profession is open to them for which such education is indispensable, and medicine is most definitely available for this purpose." The fellowship of common membership in a profession, Jacobi believed, afforded a model to women in other occupations. As women carved a place for themselves in medicine, "whose tests are more strict, whose rewards are more precise, and whose practical bearing is more powerful . . . '' the position of women in ''literature, education, art and science, will be better defined and valued.''[55]

Physicians like Jacobi, who won the grudging respect of male colleagues, provided strong, vigorous role models for younger women wishing to enter the professions at the end of the nineteenth century.[56] Women doctors who married (and between one-fifth and one-third did) furnished a feminist alternative to the constrictions of traditional Victorian family relationships. Nineteenth-century feminist theory devoted much attention to the restructuring of male-female relationships within marriage, but women physicians confronted the issue in personal terms.[57] ''A woman can love and respect her family just as much if not more,'' asserted Dr. Georgiana Glenn, a wife and mother herself, ''when she feels that she is supporting herself and adding to their comfort and happiness.'' Mary Putnam Jacobi, married and the mother of two children, frankly conceded that matrimony complicated professional life, but she also believed that raising children increased vigor and vitality in healthy women and ''a good deal more than compensates for the difficulties involved in caring for them.''[58]

Professionally as well as personally, women doctors viewed themselves as having a special relationship to motherhood and family life. ''A woman Doctor . . . '' wrote Dr. Eliza Mosher to her sister in 1887, ''holds a position of greater responsibility than does a man. So many questions come to her which are never asked of men . . . and her relations to families and family life is a very intimate and sacred one.'' In their approach to treatment, most nineteenth-century women physicians took their role as teachers of hygiene with great seriousness. ''Women physicians,'' wrote Frances A. Rutherford in 1893, ''were early selected as teachers of hygiene, were friends of women teachers, helped them and mothers to see the necessity of the development of the children in a threefold manner, mentally, morally and physically. . . .'' Besides lecturing at mothers' meetings, women's temperance organizations, social purity groups, and women's clubs, women doctors taught hygiene in the newly established women's colleges and published books and pamphlets on family hygiene and female health.[59]

The available evidence suggests that their hospitals and dispensaries gave scrupulous attention to the physician's heuristic role and anticipated the hospital social service departments of the twentieth century. The New York Infirmary, for example, was one of the first hospitals founded by women to establish the position of ''sanitary visitor.'' The post usually was filled by a young graduate of the medical school who wished to gain further clinical experience. The extern was expected to go into the slums not only to treat emergency cases but also to teach cleanliness, proper ventilation, nutrition, and family hygiene. Other women's hospitals followed suit. In the Woman's Hospital in Cleveland, Ohio, interns did not confine their work ''entirely to curing the sick.'' Here, as in New York, employment had been found for those patients who needed it, and instruction was offered ''in the laws of health'' and in ''the care and diet of children.'' Hospitals run by women physicians in Chicago, San Francisco, and Boston recorded similar goals.[60]

Individuals in private practice also felt it was their duty to enlighten as well as to heal. Evelyn Garrigue, a New York physician and an admirer of Elizabeth Blackwell's reform ideas, wrote to her in 1899 that she had distributed copies of Blackwell's pamphlet, *Counsel to Parents on the Moral Education of the Young*, to her patients, and that she now had a volume circulating "among some very noble tenement house patients, slaving themselves to protect their children from the evils to which they are exposed." Garrigue felt particularly grateful to Blackwell because the older woman's pamphlets represented a "powerful aid in my work." She added, "Since coming into medicine and getting my eyes open to evils . . . I have been stirred to the innermost depth of my being . . ., and when your sister kindly lent me your 'Essays in Medical Sociology,' . . . I was able to gain a clear exposition of them with reference to the duty of the physician." It hardly seems necessary to add that it was a woman's medical college, the New York Infirmary, that became the first institution in the country to establish a faculty chair in preventive medicine in 1868.[61]

Early Twentieth-Century Professional Developments: The Rise of Scientific Medicine, the Frustrations and Disappointments of Medical Coeducation, and the Appearance of the "Modern Woman."

Nineteenth-century medical women successfully managed to secure a place in medicine by creating a professional role that was believed to bridge the gap between the public and the private. Their role applied "domestic" values to larger communal concerns and utilized the scientific and technical advances made in the public realm for the improvement of life in the home. In justifying their extradomestic activity by using the Victorian stereotype of "woman-as-mother," female medical educators and their supporters differed little from female moral reformers and other nineteenth-century social feminists who professed a home-based ideology in order to introduce significant numbers of women to activity in the public sphere.

Like other social feminists at the end of the nineteenth century, women physicians boasted a measure of achievement that offered ample opportunity for pride and satisfaction. In numbers alone they had increased several thousand and in 1900 comprised close to 5 percent of the profession.[62] Visionary women like Elizabeth Blackwell, Mary Putnam Jacobi, Ann Preston, Marie Zakrzewska, and Mary Harris Thompson could point proudly to the medical schools and hospitals located in several major cities that educated and trained first-rate women physicians. Perhaps even more promising from their perspective was the progress of medical coeducation. A number of midwestern universities had begun to accept women students. By 1900, for example, the University of Michigan had trained

394 women in its medical department.[63] The crowning achievement in this field was the opening of Johns Hopkins University Medical School in 1893. Through the combined efforts of M. Carey Thomas, Dean of Bryn Mawr, prominent female medical educators, and a network of committed feminists, the school agreed to admit women on the same terms as men. In return, Thomas and her friends gave the institution a total of $500,000 in contributions. Without this money, the medical school never would have become a reality. Thomas and her contemporaries rightly believed this achievement to be a crucial event in the history of American feminism.[64]

Other developments, too, provided cause for optimism. With the decline of sectarian medicine, 75 percent or more of women doctors were regular physicians. This development gave them as a group more credibility within the profession, which was moving rapidly toward standardization and orthodoxy. During the last third of the nineteenth century, most state and local medical societies quietly admitted women without objection.[65] Although the American Medical Association did not formally accept women until 1915, it indirectly recognized them when it received Dr. Sarah Hackett Stevenson as a state delegate from Illinois at the 1876 convention. Women physicians had also made progress in gaining admission to hospital clerkships, especially in New York, Philadelphia, and Chicago. Motivated either by custom or by law, several states had begun to appoint women physicians as clinicians or superintendents at state asylums in which women were confined.[66] In addition, a handful of women surgeons had managed to demonstrate proficiency in a specialty that was gaining visible status within the profession. Other women doctors could look with pride at the growing list of publications by women in respected scientific and medical journals.[67]

Furthermore, women physicians had taken steps to formalize professional networks among themselves. In the decade between 1890 and 1900, women's medical societies were founded in many states.[68] Those in Boston and New York were particularly strong. In Philadelphia, the alumnae association of the Woman's Medical College of Pennsylvania was especially active; in 1900 it boasted of 219 members. Because it had a policy of giving honorary membership to distinguished female graduates of other schools, this association, which met for several days annually, offered much more than mere parochial social contact. Members read and criticized each other's scientific papers, which were then published in the alumnae journal. They also shared case studies, debated such professional issues as fee splitting and specialization, and took positive steps to promote the interests of women in the profession. In 1893, a group of women physicians from Toledo, Ohio, began the *Woman's Medical Journal,* a periodical devoted to raising professional consciousness by publishing both scientific articles and material about women physicians. The strengthening of professional ties among women physicians culminated in 1915 with the founding of the American Medical Women's Association by a group of Chicago women.[69]

As the new century wore on, however, decisive changes within the organization of the medical profession and profound shifts in cultural beliefs regarding a woman's role and activity in the public and private spheres called the achievements of nineteenth-century medical women into question. More than one historian has pictured the years between 1900 and 1965 as dark ones for the progress of women in medicine, as years in which nineteenth-century beachheads were surrendered and lost to male backlash and institutional discrimination.[70]

A glance at the statistics appears to confirm such a view. Despite the enormous promise of coeducation in the 1890s, the ranks of women physicians did not continue to increase. In fact, the number of women medical students actually declined from 1,280 to 992 in the years between 1902 and 1926. Female physicians lost ground both in percentages and in absolute numbers. Moreover, the charts reveal that medicine was the only profession in which the numbers of women declined absolutely. After peaking at 6 percent of the national total in 1910, the percentages steadily shrank, and only in 1950 did women physicians again reach the magic 6 percent. It was not until the 1970s that dramatic alterations in the numbers of women in medical schools again occurred.[71]

Although the reasons for the declining numbers of medical women in the first half of the twentieth century are complicated, one significant factor, often slighted by historians, is the enormous alteration that came about in the structure and content of the medical care delivery system.

It is important to remember that the modern medical profession grew to maturity in the first three decades of the twentieth century. At the beginning of this period, issues of professionalization took the center stage, as the roles of professional associations, state licensing agencies, and colleges and universities only gradually emerged into their modern forms. In 1900, the majority of physicians believed that their economic and social position, as well as the collective status of the profession itself, warned of a crisis in medicine. Probably for the first time, the interests of various competing groups within the profession—medical societies, eastern scientific elites, midwestern general practitioners, licensing agencies, and the leading bloc of medical colleges—pointed to the necessity for consolidation and reform. Common aims included the raising of professional entrance standards, the standardization of medical school curricula, the suppression of weak proprietary institutions, and the overall reduction in the number of medical graduates. The educational goal of raising standards remained decisively intertwined with the policy of drastically reducing the number of practitioners in a field believed already to be overcrowded.[72]

By critically analyzing the medical reform movement, recent historical scholarship has contributed much toward an understanding of medicine as an instrument of social control. A few social historians also have demonstrated the medical profession's central role in promoting its own interests in these years. Doctors clearly intended to upgrade their status and income as well as their professional skills. Finally, researchers tentatively have begun to clarify what they see as a link between reform strategies and a more general ideological support for the dominant industrial classes and the specific interests of a capitalistic corporate state.[73] Viewing the medical reform movement from the perspective of this recent work provides a clearer understanding of the effect of modern medical professionalism on women.

Perhaps the most immediate problem facing the reformers was the large number of inferior schools. Working through the joint efforts of the American Medical Association's Council on Medical Education, the publicity and the public pressure provided by the *Journal of the American Medical Assocation,* and the offices of several state licensing boards, the leaders of medical reform began the process of self-criticism. Yet, pressure from within was perhaps even less significant in the long run than pressure from without. It was in this period that large philanthropic foundations backed by Rockefeller and Carnegie wealth began to use their resources to force specific changes in medical education. From 1910 to 1930 foundations donated over $300 million to medical education and research. Indeed, Rosemary Stevens has argued that these philanthropic foundations were "the most vital outside force in effecting changes in medical education after 1910."[74]

The most crucial historical event in this new alliance between scientific medicine and corporate power was the Carnegie Foundation's publication in 1910 of Abraham Flexner's meticulous study of contemporary medical education. The Flexner report made public what medical educators had known privately and had worked to correct for a decade: American medical schools labored under appalling inadequacies. Most schools accepted inferior students, provided meagre or nonexistent training in laboratory science and clinical medicine, and overproduced doctors. Only the youthful Johns Hopkins Medical School totally escaped Flexner's scathing criticism. According to Flexner's study, medical schools needed to be placed under the control of universities; preliminary education requirements needed to be enforced; curricula needed to be lengthened; and laboratory facilities needed to be improved. These changes would please both the foundations, which wanted higher standards, and the profession, which wanted less competition.

And there was more. The need to decrease the number of doctors and consolidate medical schools reflected one important aspect of medical reform; the affiliation of surviving schools with hospitals and dispensaries reflected yet another. The hospital already had begun gradually to concentrate the complex technology that became the hallmark of modern medicine within its walls. Indeed, the leading spokesmen for scientific medicine regarded the hospital as so essential to the medical school curriculum that, in 1900, the *Journal of the American Medical Association* declared, "to a large extent, the hospital, with [all its facilities] *is* the medical school."[75]

Flexner remained adamant on all his recommendations, and although his candid study did not launch the process of medical reform, which was already underway, it probably hastened the results. Between 1904 and 1915, 92 schools merged or closed their doors when confronted with higher state board requirements, poor clinical facilities, financial difficulties, or Flexner's public criticism. By 1920, only 85 out of the 155 medical schools visited by Flexner remained in existence.[76] The better schools improved their facilities through the generous help of the foundations; others were left to fend for themselves. Unfortunately, but not surprisingly, among those schools denied the largesse of the new philanthropy were the three women's medical schools that had survived into the twentieth century.[77]

The reasons for the failure of all but one of the women's medical schools to survive past the second decade of the twentieth century are complex and cannot be explained merely by raising the ugly specter of discrimination. Discrimination certainly did exist, but it is also true that medical women were hampered by the limitations of and contradictions in their own ideology, an ideology no longer suited to the problems of the new century.[78]

In a very real sense, the goals of the nineteenth-century woman's medical movement had been realized by the opening decade of the new century. Women physicians had fought for equal opportunities in medical education on philosophical grounds that unquestioningly accepted woman's dominance over the private sphere. Indeed, they never had anticipated women's participation in medicine to be on the same level as men's, nor had they expected or desired that the majority of women would leave home for full-time, extradomestic activity. They understood that the woman physician would always remain exceptional. In fact, they fought unabashedly for the rights of that exceptional minority. They fully believed that the realization of those rights would benefit society at large because women physicians naturally were better than men in treating women and children, concerned themselves more assiduously with preventive medicine, and worked, in a more general sense, to humanize the profession by weaning it away from narrow self-interest. It was only in the altered cultural setting of the twentieth century that nineteenth-century goals began to shift to a more broadly egalitarian posture.

To be sure, women physicians never demonstrated a thorough unanimity when they mustered their arguments in defense of woman's medical education. Although there was a strong tendency to emphasize their unique contributions, a few hardheaded scientists, like Mary Putnam Jacobi, coolly deplored such sentimentalism. Although Jacobi never entirely discarded the notion that women had special strengths, she feared that such an ideology led to female-centered, moralistic, separatist standards. In contrast to these, her assumptions remained fundamentally universalistic and assimilationist.[79] Jacobi's approach, however, proved distinctly less popular in the public and private thought of women doctors until the twentieth century. And, as we shall see, assimilation exacted its own price.

Ironically, despite an ideology that emphasized their own uniqueness, few women physicians favored separate education or understood the potential pitfalls of medical coeducation. With the exception of the faculty of the Woman's Medical College of Pennsylvania, female medical educators looked at the women's schools as temporary expedients. In fact, women physicians seem to have been haunted periodically by the fear that women could not maintain first-rate educational institutions by themselves. By the close of the nineteenth century, burdened with the rising financial costs of quality medical education and heartened by the prospects for equal opportunity at existing male schools, female institutions passed out of existence one by one. It could be argued that in so doing, female medical educators lost, however unwittingly, the autonomous control of institutions that, at least in the case of Chicago and New York, had provided an opportunity for a self-supporting and self-directed female community to inspire younger women to follow in its footsteps. Coeducation never fulfilled its promise, and women physicians continued to find themselves isolated as a group from the mainstream of American medicine.[80]

During this period of assimilation, the Woman's Medical College of Pennsylvania limped along, a sole dissenter in the ranks. Skeptical of the rewards of coeducation for all types of women, its faculty struggled valiantly in the face of staggering financial difficulties to maintain a class A rating with the American Medical Association. One cannot help wondering what feats this school could have accomplished had it received the $500,000 endowment M. Carey Thomas and Mary Elizabeth Garrett gave to John Hopkins. Instead, the Woman's Medical College of Pennsylvania fell victim to women physicians' collective attitude toward separate education. Over the years, more and more men took important positions on its faculty, which helped the school maintain an aura of legitimacy in the harsh professional realities of the medical world. While praising the college for its "striking evidence of a genuine effort to do the best possible with limited resources," Abraham Flexner then went on to reiterate the arguments of Dean Emily Blackwell when she announced in 1899 the merger of the New York Infirmary with Cornell University. Flexner observed:

Medical education is now, in the United States and Canada, open to women upon practically the same terms as men. If all institutions do not receive women, so many do, that no woman desiring an education in medicine is under any disability in finding a school to which she may gain admittance. . . . Woman has so apparent a function in certain medical specialties and seemingly so assured a place in general medicine under some obvious limitations that the struggle for wider educational opportunities for the sex was predestined to an early success. . . . Whether it is either wise or necessary to endow separate medical schools for women is a problem. . . . In the first place, eighty per cent of women who have in the last six years studied medicine have attended coeducational institutions. None of the three women's medical colleges now existing can be sufficiently strengthened without an enormous outlay. . . . In the general need of more liberal support for medical schools, it would appear that large sums, as far as specially available for the medical education of women, would accomplish most if used to develop coeducational institutions, in which their benefits would be shared by men without loss to women students. . . .[81]

Tension between separatism and assimilation has continued to divide women physicians, as it has other minority groups, in the twentieth century. With the achievement of coeducation, militant separatism understandably appeared to many to threaten the possibility that men would welcome women colleagues as equals. It seemed to the younger women physicians that the battle over equal intelligence had ended, and they lacked the pioneer determination of their elders because significant advances in fact had been made. Consequently, many women rejected formal contacts with professional women's associations. Others unwittingly internalized cultural assumptions that were suspicious of separatist institutions and groups. As a result, only the most militant and feminist women joined the American Medical Women's Association after 1915. Although the organization has not only advanced the cause of women in medicine but also supported such various sociomedical issues as liberalized birth control laws, medical insurance, Medicaid, Medicare, and abortion reform, its membership rolls have never attracted more than one-third of the women physicians in the country.[82]

The younger generations of women physicians, for whom sex discrimination was often so subtle that it went unnoticed, were uncomfortable with the feminist militancy of the American Medical Women's Association. Many shared the sentiments of Ethel Walker, a pediatric resident at Johns Hopkins Hospital, who, in 1940, coolly explained to Bertha Van Hoosen her reasons for not joining the organization:

I am strongly opposed to any organization or individual's attitude which sets women apart from men . . . instead of teaching them to lose themselves in their profession. . . . In the early days of women in medicine they no doubt had to band together, but now in most sections of the country if not all the quicker the woman physician can forget any feeling that she is in a class apart from her men colleagues the happier she will be and the better she and they will get along. In medical school and interne [sic] days I have seen it happen time and time again that the girls who were totally unconscious of any difference between themselves and their men confreres and who mingled with them on exactly the same footing achieved a professional equality and friendship which was entirely denied to the women who were always huddled together with other women and who continually made it plain to everybody that they were different and knew they were different. In my experience it has been the former group who did well in their profession . . . whereas the other group of women's women . . . seldom advanced. . . .[83]

The late nineteenth-century scientific revolution in medical therapeutics also produced tension within the ranks of women physicians and disarmed the arguments that earlier women physicians had used in support of female medical education. Nineteenth-century suppositions about the body had described illness as a phenomenon of the total organism. Physicians who wished to restore a patient's health did so by readjusting the body's internal equilibrium and returning it to harmony with its environment. Under these assumptions, local inflammations were indicative of systemic ills, and localized treatment was intended to remedy general physical states. Before taking action, the experienced physician weighed a bewildering complexity of factors that included climate, age, gender, and the family's constitutional idiosyncrasies. The better he knew the patient, the better his chances for success, for each individual organism displayed its own distinct features and interacted uniquely with a constantly changing environment.[84]

In contrast to this, the major theme pervading the history of modern therapeutics is that of discreteness and specificity. When bacteriologists directed their attention to specific symptoms and causes, they revolutionized the approach to disease. No longer is medication selected to effect a balance in the entire organism. Therapy is aimed at discrete entities, and the intention is to remove the causes altogether. In this view of disease, somatic considerations reign supreme, and there is little room for the social, psychological, and behavioral dimensions of illness. As a consequence, both the physician's approach to his own discipline and the public's perception of his role have changed considerably.

Whereas the nineteenth-century physician approached his patient with a predisposition to physiological holism, twentieth-century therapeutics has transformed the doctor into a specialist whose knowledge encompasses some specific symptom or some discrete portion of the patient's body. Treatment understandably has become fragmented; total patient ''care'' has become increasingly dissociated from the specialist's concerns as he busies himself with patient ''cure.'' Indeed, medicine has become so identified with this highly technical and reductionist approach that for many physicians whatever lies outside the domain of specific diagnosis and treatment lies outside the domain of medicine itself.[85]

Institutional developments in the early twentieth century reflected this gradual fragmentation in the delivery of health care. The general practitioner became an endangered species. Physicians even became alienated gradually from one another as each specialty developed its own language and body of knowledge. As doctors found it less necessary to treat patients in their homes, care shifted to the hospital, which offered a more convenient setting for the highly technical and more narrow approach to disease.[86] Gradually, nurses and social workers took on the nineteenth-century physician's heuristic role. Public health nurses, for example, replaced the women interns who had defiantly entered the slums to teach the poor how to be well. In their effort to professionalize and claim nursing for women, self-conscious leaders in the field of nursing played an important part in shifting the so-called feminine and nurturant aspects of medical care from the doctor to the nurse. In 1913, while struggling to define an independent role for the tuberculosis nurse, Elizabeth Gregg, Superintendent of Nurses for the New York City Health Department, wrote:

Physicians have not the time, neither is it born in many [doctors] to devote themselves to the detail that requires the patient, painstaking effort of a woman; and this detail tends to reveal the very causes or the contributing factors of tuberculosis more than in any other disease; so that the nurse, with her knowledge of home conditions and the family's principles of living, and with her instinctive woman's insight into the causes of trouble, is the physician's right hand.[87]

Although women doctors were not alone in their sensitivity to such changes in the field, they often lamented the passing of the "human" in the practice of medicine. Eliza Mosher, for example, a past president of the American Medical Women's Association, regretted the loss of "the sympathetic relation which formerly existed between doctors and their patients," and warned her colleagues to beware of "narrowing and concentrating their vision upon the purely physical to the exclusion of the psychic and human."[88] Others continued to believe that medical women must exert their influence in favor of more holistic approaches. In 1930, M. Esther Harding, a psychiatrist, spoke for many women doctors when she wrote to Bertha Van Hoosen, a prominent female surgeon and the founder of the American Medical Women's Association,

I have been struck recently more than once at the meetings of a Psychotherapeutic Society of which I am a member with a queer little difference between the attitude and aproach [sic] of the men and the women . . . to the subject under discussion. . . . Usually the men lead off with scientifically arranged data, followed by statistics and rather abstract theory. Then presently a women speaks up and nearly always her voice is raised to remind the group that after all the patient is a human being and not merely the subject of certain symptoms or mechanisms. And this I think is characteristic. We women are more nearly concerned with the human problem presented to us and relatively less absorbed with the collection and classification of scientific material. Let us who write about the intricacies of the human psyche, whether in its normal functioning or in its illnesses and conflicts, remember always that in any final analysis it is the human being that matters. Knowledge of disease and its detailed investigation are not ends in themselves, they are only means to an end, namely that the human being may grow and flourish.[89]

Even in the fragmented and technocratic context of the early twentieth century, women continued to preserve their penchant for holistic approaches through their specialty choices, which usually fell into the primary care fields, most notably general practice, pediatrics, and psychiatry.[90] Public-health work, especially part-time positions with low pay and little prestige, also attracted a steady stream of women. It simply cannot be argued convincingly that their involvement in public-health work was caused only by their "exclusion from other medical careers due to sex discrimination."[91] Women doctors seemed to be well suited for public-health work, and no one argued this point more forcefully than they themselves. Married women physicians, who needed more flexible time commitments in order to care for their families, were urged by leading women in the field to choose school and community work. The history of the anonymous women physicians who filled important social needs as clinical workers for the Federal Children's Bureau, part-time members of local boards of health, school physicians, and charity workers still needs to be written.[92]

Of course, the achievements of such prominent pioneers in the field as Josephine Baker, Alice Hamilton, and Ellen C. Potter inspired others, but probably the most convincing illustration of the sustaining attraction of public-health work after 1900 is found in the life of Florence Sabin. Sabin, an early graduate of Johns Hopkins Medical School, was a protégée of the great anatomist Franklin P. Mall. Her brilliant research in anatomy and histology led to her appointment, after fifteen years on the Johns Hopkins faculty, as the first woman member of the prestigious Rockefeller Institute. After her retirement from research in 1938, she became, at the age of seventy-three, chairwoman of the Governor's subcommittee on public health in her native state of Colorado and began a dramatically successful crusade for basic health reforms.[93]

Nevertheless, although many women physicians continued to regard health education as a female responsibility, technical and professional developments made medicine a very different field of endeavor than it had been only fifty years earlier. As long as medical practice remained more a matter of "art" than "science," women found themselves drawn to the work and armed with compelling reasons for claiming it as their own. Furthermore, because nineteenth-century problems of professionalization centered on the semi-private realm of licensing, legitimacy, and the decline of heroic medicine, women who attained a medical degree could still gain an official foothold as physicians. In contrast, the organization and practice of medicine after 1900 moved from the semi-private to the public and political realm. These circumstances may have made it more difficult for women to carve a place for themselves. What is equally apparent, however, is that women then found it less desirable to study medicine for a complicated set of reasons. Thus, the discriminatory donation policies of various foundations, the rapid decline of the family-based general practitioner, the fragmentation of medical care, and the transferal of medical practice from the intimate confines of the home to the impersonal setting of a hospital converged to work in various ways against the fuller participation of women as physicians in the health-care field.

Women flocked to nursing in these years. Between 1880 and 1900 the number of nurses increased from 15,601 to 120,000.[94] Another category of health workers, "physicians and surgeons attendants," showed an 86 percent increase in the census from 1910 to 1920. Because nursing generally attracted women from a different class background than that of women physicians, the declining number of women doctors after 1910 cannot be explained by the expansion of nursing alone. Statistics from these years would seem to indicate rather that social work and graduate school diverted some women's interests from medicine.

The years between 1890 and 1918 reveal sharp increases in the number of women doing graduate work. The percentage of female graduate students rose from 10.2 in 1890 to 41.0 in 1918. In terms of absolute numbers, this change represented a twentyfold increase, while the number of men attending graduate school increased only fivefold. After 1910, the census data suggest that many of these women were using their degrees in the new helping professions. In that year, women made up about 56 percent of the welfare workers; ten years later their absolute numbers had increased almost 200 percent. In 1910, women comprised 30 percent of the "keepers of charitable institutions"; by 1920 that percentage had increased to 38 percent. Again, the increase in actual numbers is impressive, from 2,250 in 1910 to 4,900 in 1920. Unfortunately, the census information cannot indicate what percentage of the total body of educated women were choosing welfare work and its allied fields. Nevertheless, it is possible to hypothesize that there is a distinct connection between the rising numbers of women with advanced degrees and the sharp increase in the number of women professionals in these occupations.[95]

The census data suggest that subtle cultural factors were at work. The twentieth century has witnessed unmistakable shifts in the primacy of essential Victorian values. Most notable among those changes have been the altered expectations surrounding the home, women, and family life. Earlier in this essay, it was contended that a prominent feature of Victorian culture was the exaltation of motherhood through the cult of domesticity. The high status afforded motherhood followed logically from the conviction that mothers were the primary agents for the transmission of cultural values. Yet, despite their own glorification of motherhood, feminists had expressed a particular personal disdain for the patriarchal Victorian family. In the nineteenth century, large numbers of educated and professional women rejected marriage in favor of the pursuit of meaningful work. Opponents of higher education for women were fond of pointing out that college women married less frequently and had fewer children than did more ordinary women, and, indeed, statistics for the years between 1880 and 1920 support these claims.[96]

In the twentieth century, however, the image of woman-as-mother gradually gave way to the image of woman-as-mate. The social and economic changes in the decades before World War I created more positive attitudes toward pleasure, individual self-fulfillment, sexuality, and women's work.[97] Probably because of this altered climate, college educated women and professional women did not continue to reject marriage with the vehemence that they had earlier. The proportion of professional women who married, for example, doubled from 12.2 percent in 1910 to 24.7 percent in 1930.[98] Joyce Antler has convincingly argued that the early twentieth century produced a new kind of feminism, previously found only among a small minority of nineteenth-century women activists. These women chose not to shun marriage but to strive instead to "work out the large issues of feminism on an individual basis." Only if we acknowledge the existence of this brand of feminism, which Antler labels "feminism-as-life-process," can we "rescue from the lost generation of feminist endeavor after 1920 some of the women whose lives might properly be called 'feminist.' ''[99]

For these women the central issue was the need to balance participation in the public sphere through professional, political, or other activities with marriage and family. In their own lives, they struggled to "work out that balance of interests between the private and public [in this case, between marriage and career] that would allow them to achieve the self-determination and autonomy that they posited as their highest goal." Although the number of married women physicians also increased during these years, it is quite likely that many women of Antler's description may have been attracted to medicine initially but ruled out careers as doctors because the work appeared too strenuous, too inflexible, and ultimately less amenable to this kind of delicate balancing act.[100] It may be presumed that their choices were reinforced by the changes in medical practice itself, which was becoming increasingly more technocratic and aggressively "male."

Finally, public feminism, which had offered nineteenth-century professional women companionship and support, passed into dormancy after 1920. Older generations of women physicians occasionally mourned the passing of a "high spirit of enthusiasm for a cause" and complained of "complacency and secure smugness" among younger women doctors.[101] In fact, until the 1960s when a revitalized feminist movement used as its motto "the personal is political" and thus focused attention on the interaction between women's public and private lives, medical women generally engaged in intimate and solitary struggles.[102]

In explaining the decline in the number of women physicians during this period, however, the unhappy effects of institutional discrimination of all kinds must never be overlooked, even though the existence of quotas was more sporadic and decidedly less universal in medical schools than historians have believed. While schools in parts of the Northeast and South proved consistently discriminatory, others, especially in the Middle and Far West, maintained commendable percentages of female students throughout the twentieth century. From 1929 on, the percentage of acceptances for both men and women applicants hovered around 50 percent. It is apparent that the diminishing number of female students after that year paralleled the diminishing number of female applicants. When the percentage of women applicants rose in the mid-sixties so did the acceptances, although some have argued convincingly that women applicants are a more highly selective group than their male counterparts.[103]

Perhaps even more insidious than discrimination by the medical schools were the tracking systems, "old boy" networks, and women's difficulties in procuring first-rate hospital appointments. In 1914, *Harper's Weekly* complained that even female graduates from such excellent medical colleges as Cornell Medical School had problems finding good internships. Twenty years later the American Medical Women's Association revealed that almost half of the nation's hospitals had never employed a woman doctor. Although a decade later that figure had dropped to 20 percent, choice residency programs continued to remain difficult, if not impossible, to secure.[104]

In many respects, institutional discrimination was merely the most visible element of a more distressing kind of exclusion. In the final analysis, women fell victim to the social dictates of a culture still characterized by extreme sex stereotyping. The vigorous, detached, almost godlike figure of the twentieth-century physician kept all but the most determined women from challenging cultural barriers. Their desire to be wives and mothers, the ambivalent feelings within the ranks of women physicians over separatism or assimilation, and the lack of an aggressive feminist movement to help them better articulate their goals made medical women an easy mark for official institutional intolerance. No reader can appreciate the significance of the lives of the individual women whose stories are published in this volume without understanding the complex and subtle cultural assumptions that they had to overcome.

The Revival of Feminism, the Reentrance of Women into the Medical Profession, and the Dilemmas and Challenges of Change

The rebirth of feminism in the late 1960s prompted a frontal attack on the social values that had prevented many women from seeking professional goals. Its ability to convince large numbers of women that professional careers did not have to conflict with marriage, motherhood, or female fulfillment was one of its most important achievements. The movement's success in inspiring young women was reflected in the application and acceptance statistics for women at medical schools across the country. While women comprised only 9 percent of the applicants in 1960, their numbers had increased to nearly 30 percent by the end of the 1970s. It has been predicted that within the next decade or two, women will constitute between 25 and and 35 percent of the profession.[105]

Although the older women whose lives are recounted in this volume fought lonely battles and often were blissfully unaware of the subtle handicaps that they were struggling to overcome, their younger counterparts appear to be somewhat more fortunate. They have benefited, if only indirectly, from the fundamental support and encouragement of a revitalized feminist movement that managed, despite occasional disappointments, to raise the consciousness of an entire society. Indeed, the influx of women into medicine has even begun to challenge the traditional images of the doctor. For the first time, women physicians are demanding power in setting health-care policy, in making decisions pertaining to medical practice, and in determining how medicine is taught. They are publicly denouncing "old boy" networks, rigid tracking systems, and their own psychological timidity. Finally, they are bringing new attitudes and new cognitive styles to clinical practice. At a recent conference at Johns Hopkins University, Dr. Carola Eisenberg, Dean of Student Affairs at Harvard Medical School, praised women's tendency to show emotion and argued that it could be done without compromising professional identity. "Strength," she urged, "is not incompatible with compassion."[106]

Yet problems persist. A woman's fundamental connection with children and family life still complicates her achievement of career goals. Throughout the 1940s and 1950s medical educators loudly complained that women medical students had a higher attrition rate than men.[107] Even more damaging was the contention that women physicians' productivity, especially among those who were married, fell far below the male standard. Recent studies have recorded significant changes in the last decade for comparative figures measuring total practice hours, but the figures for women still fall short of those for men.[108]

One study by Dr. Marilyn Heins, which found that 76 percent of the married women physicians sampled did *all* of the cooking, shopping, child care, and money management in their households, suggests that the problems facing a woman physician who is also a wife and mother have not been solved. It may be that the present generation has learned only how to handle the pressures better.[109] Also disconcerting was the evidence that marital status and family size were inversely related to career success. The most "successful" women physicians from the perspective of their profession were more likely to be single.[110] Other researchers have correlated women's specialty choices and willingness to take low prestige, part-time, and low salaried positions with their felt needs for a time commitment that can be fitted more easily to the demands of family life.[111]

Married or single, women physicians are still severely underrepresented in private practices, surgical specialties, and high-level academic, administrative, or policymaking positions. In general, patients still prefer a male doctor. Although medical school admissions committees no longer seem to be discriminating against female applicants as they have in the past, flexible training programs that can be more responsive to the female life cycle are relatively rare. There is a persistent dearth of female role models on medical school faculties. Finally, the woman student still confronts subtle psychological challenges that hamper her efficiency—challenges beyond those that she shares with her male peers.[112]

Recently, two women psychiatrists spoke eloquently of the more hidden difficulties of medical school. Although all medical students are confronted with the need to form an identity as physicians, women have had the added burden of developing their identity in what is thought of as a man's world. Women medical students struggle to cope with myths about the loss of femininity. In addition, because most women rarely recognize the pressures under which they operate, they tend to feel guilty when their personal lives lead them to make demands of a profession "generous" enough to accept them:

Women often accept the "peculiarity" of their position as doctors, and they may share the prejudices of men regarding their capabilities and the legitimacy of their career aspirations. The woman who chooses to pursue "two lives" in our culture may have to face conflicts that she is unprepared to cope with. Built upon her longstanding feelings of being less than adequate in comparison with men, she faces the burden of feeling unwanted and unwelcome in many of the fields she might choose. In addition to having very few models of achievement and success, she is viewed as if she were performing an unnatural act when her choice is a traditionally "masculine" field (e.g. surgery). The development of a woman's self-esteem and self-image cannot be measurably improved by the imposition of these additional burdens of confusion and guilt. . . . If we define success in terms of carrying through of one's goals, then we must also look at the high price the successful woman must pay in our culture.[113]

The increasing number of women physicians has not proved the medical profession's only problem in recent years. Doctors also are faced with the probability that the traditional biomedical model, which generated dramatic and significant victories in the battle against disease, may no longer be adequate for the scientific tasks and social responsibilities now facing the profession in the twentieth century. Although this model has been successful previously, heightened public dissatisfaction and the palpable challenge of holistic medicine suggest that some physicians themselves are beginning to surrender reductionist, exclusively somatic definitions of disease. Indeed, the profession may find itself in need of a means of broadening the approach to illness to include the psychosocial without sacrificing the enormous advantages of the biomedical approach. Women can make important contributions to this reorientation.[114]

The persistence of such difficulties, both for the profession and for women themselves, makes it difficult to predict what the long-range effects of their burgeoning numbers will be. Some commentators have suggested that the willingness of women physicians to choose salaried positions and their traditionally more liberal attitudes toward social issues ultimately may influence the profession's stand on national health insurance and prepaid health plans.[115] Others have hoped that women physicians will take a leading role in the reform of women's health care.[116] The long-standing interest of women in preventive medicine and the current public dissatisfaction with crisis-oriented care have led still others to predict that one contribution of women may be a more "health-oriented" medical practice. Finally, the need of married women physicians who are mothers for a more flexible and shorter work week may accelerate this trend for all physicians "as a substitute for the work-money 'rat-race.' "[117] However accurate such speculations may be, the consensus has been that major changes are occurring in the organization and practice of modern medicine and that young women physicians will play an important role in bringing them about. Friends and supporters of women physicians quietly hope that many women do, in fact, offer special personal qualities and altruistic values to their profession and that their continued presence as doctors will positively influence the behavior of all physicians—men and women alike.

Notes

1. Stephen Smith, M. D., "A Woman Student in a Medical College," *In Memory of Dr. Elizabeth Blackwell and Dr. Emily Blackwell* (New York: Academy of Medicine, 1911), pp. 3-19.

2. Mary Putnam Jacobi, M. D., "Woman in Medicine," in *Woman's Work in America,* ed. Annie Nathan Meyer (New York, 1891), p. 141.

3. See Catherine Scholten, "'On the Importance of the Obstetrick Art': Changing Customs of Childbirth in America, 1760-1825," *William and Mary Quarterly* 34 (July 1977): 426-45.

4. O. T. Beall, Jr. and R. H. Shryock, *Cotton Mather: First Significant Figure in American Medicine* (Baltimore: Johns Hopkins University Press, 1954), pp. 16ff.

5. See Richard Shryock, *Medicine and Society in America, 1660-1860* (Ithaca, N. Y.: Cornell University Press, 1960), p. 9. Also on medical professionalization, see James Kett, *The Formation of the American Medical Profession* (New Haven, Conn.: Yale University Press, 1968); William G. Rothstein, *American Physicians in the 19th-Century* (Baltimore: Johns Hopkins University Press, 1972); and Martin Pernick, "A Calculus of Suffering: Pain, Anesthesia and Utilitarian Professionalism in 19th-Century American Medicine" (Ph.D. diss., Columbia University, 1978).

6. Gerda Lerner, "The Lady and the Mill Girl," *American Studies* 10 (Spring 1969): 5-15; Julia C. Spruill, *Women's Life and Work in the Southern Colonies* (Chapel Hill: University of North Carolina Press, 1938); Elizabeth A. Dexter, *Career Women of America: 1776-1840* (Francestown, N. H.: Kelley, 1950); Mary Ryan, *Womanhood in America* (New York: New Viewpoints, 1975); Roger Thompson, *Women in Stuart England and America: A Comparative Study* (London: Routledge and Kegan Paul, 1974). For a revisionist view, see Mary Beth Norton, *Liberty's Daughters* (New York: Little, Brown, 1980).

7. See Jane Donegan's excellent study on which my own account relies, *Women and Men Midwives, Medicine, Morality and Misogyny in Early America* (Westport, Conn.: Greenwood Press, 1978). See also Edna Manzer, "Woman's Doctors: The Development of Obstetrics and Gynecology in Boston, 1860-1930" (Ph.D. diss., University of Indiana, 1979), and Richard and Dorothy Wertz, *Lying In: A History of Childbirth in America* (New York: Free Press, 1977).

8. Scholten, "'On the Importance of the Obstetrick Art,'" pp. 438-40.

9. Alexis de Tocqueville, *Democracy in America,* Bk. 3, ch. 41, ed. Richard D. Hefner (New York: New American Library, 1956), p. 244.

10. Nancy Cott, *The Bonds of Womanhood* (New Haven, Conn.: Yale University Press, 1977), pp. 5-18. Also, Lerner, "The Lady and the Mill Girl."

11. See also William Leach, *True Love and Perfect Union: The Feminist Reform of Sex and Society* (New York: Basic Books, 1980), pp. 38-63, and Norton, *Liberty's Daughters,* pp. 295-99.

12. John Ware, *Remarks on the Employment of Females as Practitioners in Midwifery, By a Physician* (Boston, 1820). See also Manzer, "Woman's Doctors," pp. 15-20.

13. Nancy Cott, "Passionlessness: An Interpretation of Victorian Sexual Ideology, 1790-1850," *Signs* 4 (Winter 1978): 219-36.

14. Ware, *Remarks,* pp. 3, 16.

15. Ibid., pp. 6, 7, 9.

16. Ibid., pp. 21, 4. See also Regina Markell Morantz, "The 'Connecting Link': The Case for the Woman Doctor in 19th-Century America," in *Sickness and Health in America*, ed. R. Numbers and J. Leavitt, (Madison: University of Wisconsin Press, 1978), pp. 117–28.

17. Ware, *Remarks*, p. 7.

18. See Donegan, *Women and Men Midwives*, pp. 164–96.

19. Charles Meigs, *Females and Their Diseases* (Philadelphia, 1848), pp. 19, 20–21.

20. Cott, "Passionlessness," p. 236. See also Charles Rosenberg and Carroll Smith-Rosenberg, "The Female Animal: Medical and Biological Views of Woman and Her Role in Nineteenth-Century America," *Journal of American History* 60 (September 1973): 332–56; Carroll Smith-Rosenberg, "The Cycle of Femininity: Puberty and Menopause in Nineteenth-Century America," *Feminist Studies* 1 (Winter 1973): 58–72. Ultimately, the increasing rigidity of this point of view provoked a rebellion from feminists. See Morantz, "Connecting Link," pp. 120–25; and Leach, *True Love and Perfect Union*, pp. 19–80.

21. Thomas Ewell, *Letters to Ladies, Detailing Important Information Concerning Themselves and Infants* (Philadelphia, 1817).

22. See, for example, Samuel Gregory, *Letters to Ladies in Favor of Female Physicians* (New York, 1850).

23. Shryock, *Medicine and Society*, p. 125.

24. Martin Pernick, "Medical Profession: I: Medical Professionalism," in *Encyclopedia of Bioethics*, ed. Warren T. Reich (New York: Free Press, 1978); and Pernick, "A Calculus," Intro. and ch. 1, pp. 1–17.

25. Jeffrey L. Berlant, *Profession and Monopoly* (Berkeley: University of California Press, 1975) quoted in Pernick, "A Calculus," p. 128.

26. Mary Gove Nichols, "Woman the Physician," *Water-Cure Journal* 12 (1851): 3.

27. See Pernick, "A Calculus," pp. 112–71.

28. Martin Kaufman, *American Medical Education* (Westport, Conn.: Greenwood Press, 1976); Robert P. Hudson, "Abraham Flexner in Perspective: American Medical Education 1865–1910," *Bulletin of the History of Medicine* 56 (November-December 1972): 545–61.

29. See Pernick, "A Calculus," p. 25; William B. Walker, "The Health Reform Movement in the United States, 1830–1870" (Ph.D. diss., Johns Hopkins University Press, 1955); Ronald Numbers, "Do it Yourself the Sectarian Way," in *Medicine Without Doctors*, ed. R. Numbers, J. Leavitt, and G. Risse (New York: Science History Publications, 1977), pp. 49–72; Joseph Kett, *The Formation of the American Medical Profession* (New Haven, Conn.: Yale University Press, 1968), pp. 97–164; Martin Kaufman, *Homeopathy in America* (Baltimore: Johns Hopkins University Press, 1971); James Harvey Young, *The Toadstool Millionaires* (Princeton, N.J.: Princeton University Press, 1961).

30. Megali Larson, *The Rise of Professionalism* (Berkeley: University of California Press, 1977), p. 133.

31. See Leach, *True Love and Perfect Union*, p. 21; and Regina Markell Morantz, "Making Women Modern: Middle Class Women and Health Reform in 19th Century America," *Journal of Social History* 10 (Summer 1977): 490–507; Charles Rosenberg, *The Cholera Years* (Chicago, Ill.: University of Chicago Press, 1962).

32. Mary Gove Nichols, *Lectures to Women on Anatomy and Physiology* (New York, 1846), p. 20; Morantz, "Making Women Modern," p. 498.

33. Morantz, "Making Women Modern."

34. Kirk Jeffrey, "The Family as a Utopian Retreat from the City," *Soundings* 15 (Spring 1972): 21–41; Bernard Wishy, *The Child and the Republic* (Philadelphia: University of Pennsylvania Press, 1968); David J. Rothman, *The Discovery of the Asylum* (Boston: Little, Brown, 1971); Regina Markell Morantz, "Nineteenth Century Health Reform and Women: A Program of Self Help," in *Medicine Without Doctors*, pp. 73–94.

35. Morantz, "Making Women Modern," p. 500.

36. Leach, *True Love and Perfect Union*, p. 21.

37. Elizabeth Blackwell, *Pioneer Work in Opening the Medical Profession to Women* (New York, 1895), p. 27.

38. See, for example, Elizabeth Blackwell, *Address on the Medical Education of Women* (New York, 1856) and her *Medicine as a Profession for Women* (New York, 1860).

39. Ann Preston, "General Diagnosis"; Angenette A. Hunt, "The True Physician" (Theses, Medical College of Pennsylvania Archives, 1851). Hereinafter papers from the Medical College of Pennsylvania Archives are cited as MCP.

40. Morantz, "Connecting Link."

41. Samuel Gregory, "Female Physicians," *The Living Age* 73 (1862): 243–49; Morantz, "Connecting Link," pp. 122–23.

42. "On the Education of Women Physicians" [1860], Elizabeth Blackwell Papers, Box 59, Library of Congress, Washington, D.C.; Ann Preston, *Valedictory Address* (Philadelphia, 1858) p. 9; Blackwell, *Medicine as a Profession for Women*, pp. 10–11.

43. Harriot Hunt's remarks in *Proceedings of the Women's Rights Convention, October, 1851* (Boston, 1852). Price, "The Necessity for Women Physicians," MCP, 1871; Saur, "Physicians and Their Duties," MCP, 1871.

44. See James J. Walsh, "Women in the Medical World," *New York Medical Journal* 96 (1912): 1324–28; Morantz, "Connecting Link," p. 117.

45. The five "regular" schools were the Woman's Medical College of Pennsylvania (1850 to the present); New England Female Medical College (1856–1873), which merged with the homeopathic Boston University; Woman's Medical College of the New York Infirmary (1868–1899); Woman's Hospital Medical College of Chicago (1870–1902); Woman's Medical College of Baltimore (1882–1909). See Morantz, "Connecting Link," p. 117.

46. See Regina Markell Morantz, "Women Physicians, Co-education and the Struggle for Professional Standards in 19th-Century Medical Education" (Paper delivered at Berkshire Conference, Mount Holyoke College, South Hadley, Mass., August 1978); Martin Kaufman, "The Admission of Women to 19th-Century Medical Societies," *Bulletin of the History of Medicine* 50 (Summer 1976): 251–59.

47. W. W. Parker, M.D., "Woman's Place in the Christian World: Superior Morally, Inferior Mentally to Man—Not Qualified for Medicine or Law—the Contrariety and Harmony of the Sexes," *Transactions of the Medical Society of the State of Virginia*, (1892): 86–107. See also Mary Roth Walsh, *"Doctors Wanted: No Women Need Apply," Sexual Barriers in the Medical Profession, 1835–1975* (New Haven, Conn.: Yale University Press, 1977); and Gloria Melnick Moldow, "The Gilded Age, Promise and Disillusionment: Women Doctors and the Emergence of the Professional Middle Class, Washington, D.C., 1870–1900" (Ph.D. diss., University of Maryland, 1980).

48. See *Boston Medical and Surgical Journal* 111 (1884): 90; ibid., 40 (1849): 505; ibid., 89 (1873): 23.

49. Edmund Andrews, M. D., "The Surgeon," *Chicago Medical Examiner* 2 (1861): 587-98, quoted in Pernick, "A Calculus," p. 131; Newspaper clipping, n.d., Chadwick Scrapbook, Countway Library, Boston, Mass., cited in Mary Walsh, *Doctors Wanted: No Women Need Apply,* p. 139. For a good discussion of doctors' fears of feminization see Pernick, "A Calculus," *passim,* and Walsh, *Doctors Wanted: No Women Need Apply,* pp. 135-46.

50. E. H. Clarke, *Sex in Education: A Fair Chance for Girls* (Boston, 1873), p. 23; also Horatio Storer, "Letter of Resignation," *Boston Medical and Surgical Journal* 75 (1866): 191-92.

51. Clarke, *Sex in Education,* p. 41.

52. M. Carey Thomas, "Present Tendencies in Women's College and University Education," *Educational Review* 25 (1908): 68.

53. Mary Putnam Jacobi, *The Question of Rest for Women during Menstruation* (New York, 1877); Emily F. Pope, M.D., Augusta C. Pope, M.D., and Emma Call, M.D., *The Practice of Medicine by Women in the United States* (Boston, 1881), p. 7.

54. See, for example, Elizabeth C. Underhill, M.D., "The Effect of College Life on the Health of Women Students," *Woman's Medical Journal* 22 (February 1912): 31-33; Mary E. B. Ritter, M.D., "Health of University Girls," *California State Medical Journal* 1 (1902-3): 259-64; Clelia Mosher, M.D., "Some of the Causal Factors in the Increased Height of College Women," *Journal of the American Medical Association* 81 (August 1923): 535-38; Elizabeth R. Thelburg, "College Education a Factor in the Physical Life of Women," *Transactions of the Alumnae Association of the Woman's Medical College of Pennsylvania* (1899): 73-87. See also Virginia Drachman, "Women Doctors and the Women's Medical Movement: Feminism and Medicine, 1850-1895," (Ph.D. diss., State University of New York at Buffalo, 1976) for a somewhat different perspective.

55. M. Carey Thomas, *The Opening of the Johns Hopkins Medical School to Women,* pamphlet reprinted from *The Century Magazine* (February 1891), Sophia Smith College Collection, Northampton, Mass., Box labeled "Physicians U.S."; Mary Putnam Jacobi, "Social Aspects of the Readmission of Women into the Medical Profession," *Papers and Letters Presented at the First Woman's Congress of the Association for the Advancement of Woman* (New York, 1874), p. 174.

56. See, for example, Josephine Baker's comments about Emily Blackwell and other women faculty at the New York Infirmary in her *Fighting for Life* (New York: The Macmillan Co., 1959), pp. 34-44; and Emily Dunning Barringer's remarks in her *Bowery to Bellevue* (New York: W. W. Norton, 1950), pp. 60-61, and Jacobi, pp. 80-81. See also the correspondence between Elizabeth Blackwell and Eliza Mosher in Mosher Papers, Michigan Historical Collections, University of Michigan, Ann Arbor, Michigan.

57. For a thoughtful discussion of feminist thought on the subject of marriage, see Leach, *True Love and Perfect Union,* pp. 38-132.

58. Georgiana Glenn, "Are Women as Capable of Becoming Physicians as Men," *The Clinic* 9 (1875): 243-45; Jacobi, "Inaugural Address Delivered at the Women's Medical College of the New York Infirmary, 1880, *Chicago Medical Journal & Examiner* 42 (1881): 580.

59. Eliza Mosher to sister, April 17, 1887, Mosher Papers, Michigan Historical Col-

lections. Frances A. Rutherford, M.D., "The New Force in Medicine and Surgery," *Proceedings of the Michigan State Medical Society* (1893), p. 4.

60. See Annie S. Daniel, "A Cautious Experiment," *Woman's Medical Journal* 47 (July 1940): 201; Blackwell, *Pioneer Work,* p. 227; "Pioneer Medical Women of Cleveland," *Journal of American Medical Women's Association* 6 (May 1951): 186–89; Edna H. Nelson, *The Women and Childrens Hospital,* pamphlet reprinted from *Hospital Council Bulletin,* 10 (January 1941), Radcliffe Women's Archives, Radcliffe College, Cambridge, Mass., hereinafter cited as RWA. Lillian Welsh, *Reminiscences of Thirty Years in Baltimore* (Baltimore: Norman, Remington, 1925), pp. 48–61 for a description of the medical social work carried out by the women physicians at the Evening Dispensary for Working Women. On the New England Hospital for Women and Children, see Regina Markell Morantz and Sue Zschoche, "Professionalism, Feminism, and Gender Roles: A Comparative Study of Nineteenth-Century Medical Therapeutics," *Journal of American History* 67 (December 1980): 568–88.

61. Garrigue to Blackwell, December 21, 1899, Blackwell Manuscripts, RWA; Jacobi, "Woman in Medicine," p. 171.

62. See U.S. Department of the Interior, *Report of the Commissioner of Education,* 1889–90, 1895–96, 1898–99, 1903 (Washington, D.C.: U.S. Government Printing Office).

63. *Alumnae Catalogue of the University of Michigan, 1837–1921* (Ann Arbor: University of Michigan Press, 1923).

64. Donald Fleming, *William H. Welch and the Rise of Modern Medicine* (Boston: Little, Brown, 1954), pp. 96–99; Thomas, *The Opening of Johns Hopkins Medical School to Women,* and Jacobi, "Woman in Medicine," p. 205.

65. The notorious exceptions were the Massachusetts Medical Society and the Montgomery County Medical Society in Pennsylvania, both of which put up dramatic resistance, only to succumb in the 1880s. See Walsh, *Doctors Wanted, No Women Need Apply,* pp. 159–65, and Jacobi, "Woman in Medicine," pp. 177–88.

66. Jacobi, "Woman in Medicine," pp. 189–96; Constance McGovern, "Predictable Failures; Women Psychiatrists and Their Patients, Pennsylvania 1880–1910" (Paper delivered at the Organization of American Historians' Convention, San Francisco, California, 1980).

67. Jacobi, "Woman in Medicine," pp. 202–4; Clara Marshall, *The Woman's Medical College of Pennsylvania: An Historical Outline* (Philadelphia, 1897), pp. 89–142, for a list of publications.

68. Cora B. Marrett, "On the Evolution of Women's Medical Societies," *Bulletin of the History of Medicine* 53 (Fall 1979): 434–48.

69. See *Transactions of the Alumnae Association of the Woman's Medical College of Pennsylvania* (Philadelphia, 1875–1921); Regina Markell Morantz, "Bertha Van Hoosen," in *Notable American Women: The Modern Period,* ed. B. Sicherman and C. Hurd Green, (Cambridge, Mass.; Harvard University Press, 1980), pp. 706–7.

70. See Walsh, *Doctors Wanted, No Women Need Apply,* pp. 178–267; William Chafe, *The American Woman* (New York: Oxford University Press, 1972), pp. 89–112; Barbara Harris, *Beyond Her Sphere, Women and the Professions in American History* (Westport, Conn.: Greenwood Press, 1978), pp. 95–126.

71. Chafe, *The American Woman,* p. 90; Walsh, *Doctors Wanted, No Women Need Apply,* p. 186.

72. Rosemary Stevens, *American Medicine and the Public Interest* (New Haven, Conn.: Yale University Press, 1971), pp. 55–73; David Rosner and Gerald Markowitz, "Doctors in Crisis: Medical Education and Medical Reform During the Progressive Era, 1895–1915," *American Quarterly* 25 (March 1973): 83–107.

73. See E. Richard Brown, *Rockefeller Medicine Men: Medicine and Capitalism in America* (Berkeley: University of California Press, 1979); Eliot Friedson, *Profession of Medicine* (New York: Dodd, Mead, 1970); Larson, *The Rise of Professionalism;* Burton J. Bledstein, *The Culture of Professionalism* (New York: W. W. Norton, 1978); Stevens, *American Medicine*; and Rosner and Markowitz, "Doctors in Crisis." It should be noted that these "revisionist" medical historians are taking part in a respectable and long-standing debate among American historians on the subject of how progressive and reformist was progressive reform. James G. Burrow has argued recently that the medical profession was in favor of social reform during the progressive era, but I would contend that the issue is still very much open to question. See James Burrow, *Organized Medicine in the Progressive Era* (Baltimore: Johns Hopkins University Press, 1977).

74. Stevens, *American Medicine,* pp. 58–68, 69.

75. Editorial, *Journal of the American Medical Association* 35 (August 1900): 501, quoted in Rosner and Markowitz, "Doctors in Crisis," p. 98. Emphasis added.

76. Stevens, *American Medicine,* p. 68; also Robert Hudson, "Abraham Flexner."

77. These three schools were The Woman's Medical College of Pennsylvania, The Woman's Medical College of Baltimore, and the New York Medical College for Women, a homeopathic institution. For the Philadelphia college's financial problems, see Gulielma Fell Alsop, *A History of the Woman's Medical College* (Philadelphia: J. B. Lippincott, 1950). Black medical schools suffered the same fate.

78. For a good discussion of discrimination see Walsh, *"Doctors Wanted, No Women Need Apply,* pp. 178–267, and Moldow, "The Gilded Age, Promise and Disillusionment," pp. 88–130, 163–90.

79. See Regina Markell Morantz, "Science vs. Art: The Medical Thought of Mary Putnam Jacobi and Elizabeth Blackwell" (Paper delivered at the American Association of the History of Medicine Conference, Boston, Massachusetts, May 1980).

80. See Morantz, "Women Physicians, Co-education, and the Struggle for Professional Standards."

81. For Blackwell's arguments see "The New York Infirmary and Medical College for Women," in *Transactions of the Alumnae Association of the Woman's Medical College of Pennsylvania, 1900,* pp. 76–80. For Flexner see Abraham Flexner, *Medical Education in the United States and Canada* (New York: The Carnegie Foundation, 1910), pp. 296, 178–79.

82. Carol Lopate, *Women in Medicine* (Baltimore: Johns Hopkins University Press, 1968), p. 17.

83. Walker to Van Hoosen, February 6, 1940, Van Hoosen Papers, MCP.

84. See Charles Rosenberg, "The Therapeutic Revolution: Medicine, Meaning, and Social Change in Nineteenth-Century America," *Perspectives in Biology and Medicine* 20 (Summer 1977): 485–506.

85. This description of modern therapeutics relies on Edmund D. Pellegrino, M.D., "From the Rational to the Radical: The Sociocultural Impact of Modern Therapeutics" in *The Therapeutic Revolution: Essays in the Social History of American Medicine*, ed. Morris Vogel and Charles Rosenberg (Philadelphia: University of Pennsylvania Press,

1979); and George L. Engel, "The Need for a New Medical Model: A Challenge for Biomedicine," *Science* 196 (April 1977): 129-35.

86. Stevens, *American Medicine*, pp. 77-97. Morris Vogel, "The Transformation of the American Hospital" in *Health Care in America*, ed. David Rosner and Susan Reverby (Philadelphia: Temple University Press, 1979), pp. 105-16.

87. Elizabeth Gregg, "The Tuberculosis Nurse under Municipal Direction," *Public Health Nursing Quarterly* 5 (October 1913): 16. I am indebted to Dr. Barbara Bates for this citation.

88. Eliza Mosher, "The Human in Medicine, Surgery and Nursing," *Woman's Medical Journal* 32 (May 1925): 117-19. See also Barringer, *Bowery*, p. 244, and Baker, *Fighting for Life*, p. 248.

89. Harding to Van Hoosen, May 6, 1930, Van Hoosen Papers, MCP.

90. L. Powers, H. Wiesenfelder, and R. C. Parmelee, "Practice Patterns of Men and Women Physicians," *Journal of Medical Education* 44 (January-June 1969): 481-91.

91. Walsh, *Doctors Wanted, No Women Need Apply*, p. 259.

92. See Adelaide Brown, M.D., *What Medicine Offered in 1888 and Now in 1938*, pamphlet reprinted from *Woman's City Club Magazine* (August 1938), Sophia Smith Collection; Hulda Thelander and Helen B. Weyrauch, "Women in Medicine," *Journal of the American Medical Woman's Association* 148 (February 1952): 531-34. For women's work with the Children's Bureau see Nancy P. Weiss, "Save the Children: A History of the Children's Bureau, 1903-1918" (Ph.D. diss., University of California, 1974) and the papers of Dr. Dorothy Reed Mendenhall, Sophia Smith Collection. Also Mabel Ulrich, "Men Are Queer That Way, Extracts From the Diary of an Apostate Woman Physician," *Scribner's Magazine* 93 (June 1933): 365-69.

93. See Josephine Baker, *Fighting for Life;* Alice Hamilton, *Exploring the Dangerous Trades* (Boston: Little, Brown, 1943); see also Ellen C. Potter Manuscripts, MCP; Gert Brieger, "Florence Sabin," *Notable American Women: The Modern Period*, pp. 614-16.

94. Rosner and Markowitz, "Doctors in Crisis," p. 89.

95. Statistics on the numbers of women graduate students are taken from the *Records of the Commissioner of Education*, 1894-95, 1910, 1915, 1918. Statistics on women welfare workers, "physicians and surgeons attendants," and "keepers of charitable and penal institutions" are taken from U.S., Bureau of Census, *U.S. Census of Population* (Washington: U.S. Government Printing Office, 1900, 1910, 1920).

96. Harris, *Beyond Her Sphere*, p. 101.

97. Henry F. May, *The End of American Innocence* (New York: A. A. Knopf, 1959); William L. O'Neill, *Divorce in the Progressive Era* (New Haven, Conn.: Yale University Press, 1967); James R. McGovern, "The American Woman's Pre-World War I Freedom in Manners and Morals," *Journal of American History* 55 (September 1968): 315-33; Regina Markell Morantz, "The Scientist as Sex Crusader: Alfred Kinsey and American Culture," *American Quarterly* 29 (Winter 1977): 563-89; Sheila M. Rothman, *Women's Proper Place* (New York: Basic Books, 1978); and John Burnham, "The Progressive Era Revolution in Attitudes Toward Sex," *Journal of American History* 59 (March 1973): 885-908.

98. Harris, *Beyond Her Sphere*, p. 134.

99. Joyce Antler, "Feminism as Life Process: The Life and Career of Lucy Sprague Mitchell," *Feminist Studies* 7 (Spring 1981): 134-57.

100. Ibid., p. 135; Frank Stricker, "Cookbooks and Law Books: The Hidden History

of the Career Woman in 20th-Century America," *Journal of Social History* 10 (Fall 1976): 1-19.

101. Mabel Gardner, M.D., to Catherine Macfarlane, M.D., February 4, 1952. Macfarlane Manuscripts, MCP.

102. See in this regard, Mabel Ulrich, "Men Are Queer That Way."

103. Lopate, *Women in Medicine,* pp. 193-95. C. Nadelson and M. Notman, "The Woman Physician," *Journal of Medical Education* 47 (March 1972): 176-83.

104. Kristine Mann, M.D., "Medical Women's Handicap," *Harper's Weekly* 58 (February 1914): 32; Editorials, "Women in Medicine," *Journal of American Medical Women's Association* 1 (April 1946): 93-95.

105. Arnold S. Relman, "Here Come the Women," *New England Journal of Medicine* 302 (May 1980): 1252-53.

106. Editorials, "What Women Want in Medicine Most—Power," *Medical News,* February 18, 1980; "Female Doctors Assess the Problems of Their Profession," *New York Times,* October 12, 1979.

107. Marilyn Heins, M.D., "Women Physicians," *Radcliffe Quarterly* (June, 1979): 11-14; Davis G. Johnson and Edwin B. Hutchins, "Doctor or Dropout? A Study of Medical Student Attrition," *Journal of Medical Education* 41 (December 1966): 1099-1269; Lopate, *Women in Medicine,* pp. 93-104.

108. For earlier studies, see Roscoe Dykman and John Stalniker, "Survey of Women Physicians Graduating from Medical Schools, 1925-40," *Journal of Medical Education* 32 (March 1957): 3-38; Florence Lowther and Helen R. Downes, "Women in Medicine," *Journal of the American Medical Association* 129 (October 1945): 512-14. For more recent figures see C. S. Shapiro et al., "Careers of Women Physicians: A Survey of Women Graduates from Seven Medical Schools, 1945-51," *Journal of Medical Education* 43 (July-December 1968): 1033-40; M. Rosenlund and F. Oski, "Women in Medicine," *Annals of Internal Medicine* 66 (May 1967): 1008-12; Carla A. Pullum "Women, Medicine and Misconceptions," *Journal of the American Medical Women's Association* 18 (July 1963): 563-65; M. Heins et al., "Productivity of Women Physicians," *Journal of the American Medical Association* 236 (October 1976): 1961-64; H. Westling-Wikstrand, M. Monk, and C. B. Thomas, "Some Characteristics Related to the Career Status of Women Physicians," *Johns Hopkins Medical Journal* 127 (November 1970): 273-86.

109. Heins et al., "Productivity."

110. Westling-Wikstrand et al., "Some Characteristics."

111. Lynne Davidson, "Choice by Constraint: The Selection and Function of Specialties among Women Physicians-in-Training," *Journal of Health Politics* 4 (Summer 1979): 200-19.

112. Marjorie Wilson and Amber Jones, "Career Patterns of Women in Medicine," in *Women in Medicine-1976. Report of a Macy Conference,* ed. Carolyn Speiler (New York: Josiah Macy Jr. Foundation, 1977), pp. 67-87; Carol Nadelson, "Women in Surgery," *Archives of Surgery* 102 (March 1971): 234-35; Jean W. Adams, "Patient Discrimination against Women Physicians," *Journal of the American Medical Women's Association* 32 (July 1977): 255-61; Edgar Engleman, "Attitudes Toward Women Physicians: A Study of 500 Clinic Patients," *Western Journal of Medicine* 120 (February 1974): 95-100; E. R. MacAnarney, "The Impact of Medical Women in United States Medical Schools," *Women in Medicine—1976,* pp. 9-65.

113. Carol Nadelson and Malka Notman, "Success or Failure: Women as Medical School Applicants," *Journal of the American Medical Women's Association* 29 (April 1974): 167–72.

114. Engel, "The Need for a New Medical Model."

115. Relman, "Here Come the Women."

116. Mary C. Howell, M.D., "A Women's Health School?" *Social Policy* 6 (September–October 1975): 50–53.

117. Howard M. Spiro, M.D., "Myths and Mirths—Women in Medicine," *New England Journal of Medicine* 292 (February 1975): 354–56.

PART I

HARVEST-TIME

1

Katharine Sturgis

PACESETTER IN PREVENTIVE MEDICINE

In 1935, Katharine Sturgis was awarded her medical degree by the Woman's Medical College of Pennsylvania, now the Medical College of Pennsylvania. She was thirty-eight years old and a divorcée with two young children. Her training had been interrupted by two years in a tuberculosis sanitarium, but despite her late start in medicine she has enjoyed a long and productive career as a researcher and specialist in diseases of the chest. In the face of misgivings about her inexperience, she was appointed Chief Editor of the Archives of Environmental Health *and succeeded in reviving the moribund journal. Over the years she has held high-level administrative positions in many organizations and has served as the first woman member of the Council of the National Institute of Environmental Health Sciences. After a number of years as Chairwoman of the Department of Community and Preventive Medicine at the Medical College of Pennsylvania, she now has retired with her third husband, who is also a physician.*

Katharine Sturgis (1921) at the age of 18 just prior to beginning premedical studies at the University of Pennsylvania, Walnut Lane Bridge, Philadelphia.

Childhood

I was born in Philadelphia in 1903, the seventh of eight children. I think that's a great advantage because, first of all, there's no opportunity to be spoiled in such a large family; in the second place, there was a great deal of independence. I had five older brothers; they were a very big influence in my life. My father was a prominent man, a marvelous man, and a community-oriented man. He had married my mother when she was seventeen, and amazingly she became community-oriented with all these children and whatnot.

Both my parents were Jewish. My father was born in Austro-Hungary. My mother was born in New York City, but she was the child of Hungarian parents, so their backgrounds were very compatible.

My father was in the private banking and steamship business. That was at the height of the immigration from Europe, and he spoke not only German and Hungarian, but I don't remember how many languages, and he spoke a number of dialects. So our home was very rich because there were all sorts of interesting experiences.

My father was a real Victorian gentleman. He had only completed *gymnasium* [equivalent to a high school education] abroad when he decided to come to America and make his way, but he was a perpetual student. When he came home from his office, which was after dinner except on Friday nights and Sundays at one o'clock—he went to his office Sunday mornings—he retreated to his marvelous library where he studied. He knew more chemistry than his sons who went to college. He was a brilliant man.

My father respected women very much. He was also amused by their foibles. He believed that woman's place was in the home. When my older sister wanted to go to Wellesley with her friends, he put his foot down, and she was a very good daughter and didn't rebel. Now, when I came along, I wanted to go to college to be premed—I was crazy about medicine—and Father didn't at all approve of this. He said to me, "If you married a poor man, you couldn't make a dress for yourself." I hated sewing. I went out and bought green and white checked gingham and white organdy and a pattern. I cut the material out and sewed it together. It took me two weeks—a very plain dress that buttoned down the back with a Peter Pan collar. I hadn't talked to my father, whom I adored, this whole two weeks, I was so furious. I put the dress on one morning, marched myself down the long dining-room table to the far end where Father sat at breakfast, and I said to him, "I made this dress." And he had a good sense of humor; he laughed and said, "If you want to go to college that badly, I'll have to let you go."

He was very formal, very strict, but he never lifted his hand. We all were so anxious to have his approval; that was our greatest goal. But every morning we would come down and walk the length of the dining room and shake hands with him, not kiss him. I was always dying to kiss—he had the most lovely pink skin on his cheeks—and as a little bit of a girl, I remember how I longed to kiss that pinky, soft skin but never had the nerve. I'd shake hands, and he would say, "Good morning Kath"—they called me "Kath"—and I'd say, "Good morning Father." And then, he would ask me a question, always: "Did you say your prayers?" And if I said "yes" rather shakily, he'd say, "Well, let's hear them again." Sometimes he'd look down at my shoes, and he'd say, "Dirty shoes are like a dirty face. They reflect your character. You go downstairs and shine your shoes." And I'd go down in the basement where there was a shoebox with one of those iron footrests, and I'd shine my shoes, come back up, and walk down for inspection, and he'd say, "That's better."

My mother, on the other hand, I perceived as a remote human being. I thought she was a social butterfly all through my childhood. I loved my nurse Katie; I had a marvelous Irish nurse who lived to be in her early nineties, and I adored her. I really loved her more than my mother. My mother knew that and was jealous of Katie.

My mother wore gorgeous clothes. She was a very handsome woman, and she had not only a woman who came and shampooed her hair and gave it a treatment every week, but when she went to the opera or something, she had a woman who came and dressed her hair. She had a woman give her a massage once a week. And I would be brought in to say goodnight to Mother—Katie always took me to say goodnight to her—and these various things would be going on. One of my clearest recollections is when I'd be brought in to say goodnight when Mother was going to the opera. I can see her sitting in her beautiful bedroom with a dressing room—you went through the dressing room, a large dressing room, before you approached the bedroom. Mother sat there in front of a beautiful bureau with a mirror—rosewood, I think it was—and Miss Nash was doing her hair, and I'd think, "Oh, isn't she gorgeous?" And I would go to kiss her, and she'd say, "Be careful, don't muss my dress"—or something like that. And I'd think, "Oh, isn't she a mess?" We didn't use that term in those days, but I'd think, "Oh, my mother is so vain." I never gave her credit for her tremendous administrative ability.

I only began to appreciate my mother after I was married and had children of my own, because she ran with such smoothness all her children, a house with thirty rooms, all the help, the laundress, the nurse, the marketing—we were totally unaware. And she was on a number of boards of social welfare organizations, and she gave musicals to raise money for them. She did a lot of charity work.

She also had some friends who were suffragettes. I was quite young—I can't remember the year when the suffragettes marched in Philadelphia—but the wife of the pediatrician we had then, Mrs. Henrietta Lowenberg, was a petite woman and very much of an active feminist. She marched in the parade, and Father just loved having her to dinner. He would gently bait her to get her to voice all her ideas. Now, at such times, the children were not supposed to interrupt the elders, so we sat and listened to all that, and I'm sure that women like Henrietta Lowenberg with their ideas must have had a subtle impact on me.

During World War I, there was a very wonderful Hungarian woman named Rosika Schwemmer who was a guest in our house. She persuaded Henry Ford to send a peace ship, you know, and I heard all that talk at our table. She was with us long enough to make a big impression on me.

When I wanted to study medicine, almost nobody I knew—no woman, no girl—had ever had any notion of studying medicine. The only woman I knew personally was Dr. Rose Hirschler, who was Chairman of the Department of Dermatology at the Woman's Medical College of Pennsylvania. She was a wonderful woman and part of my motivation to study medicine. I called her Posie, or Aunt Rose because her niece Dorothy was my closest friend in childhood. I also admired Dr. Steinbach, who was our general practitioner, a very loving, warm man. I think that he and Aunt Rose Hirschler were models for me. Dr. Steinbach made me feel better, and he was jolly, you know. When I could first, after a bad upset stomach, have something to eat, he'd say, "How about a little vanilla ice cream?" I thought he was fun. Money never entered my mind. Service appealed to me always. Dot Steifel and I joined the Band of Mercy [an organization for the humane treatment of animals], and I took care of sick animals in our area—jumping on the backs of wagons and putting the horses' prayer [a prayer from a horse to his driver beseeching kind treatment] on the front seat and reporting drivers who beat their horses. Also my concept of womanhood was and still is of giving—the Madonna with the baby at her breast. I thought medicine was giving, caring.

I think Aunt Rose was the only woman doctor role model I had. When I came back to Philadelphia after finishing my premed, my only idea was to go to Penn; all my connections were at Penn. But Penn wanted me to take another year because I had not had physiological chemistry. I went to my physician, who was a professor at Penn, Dr. David Reisman, and talked to him, and he said, "You're never going to do research, are you?" I said, "Oh, no. I want to be a general practitioner." Well, he said, "you go up on the hill to Woman's Medical. They'll train you to be a good general practitioner." So then, I remembered Posie, and went to see her. I said, "You know, I want to study medicine"; and she put her arm around me, and she said, "You come up to the College, dearie. That's the place for a girl who wants to study medicine."

My childhood was extremely happy. I was an awful tomboy. I used to race with Paul more than any of the others. In those days, we played hide-and-seek and lay, sheepie, lay, and Paul went with the toughest boys in our neighborhood. I jumped the fences, and I'd come home having lost my beautiful satin bow that Katie had tied on my golden hair, and my dress would be all dirty or maybe even torn, and she used to say, "I'll never make a lady out of you." But I didn't feel a bit bad. I wasn't interested in clothes. I wanted to go with the boys all the time.

I knew I was different from other girls. My two closest friends were Dot

Stiefel and a girl we called Sis Baum. Dot and Sis were first cousins, and the three of us played together a lot. Now, I had dolls, but I liked them in a casual kind of way; but Sis and Dot were mad about dolls. Sis and Dot would put tickets in the hands of their dolls for them to use at night while we were gone, and in the morning, they would tell me one doll spit up and another one wet its diaper. I would then get so disgusted with them and their silly prattle—because I knew from my brothers that there couldn't be anything like that—that I wouldn't see them sometimes for a month or two. I'd think, "Oh, I just can't play with those silly girls." So, I never bought their make-believe world. Yet, I was very imaginative but in a different way.

I decided on medicine very early. I guess when I was about twelve or thirteen, I thought I would like to be a nurse. But when I was thirteen or fourteen, I realized that nurses were taking their orders from doctors, and I decided, oh, no, I didn't want to be a nurse. I wanted to be the one who was at the top level. By the way, I think that's interesting because all my professional career I've had great difficulty finding women who really want to have the top-level responsibility. I never discussed this decision with anybody except Father. We were all taught to be individually responsible for our decisions.

My school years were marvelous. My father was on the Board of Education, and he believed in public schools. He was on the search committee for the new principal of William Penn High School—they had built this wonderful new building at Fifteenth and Wallace Streets—and they brought a man named William Lewis from Syracuse. Father thought he was a wonderful principal, and he wanted me to be under his influence, so I went to William Penn. And Father was absolutely right. This man was a man of great stature. He could communicate easily with teenagers; and the thing that he emphasized over and over was, "Consider yourself a committee of one. Doesn't matter what other people are doing; it's what *you're* doing." That sense of individual responsibility! He was only there two years when he was made the head of the state Department of Education, but he made a tremendous impact on me—so much so that when he left I felt the world had fallen apart. I wrote to him complaining about the new principal—that the school wasn't the same—and he took the time to answer me promptly. He said, "Katharine, you must realize that an institution is greater than any individual; you continue to give your loyalty to the school, if not to the principal."

I was very active in high school. I liked many things because the boys liked many things; so I interested myself in everything that the boys were interested in. I was very fortunate, I had several excellent women teachers.

First Marriage

I began my premedical course at Penn in 1922. But I met my first husband in 1921. I went to a debut. He blew into town and called the gal who was coming out, and she said, "Why don't you come? We can always use a stag." He saw me across the room. I was apparently a very luscious young gal, and he fell madly in love with me—very romantic. And for over a year he just pursued me. He had graduated from Penn in chemical engineering.

I eventually eloped with Arthur Guest, mostly because my family didn't like him. My brother Paul had told me, "He's not good enough for you." My mother forbade me to see him. But they misjudged me, because the best way to get me interested in a cause was to make it appear that somebody was ill-treated. And he *was* ill-treated.

Arthur knew Penn well. I was taking chemistry under one of his classmates; he came to the lab and called me out and said, "We can meet at the B & O station when your classes are over." So I would walk across the bridge, and we met at the old B & O station and sat and talked. This went on for two weeks, when I said to him "I am not deceitful; I can't live this way. I love my family, and I'm not going to see you anymore." Well, he said, "We can get married." Well, I had never thought of that. I said, "Well, how could we do that?" He said, "Look, you meet me at Broad Street station tomorrow morning at eight o'clock, and we'll go down to Elkton and be married." I said, "All right." Well, we only stayed overnight in Wilmington, and then the next morning I said, "I have to get back for class." You see, I have a strong sense of responsibility. So when I walked into the amphitheatre at the old Harrison lab—I was the only girl in the class—the boys all yelled, "Three cheers for the golden-haired coed." I thought, "What is all this?" There had been headlines in the front page of the newspaper—"Golden-Haired Coed Elopes to Elkton." Well, how I got through the day, I don't know. My family was furious. They didn't want me to come home. I called, and they said, "No, you're not welcome." And of course, this was terrible to me.

At first Arthur was working, but he lost his job. I guess it must have been Prohibition days; he was the chemist at Publicker Company, and it seems that they were making alcohol without proper permission. I finished my first year and won a fellowship to Mount Desert Island, to the Marine Biological Laboratory. I was dying to take it, but we didn't have the money for the trip or my keep up there. I wouldn't ask for help from my family. I was very proud; I thought that I'd made my bed and had to lie in it. So we went to live with Arthur's parents.

At the corner of their street, I noticed a sign that said, "Thirty-day Business College." I thought, "Why should I waste the summer? I'll go there, and I'll work all summer. I'll work a month or six weeks to earn some money. So I went up there, and then I answered an ad for a part-time secretary to the Vice-President of the Charles B. Walton Company, Tanners, down in the leather district. I worked most of the summer there, and then came the time when I ought to have been going back to college. Arthur still didn't have a job. I figured it was absolutely out of the question. So I thought, "Well, I ought to have a full-time job, then." I went to John Wanamaker's and was interviewed and got a job as secretary to one of their big buyers. So I worked at Wanamaker's. Before long my husband was working again. But I never gave medicine another thought. I have always accepted life's blows. I feel that I was so secure emotionally from the marvelous childhood I had that I just adjusted to whatever circumstances I found myself in.

In those early years I was very happy. I became a real housewife. My mother-in-law was teaching me how to keep house. I never had done anything at home—never even had made a bed! I worked full time for a while. Then I decided, "Well, now, I'm going to be a housewife, and we'll want children. I don't know a thing about rearing children; I ought to go to normal school and learn." By that time I had reconciled with my family, so I talked to Father about it; he said, "That's an excellent idea. I will talk with Dr. Baker, the principal of the normal school, and arrange it." And he arranged it.

I rode the trolley to normal school. After a while I would become carsick. Finally, I went to my doctor, and he said, "You're going to have a baby." And I said, "We can't have a baby yet. I've got to finish this year of normal school." He said, "You can't go on at normal school. These long rides are not good for you. You may lose the baby."

Again I was terribly disappointed, but these were the facts. The doctor said there was nothing to do about it, so I had to accept it. So I went in to see Dr. Baker, the principal, to return the textbooks, and he, being a very Victorian man, blushed scarlet and couldn't get me out of his office fast enough.

When Arthur was born, I was just crazy about him; and like every mother with her first baby, I was terribly apprehensive about him. We decided that a row house was no place to raise a child and that we would buy a detached house further out in the country. Arthur was working with Western Electric then. So that's what we did.

I was really quite happy. We had a lovely house, very airy. I used to wheel the baby to the end of the street where there was a big farm; then, I'd carry him and put a blanket out and lay him on the blanket to kick and play while I picked wildflowers.

But it didn't last. For a number of reasons, we didn't stay in the country but bought an old three-story brownstone that had been made into three apartments. We took the dark, narrow first floor. Then, in the spring of 1932, Arthur experienced business reverses. So I got out my old books and brushed up on this funny shorthand. The Women's University Club had a notice on their bulletin board that the Department of Surgery at Penn's University Hospital was looking for a secretary to cover a vacation. I was crazy about medicine, so that suited me fine. Well, that was another step toward the beginning of the end, because when I was finished that two weeks, Rav [Isidor Ravdin, M.D., a prominent surgeon at the University of Pennsylvania and Chairman of the Department of Surgery from 1944–1959], who was just a young man then, said to me, "How have you liked this job?" I said, "I've loved it"—you know, the surgeons would come right out of the OR and dictate to me. And I said, "I'm sorry it's going to end." He said, "It's not going to end. I've just been made J. William White Professor of Research Surgery, and I'm entitled to a secretary, and you're going to be my secretary." So I went over to the medical school with Rav, and if he was shorthanded I'd go in the OR and hold retractors! I loved it.

I had a marvelous black housekeeper, Loretta, gentle-voiced, full of wisdom, whom the children loved and who loved the children. She was a very competent cook—not such a good cleaner, but way back then I had the sense to realize you can't get everything. And they did not suffer at all from that experience because the children knew I loved them and Loretta loved them.

But when Arthur began to get on his feet financially, he wanted me to quit work. I told Rav I would quit, and Rav said, "Well, you've got to train somebody and supervise. I can't do without you, you're too important." I didn't really want to quit. I loved being around the medical staff. So I trained a secretary, but I'd go out two or three days a week and was very happy with the arrangement.

Meanwhile, a friend of Arthur's had broken down with TB without knowing it beforehand, so Arthur thought he ought to have a chest x-ray; and they found a small lesion. I didn't know anybody who ever had had TB except one girl-hood friend who had died from it, so I thought this was the end of the world. I felt terrible for him; I felt very guilty that I hadn't stayed home. I prayed to the Lord; I said, "I've been wrong. Please make him well, and I'll do everything." I really went through a terrible, soul-searching experience. So I took the children down to my sister's seashore place at Longport while I got Arthur ready and drove him up to Saranac Lake to enter Trudeau Sanatorium.

Well, the story is, Arthur fell in love with a fellow patient. That was a very common story. I decided I might as well give him a divorce. It was very rough. I really didn't cope very well. When it was all over, I talked to the children, who were by then, I think, eight and five and a half, something like that, and I said, "Now, what should we do? I could go take a secretarial job again, or we could go away to some college town, where I could pick up the pieces and try to finish premed and medical school and help other people not to go through what's happened to us." I thought at the time that the whole thing was due to the TB, but in retrospect I can see it was building up. So both children said right away, "Oh, study medicine and keep other people well." So I wrote up to Penn State, which I knew nothing about, and got myself enrolled there and took an apartment, sight unseen, and we moved up to Penn State. I spent a year at Penn State finishing my premedical course work, which had been interrupted when I married Arthur.

Medical School

I had never thought of going anywhere but Penn. But, as I said before, Penn wanted me to take another year of premedical course work, and I was already thirty-two—it was of the utmost importance to get going. I was too proud to borrow money from my family. I was getting $150 a month from Arthur Guest for the support of the children. Aunt Rose had urged me to come to Woman's Medical. But it was necessary to convince myself as well as the Faculty at the Woman's Medical that I could do this. At my first interview with Dean Martha Tracy and the Professor and Chairman of the Department of Surgery, John Stewart Rodman, Professor Rodman said, "Why does a woman with two children want to study medicine?" I explained to him that my husband had fallen in love with another woman and that it was necessary for me to make my way in the world, that I had loved medicine and had been premed before, and that the children were also interested in my doing this rather than just taking a job. Martha Tracy's main discussion was to quiz me on what I fed my children and to caution me that she didn't think they were getting enough protein. She had been the Professor of Preventive Medicine and was a sterling if somewhat rigid woman. So I started medical school in the fall of 1935.

Now, when I came to Woman's Medical, I felt no difference in the way the Faculty treated me and the way they treated others. Marion Fay [Marion Fay, Ph.D., later Dean and President of Woman's Medical College of Pennsylvania] had just come there and was Professor of Biochemistry, and she was crazy about little boys. You know, she'd never married nor had any children. She encouraged Arthur [Dr. Sturgis' son] to come to the chemistry laboratory on his way home—he was already deeply interested in geology and minerology. Marion gave him pour plates to test his specimens on. And Dr. Hartwig Kuhlenbeck [Hartwig Kuhlenbeck, M.D., Ph.D., Emeritus Professor of Anatomy, Medical College of Pennsylvania], the Chairman of the Department of Anatomy, had also just come to Woman's Medical. There had been a big upheaval; the grade A status of the school had been threatened, so all these new chairmen of departments had been brought in; Dr. Kuhlenbeck was a real "Herr Professor." My classmates were wonderful. They insisted on my becoming President of the class, and they hung out, a great many of them, at my little house that I rented for thirty dollars a month on Vaux Street, right near the school.

The only terrible experience that I had—the very first day we went to anatomy—was when Dr. Kuhlenbeck instructed us to go and get our instruments and one of three or four anatomy books he suggested. It never occurred to me that I could have gone to the bookshop and charged them. I had five cents left and was waiting for the $150 monthly check. I had blown everything I had on the deposit on the little house, and I didn't have any money to buy the things for anatomy. I thought, "Oh, here I am. I paid the deposit on half my tuition and everything, and I can't start." I had noticed some phone booths at Jimmy Buchanan's, a pharmacy at the corner of Vaux Street and Indian Queen Lane. Very dejectedly, I walked down there and went in the booth and dialed Aunt Rose Hirschler. Her nurse answered the phone, and I said, "Is Dr. Hirschler in?" I thought, "If she isn't in, I'll die."

So Posie came to the phone with her lovely, warm, supportive voice, and I said, "Aunt Rose, do you still have your anatomy book and your dissecting instruments?" She at once understood what had happened, and she said, "Yes, of course, I have them. I'll get them to you tonight." So I marched back up and said to Dr. Kuhlenbeck, "Will it be all right if I have mine tomorrow?" And he said, "Certainly; use your partner's." And Aunt Rose had undoubtedly gone out and bought a new set of dissecting instruments—she didn't have her old ones. But she sent me her old anatomy book which I wish I'd kept—somehow in the various movings, it got lost. She had hand-colored all that old, old Gray's *Anatomy*, you know. Subsequently, I bought a new book.

In some ways, the atmosphere at Woman's Medical was warm and accepting. And yet, mixed with the warmth were some rather rigid attitudes. For example, there was overt disapproval of marriage and pregnancy during medical training. You were supposed to drop out. I remember a classmate of mine, Dr. Flora— well, she was Flora Herman then; she's now Dr. Flora Herman Biele, a psychiatrist. But when she got married, in her senior year as I recall, she wore a wedding ring. Somehow the word got to the Dean, who sent for Flora—and Flora's mother was a graduate of Woman's Medical College, so they had to treat her a little differently—and the Dean said, "What does that ring mean?" Flora said, "I got married—to a doctor," and Dr. Tracy said to her, "Well, you see that you don't become pregnant." Nevertheless, I think that they accepted me despite my having children. The children were interesting children, so they didn't mind their showing up on the scene once in awhile, but I was never given one iota of extra consideration, and I think that's one reason why I ultimately broke down with TB. I had to do everything everybody else did. There was no quarter shown me. For instance, I got a very serious pnuemonia in my second year. I remember I was taking physiology with one of the best teachers I ever had, Dr. Esther Greisheimer. I was hospitalized and given sulfapyridine, one of the first sulfas, and developed a heliotrope color—they brought everybody in to see. My mother took me down to her apartment afterward to recuperate. But when I came back, I had to make up every little lab exercise and everything, in addition to keeping up with the running work and running the house. A friend of mine who was a student at Penn, one of the boys, had been much more ill than I, been out longer, and all they said to him was, "If you have trouble keeping up, if you feel that you need some coaching in what you missed, let us know and we'll help you."

I think this atmosphere prevailed because women physicians were second-rate in the eyes of many people, and especially in their male colleagues' eyes, from the time Woman's Medical was started; so the Faculty was dedicated to the idea that you jolly well had to be better than the boys. But they didn't use judgment. They needed to prove themselves because of this sense of inferiority. I believe for this reason Woman's Medical was tough scholastically and more rigid than some of the other medical schools. The students were exceptionally highly motivated. Most of them told me confidentially that they did not want to come to

Woman's Medical; it was not their first choice—only the missionary students had it as their first choice—but they wanted to study medicine so badly that where they studied didn't matter.

It was very hard to be accepted other places, and Woman's Medical played a very important role in opening the doors for such women—like me, being an older woman with two children, and there were other girls who were older who had the same problems. And then, there were the kind that were bobby-soxers who were late bloomers that the men thought were just immature and wouldn't take a chance on.

But to be honest, I think I would have done much better if I had gone to Penn because I was used to men and a man's world. I don't think I would have been as much of a leader at Penn as I was at Woman's Medical, but I think I would have had sounder training with less emphasis on making the grades. I think exposure to a much brighter faculty would have been more stimulating—although we had some excellent faculty. But they were comparatively rigid, almost all of them, until we got to the clinical years.

For me, it was not a positive experience having women doctors as role models because my whole first year I had no confidence in any of them, and when I ran into medical problems, I called Rav at Penn. I think I also might have been a little unsure as to whether women could be as good doctors as men. I remember the first woman doctor whom I consulted, Dr. Emily Van Loon, who was head of ear, nose, and throat and bronchoesophagology. I had had a terrible lot of sinusitis all my life and had something like twenty-two operations and really was miserable most of the time with this—certainly from fall until late spring. Dr. Sarah Morris, who was in charge of student health, asked me to go to see Dr. Van Loon; she wanted an opinion. With considerable misgiving I went to see her and was at once impressed by her dexterity because I was pretty much of an expert; I had been to a number of ear, nose, and throat specialists. She used a whole method of treatment that had never been used on me, which was very successful. So that first experience with a woman—I mean, she really cleaned up my sinusitis. I didn't expect to be impressed, but from then on, I began to realize that there were some excellent women physicians.

I do think that the women who went to Woman's Medical when I did had more of a love of people, were more maternal, than most of the men. I think with the men it was a vocation that they chose intellectually, but I felt that the men students that I knew didn't find in medicine the emotional appeal that the women did. Now, I did not see it in the few women that I knew who went to Penn, for instance. One of my premed classmates, Genevra Ziegler, went to Penn, and I felt she was more like the boys. It could be that that's because she was surrounded by them, but she didn't voice her feelings. Another difference that I noticed between women clinicians and men is that women concern themselves with more detail than men do. I find that very satisfying. At the time I went to medical school, it was unusual, for example, for a doctor to go into your vitamin intake, and yet Martha Tracy was worried about my children's protein intake at my interview! The women doctors realized the importance of nutrition way before any of the men I know. No one of the men physicians that I or any of my big family had, had ever talked about anything more than the diet while you were ill. So I think that women in that way concern themselves with every detail that might contribute and prevent; I think they were more preventive-oriented.

I didn't have child-care arrangements during medical school. The children were on their own. I remember the first Saturday that I had to go to class in medical school. I thought I ought to do something about Nancy, because she was so young. She must have been only seven or eight. Anyhow, she was interested in artistic things, so I found out that the then School of Industrial Art, which is now the Museum School of Art, had a Saturday morning class for children. But I couldn't take her. With great trepidation, I coached her and gave her the money to take the trolley. She had to walk from our place down Vaux Street to Midvale and take the trolley and get off that trolley and take the one that went over Wayne Avenue and landed her at Broad and Erie; then, she had to go down in the subway and take the subway to Broad and Pine. I gave her the money for tuition and told her she'd have to buy paper. I worried all morning. I could hardly wait to get home; our class lasted until one. I got home, and she was happily drawing on her paper—Nancy had done it all.

In my third year in medical school, I was overworking terribly. I didn't have enough money, so I was teaching Sunday School for ten dollars a week, I was running the bookshop—doing anything extra to earn a few dollars to make things a little better for the children. Now, somebody should have said, ''How much do you need? We'll make you a loan''—but I didn't ask. I always have operated on this thesis, which I drank, not with my mother's milk, but with my father's philosophy, that you are responsible for yourself. But the problem was, I broke down with TB.

That was the most terrible thing I ever went through, because of the children. We had struggled so together, and we were very happy, terribly happy. Arthur would come home from junior high school, dragging a little crate, a wooden crate that he'd seen, and break it up and pile the wood up because we were so broke sometimes—we once had the electricity turned off—and sometimes we ran out of coal, so we'd have the wood with which we could make a roaring wood fire in the furnace. And we really took it as a joke. We loved it. We had candlelight; we said, ''It's beautiful.'' We were completely happy, but when I developed TB, we were helpless. I knew I had to go to bed, that's all I knew, and I went right to bed. Arthur Guest took the children.

So I spent a year at the Trudeau Sanatorium in Saranac Lake, but I didn't get any better; I got worse. Then my brother, Sam, who was on the board of Eagleville Sanatorium, moved me down to Philadelphia again. Eagleville had an

entirely different atmosphere—you jolly well better get well or get out of there if
you didn't cooperate. Suddenly, I relaxed because here was somebody who was
telling me what I was to do.

I spent a year at Eagleville; I was very lucky. Dr. A. J. Cohen was the first one
to give pneumothorax* in Philadelphia; he had gone to Germany and learned the
technique. He induced a right pneumothorax as part of my therapy. I am reasonably certain that without it I would have gone on downhill, because I just
don't heal. But by the summer of 1940, I was asking to come back to Woman's
Medical half time, so that I could go to bed half the day.

They gave me a very rough time about it. Again, I feel that many of the
women on the Faculty were extremely rigid and myopic and not loving people.
Catharine Macfarlane, on the other hand, was a woman of vision. She was acting
Dean at the time I came back. A lot of people felt she was an old battle-axe, but I
didn't. I think she was responsible for letting me come back. She was one of the
biggest women; she was not petty. She was a woman of action. Granted, she had
a hot temper, but hot tempers in surgeons were fashionable in those days, and she
had had a little more struggle to get where she got than, for instance, I have had. I
never had any struggle once I graduated, and I think she did. But I was a great
admirer of Macfarlane's.

Nobody was close to Catharine Macfarlane. That was one of the things from
which she suffered. When she was dying, her doctor called me and said, "Do
you know that Kitty Mac is in bad shape?" I said, "No, I heard she was in the
hospital." He said, "She's in bad shape. I think that if you want to see her,
you'd better come in." Sam and I went in, and she looked up—I always called
her Kitty Mac, but she always called me "Doctor"—and she said, "Doctor, did
you know that I wrote my autobiography?" I said, "I heard you did." "Well,"
she said, "I can't get anybody to publish it." I said, "I'm not a bit surprised."
She said, "Why?" I said, "You probably made yourself into a benign, nice, old
lady, and you're not. You're full of fire and vinegar."

Internship

Anyway, thanks to Macfarlane I finished medical school and went to intern at
the Woman's Medical Hospital. All my life I'd wanted to intern at Philadelphia
General, but I felt the work would be too hard, and I didn't want to break down
again. After all I'd been through, I felt that my own school would take better care
of me than a strange place. I thought, "They know what I've been through here
at WMC. They'll take care of me." But I was wrong.

The first weekend I was put on the heaviest schedule you can imagine; I didn't
have my clothes off from Friday until Monday. It wasn't very long before I came

---

*Injection of air into the pleural space, used in the treatment of tuberculosis to collapse the
involved lung.

down with pneumonia in my good lung and darned near died—was critical for about four days. Then, I said, "I just can't work this hard." I had to beg the Medical Director of the hospital to let me stay on an extra six months but take me off night call every other night; I had to get some sleep. My internship year made me very sour about WMC.

During that first weekend as an intern, I had a very painful introduction to being a doctor. I was very fatigued. I had a pneumothorax, and I was still not really in robust health. A little girl was brought in from the housing project across the street from the hospital; she was convulsing and was unconscious. She was just a little bit older, maybe a year older, than my own daughter—a beautiful little girl. And I worked on that child so hard. . . . It was a Tennessee family that had come up here—the father got a job at Midvale Steel—and in order for the little girl to be admitted to the public school system, she had to be vaccinated. Well, it turned out ultimately that what she had was postvaccinal encephalitis, which is very rare. She died of it. And as she was dying, I was unable—I had to run behind the screen intermittently because I was so heartbroken—I realized I was losing her. I'd had every consultant I could lay my hands on. We'd done everything we could, and I couldn't save her.

Of course, in a way it was a very good first experience, because it certainly showed the inadequacy of medicine. The parents decided to return to Tennessee because they had a younger son and they were not about to have him vaccinated; and I didn't blame them. But that was one of the most terrible experiences I had during my career, especially as an intern; because this child had been playing hide-and-seek, and when she didn't show up, the other children found her convulsing where she was hiding and brought her in. She lived about maybe twenty-four or thirty hours with us doing everything that we could think of for her. We could not find out what was wrong until later on. I was very emotional about that, though I didn't show it too much to the mother.

Later on, I was able to control my emotions, but I never tried to create a distance with patients. I always tried to achieve closeness, because I feel that a sick patient needs to know that his or her physician cares very much.

I learned some hard lessons that year. Despite the difficulties, however, I was doing very well professionally. I had gone and talked it over with A. J. Cohen; I was hoping he'd offer me a residency at Eagleville. But he said to me, "You're entering a dying field. TB's going to be cleaned up within the next few years." Well, he didn't see that emphysema and lung cancer were increasing. It was quite a while before TB problems lessened, and there's still a TB problem. At any rate, A. J. didn't offer me anything. I didn't realize then—I did later—that he really loved me, and he was giving me his soundest advice.

Instead, I had this fascinating experience: I had done a research project my senior year. Each senior at the time I was at medical school was required to do a piece of original research in preventive medicine. Dr. Sarah I. Morris, a very able woman, worked very hard with us on these papers. I was deeply interested in TB patients, so I studied the ultimate fate of several hundred patients discharged back to the city of Philadelphia from state tuberculosis sanatoria. Dr. David Cooper had been Director of Tuberculosis Control at that time and was amazed at my work. So he called me while I was interning and said, ''Have you any plans for when you finish your internship?'' I said, ''No.'' He said, ''How would you like to come with me and become my associate?'' Well, I was thrilled to pieces because he was a professor at Penn, one of the finest.

But I was scared to death of him at that time because he was quite difficult in many ways. And I said, ''I'd love it, but I've about decided to go into chest disease, and I feel I need some more training.'' He said, ''Have you thought where you'd go?'' Well, what I had done was look through the JAMA [*Journal of the American Medical Association*] issue that lists all the residencies, and the only one that paid anything—$5,000 a year—was Herman Kiefer Hospital in Detroit. I thought, ''If it's any good and it pays, that's for me,'' because my family had paid all the bills connected with my illness and I wanted to pay them back. So I said, ''Well, I was thinking about Herman Kiefer.'' He said, ''You couldn't do better. I'll write you a letter of recommendation.''

Residency

My experience at Herman Kiefer was marvelous. It was a complete antidote for the years I'd spent at the college, Woman's Medical. The head of the tuberculosis service, who was my chief, sent for me the first week I was there and said to me, ''What the hell is wrong with you? Don't you know what a good doctor you are? You call me and ask for permission to give an aspirin. Now, you go practice the good medicine that you practice, and stop asking for permission. . . .'' You see, I had always, up until I went to Woman's Medical, had tremendous self-confidence. At Woman's Medical, you were treated like a child. Everything was checked and double-checked, and you were required to fulfill every minor item. I was always the person that did ten times more than I had to do, you know. Over the years it beat me down, and what with the TB experience and parting with the children, I really had lost the superb self-confidence I had originally had. At Herman Kiefer I regained it.

There was one other woman resident at Herman Kiefer when I was there; the rest were men. I never looked into that because, as I tried to point out, I never looked at people as men or women or black or white. In our home we had black guests at the dinner table as well as white, and I never thought of a person as a woman, or is she reacting as a woman?

Now, the other woman who was there was black, but very, very light. Her name was Maureen Weaver; she was a Rockefeller Fellow, a brilliant woman. I remember practically the first day I was on duty, we had a chest conference, and afterwards she said to me, ''Let's go to dinner together''; and I said, ''Fine.'' She came to my office; I had charge of the men on the third floor—somehow I was always thrown more with men than women—and Maureen came and said, "Are you ready to go?" I said, "Yes." And she said, "Let's go to that wonderful Swedish restaurant." I said, "Where is it?" She said, "I don't know." I said, "I'll ask Paul Chapman"—he was our chief. So we went to his office, and he tried to discourage us. He said, "It's terribly expensive there. Are you sure you can afford it?" We went there, and she said to me, "This is a wonderful experience for me because you're so fair that with you I can pass." Afterward, Paul Chapman said, "I had a fit at your going out with a Negro woman to an elegant Detroit restaurant right after the race riots." They had just had race riots. So I was introduced through Maureen to a lot of Negro problems, black problems—we weren't calling them black then—that I would never otherwise have encountered. It was a very interesting experience.

Research, Preventive Medicine

After my year's residency at Herman Kiefer, I hoped very much that Paul Chapman would ask me to stay on, but he didn't. Instead, I received a phone call from Washington saying, "I'm calling for Dr. Hilleboe." Dr. Herman Hilleboe at that time was head of tuberculosis control for the United States Public Health Service and looked up to as a brilliant up-and-coming physician. I was very flabbergasted at this phone call from Hilleboe, who I didn't think knew I was alive. The essence of the phone call was: you are going to receive an invitation to go back to Philadelphia and head the mass chest x-ray survey there, and Dr. Hilleboe wants you to accept it. I thought it was strange. I went to Paul Chapman and asked his opinion. He said, "I think it's a mistake for a physician ever to lay down his stethoscope"—but he never said that he would like me to stay. In later years, it turned out that he fully had expected me to stay on and was very disappointed that I even considered going to Philadelphia; but he was rather shy and felt I apparently didn't want to stay. We've been lifelong friends since. Anyway, I was very disposed to take the job. And the men who interviewed me were the men I'd looked up to with great awe: Eugene Pendergrass, Ed Chamberlain, Dave Cooper, the top physicians, internists, and radiologists in the city here. They offered me—I think it was $4,000 a year, with permission to do a little teaching on the side at Woman's Medical, where I thought I would like to teach. Even though it was less money than I'd been earning at Herman Keifer, I thought the opportunity to return to Philadelphia was great. That's how I came back.

At first, my interest, of course, centered on tuberculosis and tuberculosis control. While I was a resident at Kiefer, in my "spare time," I did a study in Detroit of tuberculosis patients, similar to my senior thesis. Then, Dave Cooper, who had become my closest colleague as the years went on, and I did a study of the relationship between diabetes and TB. I had noticed cancer cases as I followed cases that I thought were TB; that began my interest in lung cancer. As I got more and more deeply interested in lung cancer, we started our big Philadelphia Pulmonary Neoplasm Research Project.

My interest in environmental issues followed logically. From our father and our mother all eight children had a tremendous interest in the good of human beings and in community affairs. Every one of us became involved very deeply in community activities. One of the ways I made the decision to accept this job with the mass chest x-ray surveys was the realization that, however devotedly I worked on my patients at Herman Kiefer, as soon as one was discharged there was another one to take the bed. I began to come to the realization that prevention was the answer, that curative medicine was very inadequate. I took Paul Chapman's admonition not to lay down my stethoscope; that's why I continued in clinical medicine as well as with the mass chest x-ray surveys. But I was constantly thinking of the implications for the community for people's welfare, and that's how I got interested in occupational medicine.

Incidentally, when I went into preventive medicine I suddenly became aware that this was a very unpopular subject. Medical students are too immature to respect anybody who can't make with the stethoscope. So I think the Department of Preventive Medicine was absolutely the lowest department in terms of respect when I came in as chairman at Woman's Medical. I don't think I fully succeeded in raising the interest in preventive medicine that I had hoped to, largely because I wasn't allowed to do the innovative things that I think would have commanded students' interest. But I do think that I tried very hard to dramatize and to give clinical orientation to all the principles of preventive medicine.

Part of the problem with the lack of student interest in this field lies with the medical school admissions policy. Often, the wrong people are chosen. Too much emphasis is placed on scientific ability rather than on a well-rounded human being. And I certainly don't disagree with the fact that it's impossible to go through medical school without scientific ability, but I don't think you have to have all "A" students in the sciences, and I don't think the MCAT [Medical College Admission Test] scores are the last word. I have seen too many people who scored very high in every way all through medical school who, in my opinion, were not fit to be trusted with a human being. They had too little value or understanding of people.

Interestingly enough, I think women have always been concerned with the preventive aspects of living. In other words, come hell or high water, if you're a housewife, the meals have to be prepared, the beds have to be made, the baby's diaper has to be changed, and so on. Women have been responsible for the mechanics of living, many of which are concerned with prevention. Pediatrics has been, I guess, the first and the outstanding example of preventive medicine, with the periodic well-child conference. And yet, there are really brilliant men in the field, like Allan Gregg whom I had the joy of meeting in 1952, very early in my career. I didn't know who he was, so I had a very close friendship with him for a week; I would have been petrified if I had known he was Vice-President of the Rockefeller Foundation. He was the first one who had an enormous impact on me in my new field of preventive medicine because of a remark he made as we walked together to a meeting. He said, "You people in preventive medicine are responsible for the overpopulation of the world, and you jolly well better take the steps that are going to solve some of these problems." That was the first time I ever heard of the population explosion, and it was as though the ground gave way under my feet and a chasm opened. I thought, "My God! What a field I've gone into. The whole world is involved here." It shook me up terrifically.

That was at the Colorado Conference of the Professors of Preventive Medicine. At the end of that conference, in the summary session, everybody was saying, "Why doesn't anybody love us? What's the matter with us?" and then, finally—this is when I found out who Allan Gregg was—John Hubbard [John P. Hubbard, M.D., George S. Pepper Professor of Public Health and Preventive Medicine, University of Pennsylvania School of Medicine] turned to him and said, "Dr. Gregg, would you have a few words to say?" Allan Gregg got up, and the essence of what he said was, "You don't understand what your problems are to begin with." And he made a very picturesque talk about when the glaciers had made all these mounds in northern Michigan, and some people thought they were Indian mounds and various things and it took somebody with real wisdom to realize that they had been carved out by glaciers. He practically said, "You people are too myopic."

So then, again, my self-confidence returned, because that's what I felt. I thought, "If I had the courage I'd get up and say, "Nobody loves you because you don't have the goods to deliver. You're worrying about what people think about you instead of realizing this crisis requires preventive medicine." So when Gregg got up and talked like that, I thought, "I can forget all those great names in preventive medicine. They don't know any more than I know." So that rid me of my inferiority complex in preventive medicine.

Unfortunately, neither our profession nor the public has yet recognized the fact that we will never have enough clinicians for the sick unless we turn off the parade of illness. The public has glimpsed this, and they're fed up with illness. They're fed up with impulsive starts and stops, like the swine flu vaccine campaign. But there's a lack of sustained interest. There's too much faddism in medicine, as in women's clothes. There is a great need for sober, deliberate thinking through. We need to recognize that there is often a necessity to make decisions before all the facts are in. Asbestos is currently a good example of this dilemma.

Teaching

In 1945 when I returned to Philadelphia, I reaffiliated myself with Woman's Medical. I also taught at the graduate school at Penn. I came back to Woman's Medical with mixed feelings, but I always felt this was my alma mater. I also loved Marion Fay very deeply. I felt she was a brilliant teacher, though one of the few "C's" I got in medical school was in biochemistry. But I felt that was all I deserved; I was not a brilliant chemist. I couldn't think chemically, and I still can't. So I never held that against Marion. It was when Marion became Dean that she got after me to take the chair of preventive medicine. I said, "I don't know anything about preventive medicine." She said, "Find out." So I decided to go down to Johns Hopkins. I took that year for my master's degree in two parts: the first was in the fall of 1952, and the second was the spring of 1954.

As I look back, I never really was completely at home at Woman's Medical because I was a crusader, a pioneer, and my wings were clipped. I was always more comfortable with the men at Penn. They were of greater scholastic and intellectual stature than the men at Woman's Medical. At Woman's Medical I had all kinds of ideas, and nobody to back me up. Nevertheless, the teaching remained important to me. I feel teaching is your immortality, the immortality of a physician. Patients go on and die, but the fires you light in students go on forever. I've had a half dozen or more students whom I've had the joy of influencing. To me, that's my professional immortality.

Second Marriage

I had met Joe at Eagleville where, following pneumonia, his internist saw in his x-ray evidence of old TB. He'd had a serious pneumonia. So the internist had him see Dr. Lou Cohen, the brother of my doctor, A. J., and Lou said, "I think you'd be very smart to spend a month or six weeks at Eagleville, where we can study your sputum and make sure the pneumonia didn't light up your old TB." Joe was an up-patient all the time, and he was interested in birds; he saw a beautiful bird and asked everybody what it was—nobody knew. Somebody said, "There's a medical student up in the hospital building who is interested in birds and has lots of books on birds with her. Maybe she'll know." And that's how Joe and I met. It was a rosebreasted grosbeak. It was a very lovely way to meet.

Joe fell madly in love with me, and for four years, he pursued me. I was terribly worried about the children, so I wouldn't marry him. When I went to Detroit on my residency, the war had come along, and my son had been drafted—he had wanted to enlist, but he wouldn't because he was saving money for his sister to go to college—so he went into the air force and was at Officer Training School. He wrote Joe a letter in which he said he was going overseas soon and he knew how much Joe loved me; why didn't we get married? Joe sent me this letter—just put a big question mark over Arthur's letter and sent it to me—and I thought, "Well, if Arthur wants this so much, then I'll go ahead and marry Joe."

Joe had been a very successful stockbroker in New York, living in northern New Jersey. He survived the first crash, 1929, and thought he was very smart to buy in on margin. Then the 1933 crash came, and he lost his shirt. He called his wife to tell her, and by the time he wound up what he had to do and got home, she had moved out lock, stock, and barrel. The house was empty. Now, I didn't know all this for a long time. Joe never told me anything about it, and I didn't ask. Joe was a remarkable man. He never said ill of any human being, not even this wife who had walked out on him. He couldn't listen to anybody, including me, criticizing. He would always have a generous word, possible extenuating circumstances. If there were no possible extenuating circumstances in a discussion about someone under criticism, Joe would get an attack of asthma. He rebelled against being unkind to any living thing. He understood birds and dogs and beetles and all kinds of things. He was a very deep, quiet man.

If it hadn't been for Joe, I would never have made the success that I did. Shortly after we were married in 1945, I persuaded him to give up work because I realized his emphysema was worsening. So he lived in my life and was very proud of me, and he believed I could do anything. For instance, when Marion Fay asked me to take the chair of preventive medicine and I went down to Hopkins, Joe became quite ill, and when I got back, I said to him, "I'm not going to go back. I'm not going to leave you." And he said, "You sit down and listen to me. You cannot live your life in anticipation of my death. You must go on. You know perfectly well from the age difference alone that you're going to lose me before I lose you. You have got to go on with your profession. You are going to be great; you're going to help many people, and you go with my blessing. If I should die while you're down there, you will know that the last thoughts of my mind were of joy that you are taking another step forward." That's the kind of man he was. He was terrific. We had eighteen years of marriage, when I didn't think he would live more than a few years when I married him.

Editor of the *Archives of Environmental Health*

This was a brand new experience, and I loved it more than anything I ever did because it put me in touch with the whole world. John Talbott [first Chief Editor of the *Archives of Environmental Health* and Editor Emeritus of the *Journal of the American Medical Association*] had appointed me on the recommendation of a friend of his who was Chairman of the Department of Preventive Medicine at Ohio State. This man had heard me give one paper and handle the discussion and had suggested me to his good friend John. But there was an outcry on the part of the members of the Academy of Occupational Medicine that I'd been appointed, because nobody in the field had heard of me.

I went up to see Phil Drinker, the previous editor. I hadn't heard of the outcry; I went up to see Dr. Drinker because he was retiring, and I wanted to find out if he had any pointers for me. I didn't realize the *Archives* was a defunct journal. When I got there, Drinker and I talked a little, and all of a sudden he said to me, "You know, I like you. Do you know what a hell of a mess you're in?" "Me?

John Talbott told me I was the unanimous choice of the committee!'' ''What committee?'' he said. ''Come into my little office here.'' And he showed me a letter from one of the deans in occupational medicine, which was so excoriating—nobody had ever heard of me; where did they get this gal? It wasn't that I was a woman, it was that I was an unknown in their field.

I felt sick. I said, ''What do you think I ought to do?'' He said, ''Call John Talbott and tell him he misrepresented everything, and you're not going to take the job.'' I said, ''I'll sleep on it.'' The next morning I decided to go to Boston to see another member of the Editorial Board. He was so unimpressed with me that he didn't even show me the courtesy of seeing me in his office. He said, ''It's almost lunch time. Do you mind? We can talk while we get our food in the cafeteria and eat.'' That confirmed Phil Drinker's opinion. When I asked him frankly, he admitted that he felt that I had no qualifications for the job.

So I went home and called John Talbott, and I really lit into him. He said, ''Well, what are you going to do about it?'' I said, ''I'm so damned mad, I'm going to show them how wrong they are.'' He said, ''That's my girl!'' Well, John Talbott was the most marvelous human being that I ever worked with. He was short of stature, and in my experience, many people—men especially—who are short have inferiority complexes; but not John Talbott. He was a giant of a man. And he backed me—backed me with the AMA Board of Trustees; he backed everything I wanted to do.

To make a long story short, I turned that journal around. It was so exciting, because we had no manuscripts. It was defunct; there was nothing in the hopper. And I feel that nothing succeeds like success, so I kept this a dark secret. Only Catherine Tomeo, the marvelous editorial secretary that I took on, and I knew the depths to which we had sunk. I would write a glamorous letter to a man like René Dubos [an eminent pathologist and renowned authority on such bacterial infections as tuberculosis] and offer him apologetically a small honorarium of $100 and get him to write a philosophical article. I would go to meetings, and if I'd hear a brilliant paper, I'd try to get it for the *Archives,* or I would ask them to write something similar. And gradually it built up; then we began to be inundated with manuscripts from all over the world.

Third Marriage

Our marriage has been very, very happy because I really fell in love. . . . This is quite different from my first two marriages. Sam had made up his mind never to remarry, so literally I courted Sam and suffered terribly on the way, but once we were married, I found I hardly knew him before our marriage. He bewitched me, that's all, the same as he bewitches everybody. I really knew very little about him. I knew Margaret Sturgis, Sam's first wife, who had taught me as Professor of Gynecology at Woman's Medical College. I admired her tremendously. She was austere—I was a little in awe of her, as all the students were. I'd met Sam several times through Margaret, but after we were married, I realized Sam and I had so many interests in common—gardens and birds and antiques and all sorts of things.

He's a lot of fun, and he's very popular socially, which almost drives one crazy; I mean, the invitations are twenty-four hours a day, seven days a week. With my heart and Sam's getting older—he's eighty-six now, and he's feeling a little unsteady on his pins—we are doing a little less of the social bit than we were. He's been perfect for this stage of my life, absolutely perfect. He's proud of me, but—for instance, he wants me to finish my autobiography—but he's psychologically unable to leave me alone long enough for me to do serious work. He just likes to be sure I'm around; he has to come in the room to see what I'm doing or to ask my opinion.

Sam still sees patients. Some still come from out of state to see him. I think the end of my life has been marvelous because of Sam, but if I had been married to him earlier, I would never have amounted to a row of pins because Sam is more of a fun person and enjoys social life, and he loves being with *me* all the time.

On Women in Medicine

I do not think that there is a special role in medicine for the woman doctor. People say that a woman prefers a woman gynecologist, and since this feminist movement, this is certainly true, but I think that that can be argued against. I really feel that any woman should be just as good in any medical field as any man. I can't see this distinction. I think there are *men* who are effeminate and women who are masculine.

In my teaching of preventive medicine, I always gave the students an opportunity to choose, as one of the areas they would like to study and conduct a seminar on, personality type in regard to choice of specialty. Year after year, certain personality types came out. People who don't love people were better off in a field like anaesthesia, where they're dealing with unconscious people. Pediatricians are more comfortable with children than with adults; they tend to be either immature or effeminate. Urologists are certain other types—may have a little homosexual tendency, because they deal largely with men. I don't think it really matters much about woman or man. I think it depends on the personality of the woman. I went into a field where there was more disease among men than women, and my men patients always loved me. I was used to men; I talked their language. Yet, I had no trouble with women either. If you have empathy for your patients, I don't think they care whether you're a man or a woman.

I'm not sure that this emphasis on the need to have women, like the need to have blacks, is doing us much good. For instance, I was the first woman to be appointed to the Council of the National Institute of Environmental Health Sciences, and I feel reasonably certain that what they said was, "We've got to find a woman in the field." Well, I had been Chief Editor of the *Archives of Environ-*

mental Health, and so I was a natural first appointee. I am not sure that that's a sound way for women to progress. I think the women of ability will find their own level anywhere. What I would like to solve is the problem of the married woman, because I don't think we're any nearer a solution to it today than we were when I came into the field. I think it's up to top management—whether it's a medical school management or a university management—to realize that a husband and wife are a team. Now, I'm a little confused here, because there's increasing divorce, right? And the question is: Are they really a team? Where a husband and wife are a team, it seems to me that top industry is smart in the way they handle things: they don't just interview the man and give him an appointment. They invite him with his wife, and they evaluate the wife because they realize that the wife's behavior is going to influence the husband's behavior; and if she's unacceptable, they don't invite the man. Now, it seems to me in academic spheres, or where the wife is a professional, that the top management—I'm using that, you know, for all opportunities, academic as well as industrial—has to take both husband and wife into consideration. Just as they interview the wife of an executive because they want to be sure she is not a social drawback, or sickly, or some such thing that may have an impact on the performance of the husband, in the same way, it seems to me, they ought to consider the profession of the wife, so that she will be happy and have an opportunity. That is a very complicated situation and may be beyond our current capacity to solve.

I want to say one other thing about women in general, not medical women. I think they're hypersensitive, and for that reason, they tend to be poor losers. I think that's one of the most difficult things for men to cope with—women bursting into tears, their being hurt or insulted, instead of talking back and arguing it out or forgiving it or forgetting it. It certainly helps if a woman can be one of the boys. The boys would never tell an off-color story in front of a certain type of woman. They would not want her at their late hour caucuses because they'd have to keep considering her. With me, I got invited to their rooms and still do—the gang all going up there. Nobody ever stops to think that I would take any offense because they feel the truth, that I understand men.

I've got quite a reputation at the Laennec Society as its first woman member. When they took me in, they said, "Our banquet is ruined because we have a woman here." One of the boys got up and said, "Let's call on her." I thought, "Boy! You've got to make it this time." I don't usually tell these stories; I had the hardest time to think up one that would be appropriate. But they loved it, and from then on, they thought of me as a raconteuse.

Another problem is that women don't help each other. When a woman begins to rise, she is as apt to encounter jealousy as commendation. Now, there are certain warm, wonderful women who are thrilled with all the accomplishments of their sisters. But there are other women who are secretly envious and who do all they can to make it difficult. I don't think you find that as much among the men. I consider that I have a deep interest in women and in understanding their problems, but.... I may be wrong in my conviction that the more aggressive activists are taking the wrong methods, because people whom I respect very much feel that this is necessary in order to make great gains. But I believe that if you have ability and if you are willing to take criticism, then you reach your level the same as mercury in a manometer. I don't think men want to keep women down; I've never found that at all. I guess that's enough to say about it.

I have never been active in the American Medical Women's Association because I never saw the need for it. I always felt it was a biased organization, that it sort of had a chip on its shoulder—"us poor women"—and I have never felt that. I have never felt it, nor have I looked for it, nor when I encounter it, have I acted upon it.

Now, myself, I was never aware of having any difficulty as a woman, except for one or two experiences. One that stands out was in 1952, when Jefferson Medical College opened a new chest hospital at Broad and Fitzwater. The man in charge, Dr. Burgess Gordon, said to me, "Would you apply for visiting chief post at Barton Memorial?" Well, it used to be that I would make a remark like, "Now, you know that they're not going to take a woman"—because Jeff had no women at that time. But then I developed the philosophy that instead of arguing ahead of time, go ahead and then let the onus be on the man who asked you. So I filled out the application with no idea I would ever be appointed. That was early in the spring, and the hospital was opening about June, as I recall. The first thing I knew, Burgess called me up and said, "You were appointed, and you're in charge of the first service July and August." Well, none of the boys wanted to work through the hot summer, you know. And I thought, "Dear me, what am I going to do?" So while I wanted to say, "Well, thanks, I'll take September and October," I said, "Well, that's just wonderful."

I remember one other time when I really did not receive a great opportunity because I was a woman. It was very meaningful to me when I was made Vice-President of the American Thoracic Society because those were my peers; those were the men who really mattered to me. They were the leaders in my chosen field of chest disease. There was a big groundswell for me to be the first woman president. Dave Cooper was very anxious for me to be the first woman president, but he was basically very shy, and the other members on the nominating committee were his best friends. Everybody knew that we wrote together and did research, and it was like he was asking for himself. When Dave timidly asked, shouldn't I be moved up, the chairman of the committee and a great leader in U.S. chest work said, "We don't want a woman."

One thing I am very aware of about women: I practically killed myself never to let anybody down because I was a woman. For instance, I belonged to the physicians' motor club. I was extremely careful in the way I did my driving— never to rush a light, never to be impolite to another driver—because I always was aware that I was labeled a physician by that little metal tag on the car. So everything I undertook, I was always keenly aware that whatever behavior I displayed had the potential of reflecting on all other women, and I never wanted anything I did to make it more difficult for another woman. I had to deliver the goods because if I didn't, somebody prejudiced might say, ''It's a woman that did it.'' I didn't do it because I was afraid for myself. I felt this strong moral obligation not to shut the door for some other woman who might not have the good luck that I had.

On Her Life

If I had my life to do over again, I would have finished medicine when I started it. I would not have eloped. On the other hand, I have two marvelous children from my first marriage. They're the most wonderful accomplishments of my life. I am a strong believer that whatever happens is for the best. I don't kid myself that my career has made any major contribution to medicine, but as far as I personally am concerned, I've loved every minute of what I've done. I only wish that I had had more years in the field I love so much.

Wynnewood, Pennsylvania
July 11 and 12, 1977

2

Alma Dea Morani

PIONEER PLASTIC SURGEON

In 1947, Dr. Alma Dea Morani, one of the few women surgeons of her day, became the first female member of the American Society of Plastic and Reconstructive Surgery. Most of her career has been associated with her alma mater, the Medical College of Pennsylvania, where she remains active. She also has been involved extensively with the Medical Women's International Association. She inherited her artistic talent from her father, an Italian immigrant who earned his living casting monumental statuary for public buildings, and her sculpture has been exhibited publicly on numerous occasions.

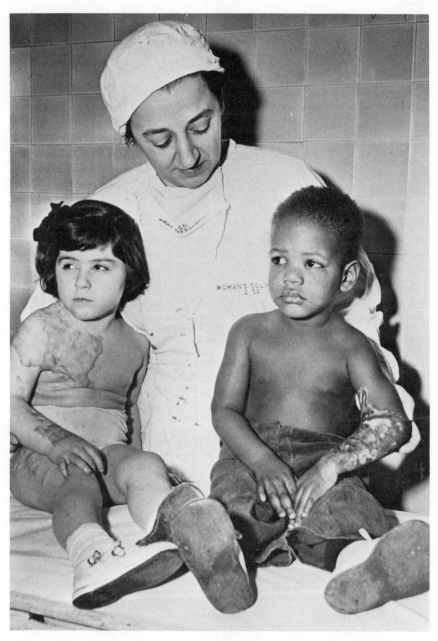

Alma Dea Morani (1951), examines two children in the pediatric ward the day before skin-grafting operations, Woman's Medical College, Philadelphia.

Childhood

I always worshipped my father because I thought he was such a talented man. He was very handsome, with a curly brown flock of hair, and he had a pointed beard and moustache very much like the Victorian gentleman you see in pictures. He was always trying to make a sculptor out of me because that's what he was, and that's what his father and grandfather had been. But somehow I didn't feel that being an artist was a very secure way of making a living. In our house we were either doing very well, when he had a commission and earned a great deal of money, or we were doing very badly, when there was no work in between commissions. So it was a matter of eating goose or apples.

As I see him now, my father could not have been anything but what he was. He was raised in a lower middle-class home in southern Italy, where women were pretty much chattel. Women were the housekeepers and the ones who made the babies and kept the men comfortable. In his age and station in life, there were not many educated women, quite contrary to my mother's background.

My mother came from a noble Italian family. Her family, the Gracci family, was considered one of the four leading families of the medieval city called Siena. She was a very intelligent and brave woman. She realized early in life that knowledge is the only hope for the world. She was always seeking more studies and more travel, which she did a good deal by becoming a governess to children of important people. She was such for the Italian consulate to Germany.

My mother taught my father a great deal. He was a talented man without much academic education. My mother, on the other hand, was one of the very few women who had a good academic education—very unusual for her period. He respected that. In fact, he would seek her counsel in many of his decisions. So she converted him to an awareness that women could have a brain as well as a body. She also made him reason out his problems rather than just react emotionally, as artists frequently do.

My father was called to the United States to fulfill a commission. He was what you would call an imported sculptor, which in those days was done rather regularly. Men who had exhibited in Italy and had gotten somewhat of a national reputation were then brought over to New York to do some of the big sculpture works. So after my parents were married in Siena, Italy, they came on their honeymoon to America because Dad had this huge order to make some religious monumental figures, which would take several years. I was born in 1907 in New York City in the area that is now Greenwich Village.

Mother didn't like New York and the ignorant Italians she met there. She felt unhappy with the lower-class Italians who were pizza vendors and laborers. She also wanted to show off her first child—me—to her large Siena family. My father couldn't leave his important commissions in his art world, so my mother and I went back to Siena, where I remained for nearly three years, from age one to four. So I learned to speak Italian before I learned English. When I came back, I was nearly four years old.

At the time, my father had been commissioned to be a teacher at the Cooper Art Institute in New York City, and he was making rather a good reputation doing bust portraits of famous men. He also worked with the Roman Bronze Foundry (which still exists in New York today), where he would be the touch-up sculptor on important monuments. By that time, I think my mother had decided America might be all right to raise her daughter in. Things were a little better financially with my father, and they moved from the horrible ghetto area of the New York Lower East Side to the Bronx. Moving to a different section made my mother accept living in America. Also, she loved my father and wanted to live with him and enjoy her family.

My mother believed that a woman's place is, first of all, to be a mother. She felt that a career was also wonderful but that it should be secondary. Throughout my later years, I recall my mother saying many times that she felt a little sad that I had never married and produced some children because she thought that was one of the great privileges of being a woman. On the other hand, as she often said, "You gave everything to your career, and that's been a very successful one. Maybe that's just as good."

My mother worked later on, when I was in high school. She taught Italian to an evening high-school class of adults. Occasionally, she had private students. My father had become sick with a gastric ulcer and didn't work for about a year or two, and during that time, my mother really supported us. I had great admiration for her courage, to go out late at night and teach the Italian language.

Everybody always talked about Professor Morani, the great sculptor, but not many people really appreciated what my mother had done and was. I did not until my later years, when I started going to college. Then, I began to realize my mother was really a very brilliant woman who spoke four languages very fluently, who was not only a good mother and a cook and ran the house and everything else but who was always reading, was always better informed than my father. As I frequently have said in the last years, I hope I inherited my mother's brain, my father's talent.

I had two sisters and one brother, all younger than myself. My relationship with the girls was fine. They were younger. I helped to take care of them—they were sort of my children. With my brother, I think there was always a certain competitive spirit. I remember a lot of family arguments when I felt he wasn't doing his share. As a boy who was four years younger than I, he could stay out late at night. I had to be in by ten or eleven o'clock at night. I resented this very much and called it discrimination, which it was. We had one or two family arguments when I thought my mother was giving him preferential treatment. On the other hand, I was well aware that my father was giving me preferential treatment, so I think it evened out.

My brother was influenced to go into the art world because of my father. He became a mural painter. It is only in the last few years that he's retired. My sisters were only a year apart and were almost like twins; they did everything together. They married two men who were also very close together, and they had a double wedding. They now live next door to each other. I see them only occasionally.

My mother was a Catholic and more or less devout but became less so as she grew older. My father had very little use for religion. He'd shrug his shoulders and say, "Oh, it's just a wonderful fairy tale." But I was raised as a Catholic and remember going to catechism classes after going to public school. I made my first communion; I was confirmed. I did like most other children—followed the rules and went to church pretty regularly on Sundays—until I got to high school age. Then, I began to do a little serious wondering about religion and began to wander away from it. There were many statements in the dogma of Catholicism that I felt were rigid and impossible to keep.

My father had a sister who came to visit us, and for a year or so, she and her husband were part of our household. I remember when her husband died. The memory of that funeral remains very strongly with me, though I was not more than six or seven years old. I'd never thought of death before then, but when this woman carried on hysterically and tried to throw herself into the grave when the casket was being lowered, I realized that death meant something is taken away. It was a sad experience which made me think a great deal more about death. Since then I've been trying everything I can to avoid it and to have other people avoid it.

My earliest friends were mostly girls of my age, and some of them were the children of these Italian people who had been friends of my parents. Because we lived in the same apartment house in the Bronx, I shared time and play events with them. There was only one who was a little boy, and I remember him, strangely enough, because he had a tapeworm. The doctors were giving him medicine to get rid of the tapeworm, and we all thought that was a very great thing, like a miracle. Finally, the tapeworm was passed and put in a jar, and we all viewed it as if it were something remarkable.

Between ten and twelve I became what my mother used to call "the worst tomboy on the street." I was always running with the boys. They had little gangs, and I was the leader of one little boys' gang until I got hit in the head with a rock. I'll show you the scar! The girls didn't play my way. They were always playing with little dolls or dishes or sewing, and those things didn't interest me very much. Once for Christmas I was given a beautiful, big doll. She had blonde hair, and she would open and close her eyes. My mother thought that was a wonderful present and that maybe now I'd like to be a girl instead of trying to be a boy. Well, a week later I took the girl doll and went upstairs on the stairway to the roof of this apartment house and cracked the head open to see how the eyes worked.

I don't know where the idea originated, but I always felt I was superior to the other little girls. Somehow I had more whatever it is—I was stronger; I was brighter; I could do things better; I could compete with the little boys. I'm sure there must have been times when I wished I were a boy because I felt that, being a female, I was held down. I wasn't allowed to do many things that boys did. But, on the other hand, there were some nice things about being a female, too, and I wanted the best of both worlds. I remember thinking, "I'm going to do everything that boys can do, only I have to do it better because I'm a girl." And you know, I was right.

It might be interesting to tell you my first experience in a hospital. I got hit in the nose with a stone during a fight, and it started to bleed. Next thing I remember, they carried me to the Bronx Hospital emergency room. To a child of ten or eleven, this was a frightening experience, yet it turned out to be very important because fortunately the doctor who handled me was very gentle and talked and reassured me. I was afraid they'd have to operate and fix my broken nose. Instead, he said, "It's only a cut in the skin. We don't even have to put stitches." I was so relieved. I thought, "Well, now, that doctor is a very good man. I think I'd like to be a doctor."

I joined the Girl Scouts my last year of grammar school. I was attracted to Girl Scouting because, first of all, the Girl Scouts had hikes where they got out in the woods. I hated living in an apartment house in a city. I loved the outdoors, and I felt you were healthier and happier outdoors. I knew the Girl Scouts had a summer camp, and that meant too that I could get away from the city for a couple of weeks in the summer. I liked the uniforms; I thought it was fun to be dressed up with medals and all kinds of things on you. Also, I had a compulsion to always try to learn, and I knew that the Girl Scout captains taught you courses and gave you instructions in many subjects. So here was the ideal combination for me—I would learn, and I would get outdoors. I got to be the patrol leader within a few weeks. Then, I took up many subjects because I'd decided I wanted to be an Eagle Scout. Well, an Eagle Scout meant you had to have thirty-three merit badges. I earned thirty-two and never made the thirty-third!

The captain's name was Anna Saunders. She was a fine, intelligent, cultured, and dignified person who immediately gained my respect because she knew so much. She was always bringing different books for us to study from. She would give us a problem and say, "Now, what would you do?" I soon found out that you had to figure out there were two or three ways to do it, but which was best? That was what I call learning to think for myself. She was practical. She inspired me.

By this time, I was in high school and very busy with a general course. But I decided that wasn't enough, so I went to high school at night and took a commercial course. I thought, "This is just what I need, because I'll have two high school diplomas, and I can get a job anywhere." I always felt you had to be able to make a living, and I calculated—I think for a child rather shrewdly—that if I had both, I could certainly always make a living. After two years, the high school authorities caught up with me, and they wouldn't let me finish my commerical course high school. So I only got one diploma, but I ended up knowing stenography, bookkeeping, and typewriting.

When they stopped me from doing that, I got a job as a dental assistant. The dentist was Dr. Harry Goldstein. His office was on 116th Street near Second Avenue. I would get through day high school at twelve-thirty in the afternoon. One o'clock I'd get home for a quick lunch. Then I'd grab the Third Avenue elevated and go downtown to Dr. Goldstein's office from two o'clock to eight o'clock at night. While he went out to his lunch, I would do my homework on the dentist's desk. Then when he came back, we'd have patients from four o'clock to eight o'clock, and I would sterilize his instruments, take the plaster impression, keep the records. He never let me collect the money; he did that himself. But I learned a good deal about teeth because I was always asking questions. He was very pleased with me, chiefly because I was a good interpreter. I had the Italian language at my fingertips, and many of his patients were Italians who spoke very poor English. I kept that part-time job for two years.

Strangely enough, I don't think I had any male friends in high school, because I was so busy with my day high school and my night high school and then with my job as a dental assistant. I had a few dates, and I thought they were a waste of time.

My high-school biology teacher, who was a fine little English woman who had taught for her whole lifetime, asked us to write a composition about what we would like to be. I think she noted that I was a little undecided. We talked about it, and she said, "Well, why don't you think of studying medicine?" I believe that is the first time I seriously considered the idea.

One of my joys was to be a good horsewoman, and I used to teach horseback riding after I'd learned its elements myself. Once I had two sisters I was trying to teach, and with one of them her horse ran away. I ran after her, and I fell off my horse and broke a wrist. Of course, I went home with a bandage and tried not to tell my parents because I was afraid they would raise hell. But my smart mother decided the wrist had to be seen, and she sent me to a friend of hers who was a woman doctor. She kindly put a bandage on my wrist and had it x-rayed and put a cast on me, and I went to see her once a week for several weeks. I much admired this quiet, dignified lady doctor who finally said no, she would not charge me because my mother was her teacher. That impressed me. That was the first contact I'd had with a woman doctor. I don't think I'd ever seen or heard of one before then. Everyone I had talked to about studying medicine had said, "Oh, well, there are so few women doctors, it's almost impossible to become one," which, of course, made me decide that's exactly what I would have to do.

I had worked as an assistant to the nurse in Girl Scout camp, and I could see immediately that whenever the nurse had a real problem with a child getting hurt or someone sick, she had to call the doctor. I figured that the only thing the nurse did was inspect our hair for nits and be sure that we kept our toothbrushes around and that we didn't get too dirty. To me, the nurse was nothing but a schoolteacher kind, and I didn't feel that was much in the way of practicing medicine. I was interested in repairing people—that's the word that always was with me, to repair the injured. The real action had to be a doctor, and I couldn't think of being a nurse, who was only a third-rate assistant doctor.

I also knew from the beginning that if I was going to be a doctor, I couldn't just be a doctor at a desk; I would have to be a surgeon. So I worked as a volunteer at the Bronx Hospital, and I remember going into the operating room with the excuse of bringing in some supplies. Then I stayed. Fortunately, it was only a transfusion that they were giving, and I thought, "Aha! I've seen my first operation, and it isn't so bad. I don't see any blood on the floor, and the doctor is talking to the patient. It isn't half what people think. I'm going to get into this operating room as much as I can." And I did.

When I decided to go into medicine, I told my mother right away. I didn't tell my father because my mother was much more understanding and more supportive. My father always thought I was sort of an unruly daughter, and he didn't quite approve of my trying to become a doctor. That was only in the beginning. After I really got into premed and medical school, he very much approved.

I remember an Italian friend of my parents, a master carpenter of some sort. He used to come frequently, and he would always shake his head and say, "I wouldn't let my daughter be a doctor—it's too hard, and it's too dangerous." He tried to discourage me. He used to take me to the movies on Saturday afternoon and try to talk me into being a schoolteacher or anything but a doctor. I just couldn't listen to him. Finally I told my mother, "I don't want to go out with him anymore."

My Girl Scout captain, of course, was very pleased, and so were a couple of my schoolteachers, that I, this little Italian girl, had decided I wanted to be a doctor. I went about saying it like I had just been decorated. But strangely enough, everybody accepted it. They didn't just laugh at me and say, "It's impossible." They began to think, "Well, maybe she will."

College

In high school we had been told that there were two very good premed courses. One was Columbia University; one was NYU. The tuition was a little more reasonable at NYU, so I applied and was accepted at NYU.

At that time, women were rather scarce in premed division, and the eight of us, the first few months, stuck pretty close together. Then, I noted that many of the group soon developed boyfriends and began to separate. There were about three of us who stuck as close friends and studied together and were in the same classes. Others began to change classes and take different courses. Finally, I think several of them just got out of premed. One married, and one got sick—I forget what happened, but four of us out of the eight finally finished the three-year premed course.

Of the three of us who stuck together, the other two were both Jewish girls, one with a family in Brooklyn, one with a family in the Bronx near my home. The one who lived in Brooklyn had a great deal of pressure on her to keep dating because her mother wanted to see her married, as she finally did. She never went on to medical school. The one from the Bronx, Hilda Fliegel, is still my very close friend. She went through medical school with me.

At NYU the competition was terrific because of the numbers and because we women were sort of washed out in this huge panorama of males. In chemistry lab, they had eight to a table, and they would put the two women way back in the corner table, as if they were ashamed of having us in their class. And while we did our work as well as the men, we would be the last ones to be examined or the last ones to be quizzed. There were a lot of little discrepancies and discriminations of which we were conscious.

I felt that the men were going into medicine because they thought they'd make a lot of money. Several of the men in our group were always talking about buying new clothes and having a beautiful car or taking out girls to expensive places. I felt that these boys were not going to be good doctors, they were going to be good merchants of medicine. The girls, on the other hand, never talked much about money. They were more interested in being the mothers, the friends of the sick, the healers—the natural role which I always felt women take in the practice of medicine. Perhaps I was as guilty as any, because I used to say, "Well, I'm going to be a surgeon, and a surgeon makes more money than you general practitioners." But money never seemed to be the goal. The goal was to be a good, useful doctor.

Medical School

During our last six months in premed, Hilda and I began to think about where we would go to medical school. We knew we would pass; we knew we would finish in three years and not get our degree, which was a B.S., until the end of our first year of medical school. We both felt rather smart that we were going to finish in three years while everybody else took four. So we decided to stick together. Hilda at that time had developed a boyfriend, but he didn't see much of her because he was busy being a premed student at another college.

To make a long story short, Hilda and I looked through the catalogues and thought of many medical schools. We finally decided we both wanted to get away from our families, away from the crowded, noisy environment of a city like New York, and Washington Square College—where you had to stand in line for ten minutes in the morning to get on an elevator to take you up to the seventeenth floor to a lecture hall, where you had to stand in line for twenty minutes to get into the cafeteria to eat, where you were only a number and the professor had 125 in the class.

We also decided we preferred an all-women's school because we were tired of being engulfed in a coed school where the coed portion of us was 8 out of 125. We wanted to get away from all these men who teased us and who made us feel like we didn't belong there. Even the male professors at NYU—only one of them had anything nice to say about these premed women; the rest of them talked down to us. Then, we heard of the Woman's Medical College of Pennsylvania, and after much discussion, which included our families, we applied and were admitted to dear Woman's Medical College.

The Woman's Medical College between 1928 and 1931 was to us a marvelous institution. It was like a second home to us women from all over the country— and we had several foreign students, some of whom were fascinating and good friends of mine. The Medical College then was a small, private institution, where everybody was supportive and friendly. The Faculty was interested in you as an individual and would invite you to their homes for an occasional meal. There was a feeling that the Faculty at that time was really interested in making you a doctor. They knew you by name; they had met your parents. There were Friday afternoon teas that you could or could not attend; there were many little functions for so-called foreign students—and I soon found out that if I called myself a foreign student because I spoke Italian, I could get in on a lot of free receptions and parties!

One of the first things we were shown were the wonderful records of some of the medical mission women who had graduated. Those names that are now on the plaques in the hallway were real people, and we met some of them. We were all very impressed and some inspired. In fact, several of the girls in my own class, which was a small class of twenty-five, did go into the mission field. In those days, I think the women who were studying medicine felt it was sort of a mission, whether it was in this country or elsewhere.

At the time we came in 1928, the Faculty at the Woman's Medical College was predominantly female. True, there were no females in the Department of Surgery, which happened to be my love, but there were professors in pathology and pharmacology and physiology, in medicine, in gynecology, and obstetrics—these were all women, and it was a woman's world. The men were perhaps 45 percent of the Faculty. I remind you that as of the latest census in this Woman's . . . now the Medical College of Pennsylvania, the percentage of male faculty has increased to 68 or 70, and the females have dropped down to near 30. But at that time, there were wonderful faculty women like Dr. Catharine Macfarlane, Professor of Gynecology; there was Mollie Geiss, who was Professor of Pharmacology; there was Jane Sands-Robb in physiology; there was a wonderful anatomist named Mary Bickings Thorndike. All of these women were fine teachers and fine physicians, and many of them had their own families and children besides, proving to us that it could be done.

But there was no woman surgeon per se, so I had my own problem trying to find an image to relate to. I could never find a woman who would say, ''I'm a surgeon.'' There were gynecologists, but I wasn't interested in that end of surgery. I wanted to be a general surgeon. It was only later that I developed a desire for plastic surgery.

The reason that the Medical College didn't encourage women to go into surgery was very simple—because the men were the surgeons, and the men had never trained a woman in surgery. In fact, it never occurred to them that any women wanted to be surgeons. In those days there were no residencies, practically. You became an assistant to an accomplished surgeon and took a preceptorship, which is what I eventually did. When I was in medical school, Dr. John Stewart Rodman was Professor of Surgery, and he had two male associates, or assistants. They were all on the Faculty, and all the surgery we learned came from these three men. There had never been a woman. In fact, I suppose I had guts when I finally said to him one day, ''Well, Dr. Rodman, I would like to be a surgeon.'' He said, ''Really? Well, I'll have to think about that.'' But he knew I was a good student, and finally it came about that he thought enough about it that, after I finished my internship, he wrote and invited me to be his third assistant. So I was a pioneer there. But if I'd gone to a coed school, I don't think I'd have had a Chinaman's chance. There wasn't the competition, which I knew there would be in a coed school, or a big medical center.

I remember the Depression vividly because I started medical school in 1928. I had saved enough money when I worked as a dental assistant during high school to pay for my first year's tuition myself. My father was very proud when I told him I had enough saved for the first year, and he could now start saving for my second year. My parents would send me a money order of thirty dollars every two weeks, and the fifteen dollars a week was supposed to be enough to take care of a little rent and food. When the Depression was at its worst, I was rooming with a schoolmate named Elizabeth Veach. Her father was a Presbyterian minister, and they had very little funds. But the two of us managed to eke out a living in a three-room apartment on North College Avenue—that's where the medical school was then. At certain weeks I wouldn't get my money order, and other months she wouldn't get her check. So we sort of supported each other. At that time, I did give a few lessons to some of the foreign students in my medical class who needed help in anatomy and pathology. I was particularly good at that, and I used to earn a few dollars or get a few free meals. Then during the summers, I would earn a little more.

In my fourth year in medical school, my father was out of work and not well, and he said he couldn't afford to give me the tuition. My mother at that time said she couldn't help either, and I was hard-pressed to find—I think it was five or six hundred dollars to pay for my last year in medical school. However, I had worked that summer up at Mercer, Pennsylvania—I was what they called a junior intern in a small private hospital. I had met a very kind and older doctor there who used to give anaesthesia, Dr. George Yeager. He taught me a great deal and took a fancy to me because he thought I had a wonderful pair of hands and the courage to become a woman surgeon. Then his wife died, and he was very much alone. Many times he would take me out to dinner or to the theater, and he was always a perfect gentleman. I much admired Dr. Yeager, and when I came back for my last year of medical school and didn't have the money, I asked Dr. Yeager. Believe it or not, he was thrilled to give the five hundred dollars I needed. He never took it back, even though I offered it to him many times. He died in 1962.

Hilda married immediately after finishing medical school, but unfortunately her marriage didn't last very long. She had no children, and there was a divorce after three or four years. Then she married again, and this time she was fortunate and had two children. Then, she lost her second husband, so now she's alone. She was one of the first female urologists in the whole state of New York and New Jersey. In the last ten years, she specialized in pediatric urology, which is quite a refined specialty.

I myself never had a feeling that I had to make a choice between marriage and medicine because I had decided in high school that if you're going to make a good surgeon, you just have to do that and nothing else. Marriage had never appealed to me, anyway. I suppose I looked upon it as a risk. I still do. But Hilda felt—I suppose because of her Jewish family, and the pressure of her two sisters who were married, and her mother and father—that she probably should be married but that she could do both. She said, "Well, it's going to be very hard, but I think I can do it because I'm going to take a special field where I can control my patients and just work when I have time." So she succeeded, but I never had the problem because I never considered marriage.

Internship

At that time, most hospitals did not admit women as interns. I applied only to those schools that accepted women, and there weren't very many. I also was conscious that I would like to earn a little money and also get surgery, which was my fundamental aim. I could have stayed here and spent a year at the Medical College of Pennsylvania, but I felt that I needed a change. After four years of medical school, I wanted to get away and get the feel of some other hospital. My father came through with an unexpected connection with one of his friends, a famous Italian doctor who was head of the Saint James Hospital in Newark, New Jersey. He said they had never had a woman intern, but it was a Catholic hospital and a good one, and would I like to apply for that? When my father suggested it, I said, "Well, I don't know. A Catholic hospital means a lot of nuns. I'll probably get in trouble with the nuns because I don't go to church very much." "Well," he said, "they pay fifty dollars a month, and you could live near enough to come home weekends." So that settled it.

To my surprise, it was a pretty modern hospital. It had about 150 beds, which was as big as the Medical College Hospital. It had a good staff. I took the internship after going to visit the hospital and meeting the Mother Superior and talking with Dr. Joseph Carboni, who was the chief medical man. They told me I would be the first woman intern, and I would sort of be on trial, because if I was a good worker and acceptable, they would then take other women interns. I thought, ":Here's my chance to do something for other women."

It turned out to be a very useful year—exciting, pleasant, in many ways one of the finest training years I've ever had. I was a very happy young doctor because I felt I was being treated as an equal. There were only two other interns, both Italian boys. They were only interested in medical things and heart conditions. I was the only one interested in surgery, so it worked out to everyone's advantage. They did my medical things, I did their surgical work. The all-male hospital staff, of course, were a little curious about this first female intern, but after I showed them I was a good worker and reliable and willing to put in the extra hours, I became quite popular with the male surgical staff. They would ask me to come and assist them. Pretty soon I had the privilege of doing most of the first-class assisting on major cases. As an intern I did six appendectomies, which is unheard of.

Here again, my languages came in strong because I had many Italian patients there in Newark, New Jersey, and I would be able to speak Italian to some of these old ladies who were there as patients. I don't think anyone ever objected to having a woman intern do their dressings or do their case histories. In fact, I recall one man who was terribly injured, and I kept dressing his leg wounds for months. He would say, "I wish you would not let the men do it, because you're more gentle. I want you to do my dressings." It was one of the great defeats I had as an intern to lose that patient.

None of us interns were very good Catholics, as much as the nuns wanted us to be. But they allowed us to go only occasionally to church, and some of the finest friendships were made with some of the nuns and some of the priests. Father Murphy, who was chaplain for the hospital, was a character who was always asking us to come and play bridge with him. Then he'd always bring out a bottle of whisky during those days of Prohibition. I remember I did object to being told by the nuns that I should wear a slip under my white uniform, that I should not smoke, that I should be home and in bed by 10:00 or 11:00 P.M. because I lived in the nurses' home. I resented these things because the men, who were doing the same work I was and at the same salary, were being allowed things that I was forbidden. But my internship year was full of delightful experiences. I can't really think of any bad ones, except my occasional forays with the Mother Superior.

Early Career

In 1932, I came back to the Medical College and spent five years working with Dr. Rodman. I started as third assistant, but after the second year, I became second assistant, and after the fourth year, I guess I was the first assistant, although occasionally his men would come back and help him. But I worked myself up to the level where I was doing a good deal of teaching, I ran the surgery clinics, I was on call day and night for emergency work, practically without end. One weekend a month would be mine. But these were the formative years, when I got a world of experience.

I soon gained the respect of Professor Rodman, although there is one funny anecdote which I think is revealing. There was another surgeon at the Woman's Medical College named Hubley Owen, who was a police surgeon for the city of Philadelphia, and occasionally he would send some of the more difficult cases up here as teaching cases. I cannot forget this one woman who was brought in because she was the wife of some police chief. She was a middle-aged, obese, grey-haired Irish woman with horrible pains in her belly and had been diagnosed appendicitis. When she was brought to the Woman's Medical College, Dr. Rodman and I examined her, and he said, "Well, there doesn't seem to be any choice. She has a rigid abdomen. We'd better operate on her and take out her appendix—it's probably an abscess."

Well, I examined the woman, and I noted some things that made me doubt this diagnosis of appendicitis. Finally, when we were scrubbing up, I said, "Dr. Rodman, you know, this woman could have something else. She could have a pancreatitis." He said, "Now, what makes you think that?" I said, "Well, she has this circumoral pallor"—it's a white pallor around the mouth—"and she is in shock, and she is obese, and her history shows that she has been an alcoholic. That's the kind of patient who develops pancreatitis. He said, "Morani, that's a lot of nonsense. This is an appendix, and let's take it out."

So we opened her up, and to everyone's amazement, it was not an appendix; it was a pancreatitis, acute. She had really digested her own pancreas. She died within two or three hours; all we did was open and drain and close her. So at the autopsy, of course, I went to see what was going to be shown, and the pathologist said, "No question, this woman had an acute pancreatitis." Dr. Rodman said, "Well, my associate!" I had suddenly been promoted to associate because I had made the right diagnosis. But, privately, he said to me, "You know, if you fell down a sewer, you'd come up smelling of violets. You're just lucky."

It was interesting to see the evolution of our association because although he never called me "Alma"—it was always "Morani" or "Dr. Morani"—he finally said, "Well, now, Professor, I'll take you to lunch." So I became a professor after about ten years at WMC.

In 1935, we opened a hand clinic at the Medical College. It was my idea, and I had to struggle for two years to get permission from the surgeons and the board to open up a new clinic. Much of my work in surgery had been compensation injuries, and a large proportion of those were hand injuries. Hand repair fascinated me because it was sort of an artistic endeavor. So I asked Dr. Rodman, and at first he said, "Oh, no, we don't have enough cases to form a clinic." But after two years, he finally said, "All right." The hand clinic met once or twice a week in the morning, and we would send all hand problems there. It was the first hand surgery clinic in the city of Philadelphia. Jefferson established one very shortly, and the University of Pennsylvania did. But ours was the first, due to my efforts.

At around the same time, they decided to have new departments of other kinds. This, of course, brought in a lot of men faculty, which some of us women resented. We always felt, "This is a woman's world, and we want to keep it this way." But there weren't any trained women in special fields like neurology and brain surgery and chest surgery and vascular surgery. These were all men's worlds, so we had to accept men. When these men arrived, they promptly brought in their men assistants and associates. The changes began then, with the growth of the medical school. Now it's full of men and all kinds of new and better departments, but the women are gradually disappearing, even though more women are studying medicine.

In all fairness, I think sometimes these men on our Faculty sincerely try to find a qualified woman to fit into a post. But there are very few women to choose from. Most of them are married, and they're going to go wherever their husbands want to go. It's very difficult for them to displace the family and come and take a faculty position just because they are women and a women's school wants them. So I was always conscious that even though we wanted to make it a woman's world and keep it that, we couldn't until we had enough women who could be qualified to train other women. I might interject here that women are not always women's friends. In many instances women criticize other women more severely than men would criticize them.

In 1938, I spent a month at the Mayo Clinic, mostly as an observer and listening to lectures in general surgery. The surgeons were very generous in allowing me to be with them, watching them, asking questions, attending some of their seminars, and even going to their homes for an occasional meal—all because Dr. Rodman, as professor, had recommended me. In fact, Dr. Mayo gave me a dog—I came back with a springer spaniel from Dr. Charles Mayo, Jr. But I remember one doctor saying, "Now, what do you want to be a surgeon for? You ought to be married and have several children." I said I'd made up my mind, I wanted to do something nobody else had done. If he didn't mind, I wanted to be a surgeon first.

Plastic Surgery Training

I had qualified for the American College of Surgeons in 1941, so it must have been 1942 when I decided to seek plastic surgery training. Part of my interest in plastic surgery was due to my growing boredom with general surgery. I found that the general surgeon always did the same thing, i.e., remove an organ, drain an abscess or infection, or try to repair an injured part, but there was nothing very creative about this specialty. All the time that I was routinely removing organs, which I'd been trained to do as a general surgeon, I felt, "It's too bad I can't do something more than just remove." I suspect that, subconsciously, it must have been a need in me to be creative, since I had no husband or children. I felt that I had to create something to justify my existence. I felt the need to produce something that was originally mine.

Then, too, my background of having a father who was an artist, and always being associated with what was called beauty, and studying art, and knowing the great masters—I think I felt the urge there, too, to try to make things beautiful as far as I could. Even with a knife, I felt that things could be made pretty rather than ugly. It always bothered me when I saw ugly scars on patients. I felt, "That wasn't necessary. That could have been sutured in a more refined way, with a better cosmetic result."

I started my training with a one-month course at the Polyclinic Hospital in New York City, which was the only plastic surgery course I could find. It turned out to be a very good basic course because I worked with Dr. Arthur Barsky, who was one of the truly great teachers of plastic surgery and who since has written several books on plastic surgery. We had a class of sixteen—two women and fourteen men. The other woman was a dermatologist who wanted to do face-lifts and cosmetic work. I was a general surgeon who wanted to do reparative, reconstructive work.

In 1946, I went to study with one of the great men of plastic surgery, J. Barrett Brown, in Barnes Hospital in Saint Louis, Missouri. It was essentially a fellowship. But it was not a fellowship given me by a medical school and certainly not by Dr. Brown who had very little use for women surgeons. It was a fellowship that was developed through the Soroptimist Women's Clubs of the State of Pennsylvania. They had given Dr. Brown, when he was here at Valley Forge Hospital working on all the war victims, a large amount of help in funds and auxiliary activities. He was very grateful to this group of women and asked them if there was anything he could do for them.

Well, I'd been a Soroptimist for several years, and I'd gotten to know the leaders of the group pretty well. I had told them of my desire to study plastic surgery and that I could not find any opening for a woman. At that time, there were only seven programs in the whole United States anyway, and when I wrote to them, they all said the same thing—either "We don't take women" or "Our openings are all closed for the next two or three years." So then, the Soroptimists got this Dr. Brown, and without my saying a word, they said, "Yes, we'd like you to train a woman in plastic surgery. We have a woman surgeon in Philadelphia who wants to study plastic surgery. Would you consider taking her?" "Oh," he said, "that's a big order." But he finally agreed to interview me.

The interview was a strange, cold one. He asked about what training I'd had and why did I want to do plastic surgery and did I know any other plastic surgeons and so forth, all of which I answered honestly. He said, "Well, I guess you can come if you want to. I don't know how useful you'll be, but you can start the first of July." So without feeling very encouraged by his rather cold attitude,

I thought, "I think I'll go, even though it may be a hard year for me. If he doesn't let me work"—because he'd mentioned he already had three men assistants—"I'll find a way to learn." So I agreed to give up my good general surgery practice here in Philadelphia for one year and go to Saint Louis.

Well, Dr. Brown said he would take me on for a year, and he did but under conditions that were pretty hard for me to support. First of all, no accommodations had been arranged for me, and I had to scout around and find a room to live in in Saint Louis, since I was told there was no room for me at the inn—at the hospital. And being a female, I suspect the men didn't really know quite what to do with me. I couldn't dress in their dressing rooms, and I couldn't eat meals in the men's lounge, so I had to be put in a nurses' home for meals or a lounge or a resting place.

While Dr. Brown was operating, he would lecture, and I will admit that all that he said was very true. He was a daring, imaginative kind of surgeon. Problems were brought to him that had been failures in other plastic surgery centers, and he would somehow solve them or figure out a way to do the repair work, even though it often meant several operations. There was a wonderful variety of cases; they used to fly celebrities with smashed-up faces in from Hollywood. There were many people who came with cancers of the head and neck area at which he was very adept, and a great deal of cosmetic work was going on. I took hundreds of pictures, which stood me in good stead later on.

But even though I had already become a member of the American College of Surgeons and was Assistant Professor of Surgery here in Philadelphia, I was just permitted to observe. He never let me assist him; he never invited me to go to his office and see the postoperative results. Finally, I felt that I had a right to complain to Dr. Brown. I asked to have an appointment with him, and he said yes, I could come and see him in his office. So I got to his office, and there was not another chair in his office except the one he was in. I was forced to stand up at his desk—like a prisoner being sentenced, I thought. I said that I must have been under a misconception, since I thought I'd come there for a fellowship and that I would be allowed to assist with some of his operations and not just be a distant observer. I suspect it took him aback because he hesitated for a while, and he said, "Yes, I suppose I have been neglecting you. You may now assist on Saturdays"—when "the boys" were off on weekends.

So my first step was in getting to assist either Brown or one of his other team men on Saturdays. Usually that was the day of small schedules of only three or four cases going on, while other days there'd be as many as twenty cases a day. However, I found my own solution. I met many general surgeons who operated on the same floor in different rooms, and many of them invited me to come and watch general surgery operations in the afternoon when the plastic surgery schedule was over. So I proceeded then to get a double education—I did plastic surgery in the morning and general surgery in the afternoon. I also made contact with some of the medical students there in Saint Louis. There were a few women who sympathized with my position and invited me to come to the anatomy lab and work with them, so I got in some anatomy dissecting sessions.

About the end of the first half of that year, I had watched a great many operations being done on hemangiomas, which are blood-vessel tumors in the skin. At that time the only treatment for them was to cut them out and put in a skin graft. X-ray didn't work, and there wasn't any other thing being done at the time. But wherever you put a skin graft you're putting a patch, and it's always discernible. I'd often thought, "Why couldn't we find some method to destroy these excessive blood vessels?" An x-ray man in Saint Louis told me they had been injecting radioactive sodium phosphate solution into tumors that were blood vessel constructed, and they would shrink. I thought about it a good deal and talked it over with some of the x-ray men, and they said, "Well, it sounds logical and reasonable. Why don't you try it?"

So I asked for a second appointment with Dr. Barrett Brown. Again I stood in his office—and this time I walked out and got myself a chair and brought it in and sat down next to his desk. I think he was a little surprised, but I felt I had at least a right to sit while I discussed my theory with him. He listened patiently. All of a sudden he opened his eyes, and he said, "You know, that might be a very good idea. We'll try it." I said, "Now, wait a minute, Dr. Brown. If I thought this up, and this turns out to be useful, I would like to be the one to try it, if you will supply the patient." He said, "I'll think that one over." A week later we found a patient who had a huge hemangioma on one-half of the upper lip. All the men came around to see me inject this solution into this lip. Dr. Brown seemed very excited about it. He said, "Well, now, go ahead, go ahead, put it in very slowly and fan it out"—which I did, and one of my friends took a picture of this exciting moment.

Well, the story, I suppose, is like all inventions—it worked partially. Within ten days the lip was very hard and swollen, and the patient said he'd had a lot of burning sensation. But when he came back, the color, which had been a deep red, was now only pink, and the thick lip was less thick. So I felt that we'd been partially successful. Dr. Brown said, "Well, I guess it did give him a little improvement. We'll work on it later on"—and completely forgot the whole idea. But years later I noticed that in one of his articles it was suggested that this was a treatment worth trying.

I think the year in Saint Louis was one of my most depressive periods. That year was sort of like going to the wars. You had to do it, and you had to follow orders in order to survive. But when it was all over and I assessed what I had done, I had had a wonderful year.

By a stroke of good luck, I met two Philadelphia plastic surgeons at a plastic surgeons' meeting in Kansas City that year. I told them what I was doing, and they thought that was wonderful—then I could come back to Philadelphia and help them with plastic surgery. I was later invited to join the American Society of Plastic and Reconstructive Surgery, and I'm sure my two good colleagues here in

Philadelphia were responsible for that invitation. Having become the first female member, I felt a moral responsibility to be seen, to attend all meetings, which I did. I was very faithful.

Later Career at the Woman's Medical College

It was very difficult to get started in plastic surgery because it was a new field and they had never had a plastic surgeon at the Woman's Medical College. By 1948, Dr. Rodman had become ill, and he'd more or less retired. A new man had become Chief of General Surgery, Dr. Kraeer Ferguson. He was a very qualified and competent general surgeon. But here I met another man who had little use for woman surgeons. When I told him that I wanted to have my own department and just do plastic surgery, he said, "That's impossible. While I'm the chief surgeon, everybody will be under my edict. You will be a general surgeon under my department and do plastic surgery."

So we went on for a few months in a *status quo* situation. Finally, I decided I had to make a living, so I did an appendectomy or a hernia or something. He called me in to say that that wasn't going to be allowed. I promptly replied, "Dr. Ferguson, I have my boards in general surgery just as much as you do. I have a right to earn a living. I have a license to practice medicine and surgery, and I have to do a little general surgery to pay my rent. If you don't allow me to make a living, I will go to the Board of Managers of this hospital and state my problem." He just walked off in a huff. After that, he hardly spoke to me, but he didn't complain if I did a little general surgery.

At that time there were a great many women physicians in this city who had big practices. When they knew that I was doing plastic surgery, God bless them, a lot of them sent me what they could, and I began to do a little cosmetic surgery in the way of noses, ear repairs, even an occasional face-lift. Within a year or two, I had developed enough referral work as a plastic surgeon.

Most of my patients were female, and predominantly females today seek the plastic surgeon. I would say that the average was middle class. There were a few of the lower class who couldn't afford to pay for their surgery but gave me good variety and experience. There were the same few up in the upper middle class who paid me large fees for cosmetic work. I never had any problems with the patients because I was a woman. They accepted me right off. I was always pleased when a man patient would say, "I never had a woman doctor, but you're all right." The most grateful patients in the world are those that you reconstruct or improve in their appearance. They not only pay their bills, they come and bring you gifts; they become your children; they keep in touch with you; they call you. If the least little accident happens to that part that you made, they're back to see you as if you were the mother of their nose.

The Department of Surgery has never had a woman professor of surgery at its head, so the men just appointed more men—after Dr. Rodman was Dr.

Ferguson, and then, when he died, it was his associate, Dr. Cooper, who is now head of surgery. These men surgeons never really made an effort to attract qualified women. I don't think the Dean's or anyone's desire to put women in favored positions would have influenced the men who made the final choice. They could always rationalize their decisions and choices. As I see it, especially with surgery, they were all feudal lords who ruled their kingdom, and they were a little bit afraid of letting in women.

I fought vigorously to get a woman plastic surgeon on the staff here. She was qualified—she had done her general surgery and passed her boards and was studying plastic surgery. And sure enough, even though she was first accepted, six months later she was refused. An orthopedic surgeon said he wouldn't work with her on the staff, and the Professor of Surgery felt he had to keep his orthopedic surgeon. That woman is now practicing plastic surgery in Philadelphia but has nothing to do with the Medical College of Pennsylvania, where she logically belongs.

I had mixed feelings when the college went coed. I didn't like it, because I guess in a sense I've always been a moderate feminist. I felt that this was the stronghold of women in medicine in this country, and we should have kept it that way. On the other hand, I felt that bringing in male medical students might make the course more exciting and interesting, and also, perhaps, bring in a different point of view for the female medical students. I had no objection to that. I had objections to the volume of men entering because I felt it was an invasion and that if you brought in ten or twenty, in the next few years it would be forty or fifty, and maybe twenty years later it would be mostly a male medical school like the 180 others. But, of course, time marches on, and now I see that what I feared has happened. There has been an invasion of men—true, many of them fine teachers, qualified, experts in their field, and they've made the school a medical center that demands respect. But growth has its price.

Teaching has always been very important to me. I felt that if you have something to give, you ought to give it. I suppose I have too much self-confidence, but I think I'm a good teacher. Some of my highest moments are when students come back to ask my advice, to talk about their problems, to keep in touch. It's like having a group of children who have wandered around the world. I now have many, many who really think about me as their godmother.

I was never really interested in doing research. I suspect this is true of most surgeons. You want immediate results, something that gives you that immediate gratification, which is what we're essentially striving for.

In 1976, the dear Medical College of Pennsylvania finally gave me an honorary degree. I say "finally" because I had hoped this would have happened before, but one does have to wait for recognition in one's own land. I suspect the thing that made it finally come to the attention of the board was the fact that I had made a rather substantial contribution to a laboratory for research in surgical immunobiology. Let me not be completely unselfish about that—this was a new field and a new research lab, and since it would have my name attached to it, I felt in a sense that I was creating my own memorial.

International Medical Work

In 1972, it was my privilege to bring family planning to the women physicians of the Far East. From 1972 to 1974, fates made me the President of the Medical Women's International Association. It was expected that a president would bring some new ideas and some new programs into the association, which numbered over twelve thousand women physicians. So I felt a great responsibility to do something different, to do something worthwhile, to put this organization on the map—because it had been, oh, quietly meeting. The women would talk to each other, but they'd never had much publicity, they'd never had many funds. They just kept to their pseudoscientific social club by which women physicians could travel and enjoy the cultural events of other countries.

My first thought was that I would have to get some money because you can't do anything nowadays without the large fund, and so I applied for grants. I finally made good contact through a gentleman friend of mine who worked in Washington, D.C., with the leaders of the Family Planning International Assistance Group. It required a lot of time, thought, energy, and some expense on my part to persuade the powers of FPIA that I had a group of international medical women who could put on a wonderful family planning program to educate women physicians in the Far East, but I finally succeeded.

The grant was for $50,000, which was like a fortune to my little organization. But, of course, I had also acquired the responsibility of seeing that this program would be well done, that it would be a credit to women doctors around the world as well as to the international association. Well, it took months of correspondence to select the women physicians from seventeen countries in the Far East. But they came, and they came willingly, to Manila to be educated in family planning in all its various methods. The echoes are still going on. I still have letters from women whom I met there from Malaysia, Indonesia, Korea, Taiwan, the Middle East, Egypt. Of course, the largest percentage of the women attending were Philippine women doctors who came from all the tiny little islands. Then, they went back to their little country or village to practice what they had learned. Now family planning is really accepted all through the Far East, and I am proud of having had something to do with it.

Later I had another opportunity to work in the Far East. One of my trips with the international medical women was a tour into Hong Kong and Taiwan, where we had the privilege of meeting Madame Chiang Kai-shek. One of her close friends was a woman physician of Taiwan, an ophthalmology surgeon, and this Chinese lady became a good friend of mine. I met also a Chinese woman general, who was head of all the nurses in Taiwan. These two Chinese women wrote to me, and within a few months we developed a good correspondence. They said, "Why don't you come back here and teach?"

Well, that intrigued me. I got to thinking that it would be very nice to offer my services to these Chinese people. Pretty soon a letter arrived inviting me to come and be a Visiting Professor of Plastic Surgery, because they were just setting up a plastic surgery department as part of the National Defense Medical Center. I didn't need to think about it too long because it was exactly what I had hoped would happen. I needed to have a change of pace. I was perfectly willing to take two months and go to Taipei, Taiwan, and give my teaching services free. Their side of the bargain was that if I paid my own travel expenses, they would give me a house and servants, so I would have no expense while I was teaching there. This seemed like a great adventure, which it turned out to be.

So I went to Taiwan. They kept their bargain—I had a house and four servants, and for six weeks I lived it up. But I also worked very hard. They gave me a lot of advance publicity, and by the time I arrived there were cases waiting for plastic surgery. I had three Chinese men surgeons, some of whom had had some training, as my assistants, and we set up a really modern, first-class Department of Plastic Surgery. We did a great deal of very difficult, risky reconstructive work, especially on some of their heroes from the Matsu and Quemoy fighting. They would not let me operate on the coolie class. They wanted to save me, they said, for working on what they called "important people"—army people, teachers, industrialists, or their children. I think we did thirty-five, forty cases, and I held clinics and gave lectures and spent six very busy but most enjoyable weeks.

The Chinese soon became my friends. They gave me a name, "Orchid Lady," which was very nice. I got to know some of their families very closely. So this was my idea of one of the most delightful periods in my life in that I felt I was giving, I was well accepted, gratefully received, came home with numbers of very fine gifts, and am still in close contact with many of the Chinese men and women physicians. It was so nice that I went back two years later and again five years later.

On Current Trends in Medicine

Medical education has changed tremendously. The course that we took in the thirties would be like kindergarten today. The whole field is so much more complex because so much more is understood, so much more has been proven. The pathology that we were taught in medical schools in the thirties would be elementary today. The same with the chemistry. We used to do a blood count and the urine and maybe a blood sugar and a blood urea; now they do twenty-two tests on your blood. Medical students today have to learn a great deal more. I think they're under emotional and nervous tension because they have so much more responsibility.

Our patients, too, are different than they were in the thirties. Most patients in those days thought surgeons were God. They rarely questioned how and why we did what we did. Now the patients all expect perfection—not only in surgery but in all fields of medicine. And why? It's simple: the patient is now better educated, better informed. They read more, they have the advantages of radio, tv, free lectures, and everything else.

So the role of the doctor now is very, very different from what it was in the forties. Even the lower-class, less-informed patient knows that he must seek a specialist. I think it makes us less the doctor. A good doctor must know the whole patient. Whatever part you're treating, you still have to be aware of his personality as an individual; you still have to be their friend. Fragmentation by specialization has put all doctors off in a little cubbyhole, where they're only looking at the left tonsil or the right breast. The pelvic man does the pelvic surgery, but he doesn't go above the diaphragm. I, as a plastic surgeon with general surgery training, am not permitted to invade the abdominal, chest, or head cavities. The point is that we're all getting so highly trained in a small field that we miss understanding the personality of the patient. It makes for superior medicine technically. The specialized surgeon can do a much superior job of his surgery. But he fails in the psychological aspect, and sometimes magnificent surgery is a failure when the patient is unhappy as a result.

I see a great danger in the way that the future of medicine looms, because of the legislative effects on the way we practice medicine. At present, more and more pieces of the pie are disappearing, and the doctors have less and less control over how they practice medicine. The numerous city, county, and federal agencies are controlling more and more the practice of medicine. You are now made to conform. You have to do things a certain way, you have to do certain tests, you have to keep certain records, you have to inform the patient preoperatively, you have to do many, many things required now by law which in the thirties and forties and fifties were not necessary. This puts a lot of additional work on the average physician for record keeping, for time, and so forth.

The malpractice crisis is still with us. In Pennsylvania, at least, all doctors must have malpractice insurance to practice medicine. This is a great burden on the average doctor because it takes a great many dollars to pay for your premiums, especially in surgery. This makes it also impossible to be the creative, imaginative surgeon. You have to practice the kind of medicine that your peers do, or immediately you are liable. I find this a great handicap to a creative surgeon like myself.

The medical profession has become depressed. We're obviously an unhappy lot—talk to physicians at surgical meetings. The younger women that I've seen are well aware of the problems of the older physicians, and a great many of them say, "I'm not going to do any private practice—it's too expensive. I'm going to take a job."

I'm afraid that the public is going to suffer in the long run, because they're probably going to end up with socialized medicine, which seems to me now to be inevitable. It's just a matter of time before more pieces of the pie disappear. The surgeon or the practitioner who wants to be independent and practice as a solo is certainly on his way out. I'm one of them. Socialized medicine has many advantages. There are many doctors who will welcome socialized medicine, who will like that kind of practice because it makes their life easier. They will not be under this personal stress which we feel now in this country. They will have regular hours and regular duties. Fine, but you also become another little robot who's told how to do, what to do. You will not have any room to spread your own wings and do anything different and to be creative. That's my complaint.

On Women in Medicine

Women have decided that medicine is a natural for them. This, incidentally, was first said by Bernard Baruch way back in the thirties: "Give a woman a proper education, and she'll become a good physician." Of course, that isn't true of all women, but the women who have this predisposition to become physicians generally make good physicians because they want to be. And why do they want to be? Let's get back to the psychology of that individual. There's a need for a woman to express her womanliness, her motherliness, and medicine makes this possible. So in a sense, I think a lot of women doctors stay in medicine because they need to.

I think in many respects the women will change the practice of medicine, at least in general practice. The woman physician who has to examine a patient will spend more time with the patient, will probably ask questions that would never occur to a man. She will be more sympathetic, more compassionate, more understanding of this patient as a personality. I've long been cognizant of the extra concern, anxiety, emotional reaction that women physicians feel for their patients. They even have a tendency to get too close to them, to be too much the mother, too much the sympathizer. I knew that this was a wrong thing to do, and therefore I behaved objectively, and I tried to keep my distance. I have seen women doctors just break down and cry or fall apart when a patient died, and I thought it was a weakness to get too close, to become too much a part of this patient. I think it interferes with your efficiency and effectiveness as a physician, especially as a surgeon.

I think because women are women, they are perhaps more likely to be good doctors in certain fields—pediatrics, for one. A great many women are doing very well in internal medicine. A great many women are doing well in psychiatry. There are now a good many women who have qualified in general surgery, and there are, I think, twenty-two in the world of plastic surgery. But chiefly, I think, the average woman physician is best at being a general practitioner, a pediatrician, or in internal medicine.

Then, there are the few who are good surgeons in gynecology and obstetrics. But gynecology is still a man's world because they're by far the majority. Many patients, let's face it, have yet to develop enough confidence in women gynecologists. They say, "Oh, I don't mind going to a woman doctor for my cold or for an ordinary checkup, but if I have to have a big operation I want a man"—implying that the man has more courage and therefore will do it better.

I have felt all along that plastic surgery is an ideal specialty for the woman who has the qualifications needed—and they include, first of all, the courage to become a surgeon, but secondly, a psychological, intuitive kind of quality which makes you understand, "Now, this patient I can help. But that patient will not be improved by my surgery because she'll find another defect; that patient goes to the psychiatrist." It takes a lot of experience to decide who is the good subject for your surgery and who should be avoided because you'll make them worse.

A woman has to have a lot of self-confidence to even first make the decision to become a surgeon. I, fortunately, have never suffered from a lack of self-confidence. You have to feel, "I can do it as well as a man because I have the knowledge and capability. A man in my position would not do it any different or any better." You have to believe that you have the facts and that you are thinking—perhaps as a man but really that you are reasoning well. The system of logic that leads you to make a decision has to be right, regardless of sex. I think there are very few women who have that kind of self-confidence. I don't think you can really make them have it. They either have it or they don't. You don't create a surgeon. Perhaps the qualities that make for a good surgeon, you have to inherit. The person who wants to be a surgeon has to be a very special kind of character. It isn't the qualities that one might think—that they just have to be full of guts and bravado. There's more to it than that.

I've noted in various surgical meetings that women are now getting on their feet and being heard a little bit more. They are developing a certain amount of courage. That timidity that I spoke of is decreasing. Also, I think a certain amount of respect is being developed by women for women. The women's lib movement has made some difference. Women have a little more guts, and they're willing to take a job, where before they'd say, "Oh, I—I wouldn't dare do that." And the women surgeons, the few that I know, are being heard from scientifically with good papers and good seminar participation. The sort of thing which ten, twenty years ago was rare is now becoming more commonplace.

On Her Life

Being a single woman, I think friendships are terribly important. I find them not only enjoyable but supportive, and I find I enjoy being a friend when I can help others. I think that's one of the great privileges. I have some very close friends, and strangely enough, some of them are men surgeons whom I've been associated with for many years. Perhaps my closest friend is a woman artist who became my art teacher when I returned from Saint Louis. As a matter of fact, we now share an apartment. She is still a portrait painter and a good landscape artist and has helped me with my sculpture—and has also traveled with me.

My primary interest outside of medicine has been art—and of course, traveling. I have done a lot of lecturing on what I call "travelogues." I have maintained a very, very heavy correspondence around the world with women physicians who I thought were worth cultivating. Strangely enough, several of them are psychiatrists—which I think brings me back to the psyche—because I have always been prodding them for better reasons to understand the mind of the patient who comes with a physical defect. Some of them have helped me in developing my own perceptiveness. So women physicians around the world, as well as a few men, have been, I think, my closest friends.

If I had it to do over, I would probably have tried harder to get a department in plastic surgery. I think I would have enjoyed being the head of a department and not just a part of the whole. I also had an opportunity to go down to Florida and practice there, and I've often wondered whether that would have been a good choice. But perhaps not—it might have been a gamble, too. But everything you do is a gamble. On the whole, I don't think I would do things any differently a second time. I'm satisfied with the choices I've made. I've been lucky, too. I think a large share of what happens to you is just pure luck. It's not just wisdom, you know.

Philadelphia, Pennsylvania
January 19 and 21, 1977

3

Pauline Stitt
PUBLIC HEALTH ADVOCATE

Born to a mother who left high school to elope and a father whose aspirations for her did not extend beyond towel girl in a rest room, permanently crippled in a polio epidemic that later claimed her brother's life, Pauline Stitt needed every ounce of determination she possessed to pursue her career in pediatrics and public health. From the vantage point of a vigorous "retirement" in Honolulu (she teaches quarter-time at the University of Hawaii), she looks back on a rich life that has included high-level posts in the Children's Bureau as well as a distinguished academic and clinical career and wide-ranging outside interests.

Pauline Stitt (1958) teaching a Harvard medical student at the Harvard School of Public Health. From left to right, a mother, Dr. Caplan, a medical student, Dr. Stitt, and a child.

Childhood

I was born in 1909 in Frewsburg, which is a small town in upstate New York in Chautauqua County.

My father went to work when he was eleven or twelve years old in his father's mirror factory. He worked all his life in silvering mirrors and then in furniture manufacture. Later on, he lost the plants in the Depression, and he finally was a village postmaster and took other jobs on the side. In other words, he had an elementary school education, as we would put it today. But at that time many children just went until they were around twelve and then went out to work.

Politically he had quite strong liberal views and saw social justice as a way of living out religion. He was a Democrat, and in upstate New York at that time, you were considered weird if you were a Democrat at all. So that was one of his principal characteristics.

I felt that my father was several notches higher than other men. The thing I missed most was evidence that he felt affection for me. I think my father was a man of unusual endowment who never had commensurate education. He had all kinds of talent. When he was dying, I kept looking at him and thinking of what a tragedy it was that he had never had a chance to live up to the full potential of his endowments. I think he took out some of his frustration on those around him. He had a right to be angry.

One time he sent word from Florida that he had found exactly the right job for me. This was when I was about fifteen, and I was excited. My mother said, "Now, be careful. Don't get your hopes up. I don't trust this." "Oh, Mama," I said, "I know it's good. He wouldn't tell us he had something nice for me to do if it weren't so." It turned out to be a post for a towel girl in toilets. That was a terrible thing to hear when you're a teenage girl—that that's the level of your father's aspiration for you. He tried very hard to get me to leave college at the end of the freshman first semester. He never relaxed such efforts until it was all over and I had my degree. Up to that point, he was continually saying, "Well, my God, can't we get you to stop this foolishness?"

My mother was incredibly equipped for anybody who was a high-school dropout. Her godmother, Miss Mary Willard, taught English and English history, and she exercised her godmotherly responsibilities, as she interpreted them, by opening vistas of life to my mother. I think my mother always felt that she had blighted her life through early marriage. I think all my family felt that they had lost out on life either through their "most grievous fault" or through fate.

Well, I think that right from the day I was born she was disappointed in many ways. As a pediatrician, I have taken great pains to help mothers know that they have nice babies because I really realize that my mother didn't know what was even normal. For instance, when she first saw me and saw those normal tiny white spots on her baby's nose, she said, "Oh, my, I had thought I would have a pretty baby, but look at those terrible blights on the skin." Then, she was a blond, and my first hair was apparently very dark. She took one look and said, "Oh, my goodness! Oh, my goodness!" I think a whole lot of her reaction was, "Oh, my goodness!"

But my grandmother Davis just thought I was the best thing that ever happened. I don't believe that her enthusiasm pleased my mother too much. The alliance between my grandmother and myself got so strong that I remember one time I called to my mother by her first name, Allene, and she said, "Don't let me ever hear you call me that. *I* am your mother."

Off and on all her life my mother would stop suddenly as though waking up and say, "Oh, my goodness, what would I ever do without you? You're the most dependable, the most reliable, the most responsible person. I forget at times." Much of the time she acted as though she were trying to control an impossible world of which I was one of the impossibilities. Then, in those sudden moments, she would look at me and say, "Oh, my! What would I do without you? I don't know." When she was dying, she kept saying to me, "Such injustice! I have done you such injustice." I do not know what the injustice was, and I shall never know, for she was much too sick for me to inquire.

I think she considered woman's role a "damned outrage" but had no hope of anything ever changing. She often recited aggravating quotations like, "Man works from sun to sun, but woman's work is never done," and that other rankler, "A son's a son 'til he gets him a wife, but a daughter's a daughter all her life." My grandmother Stitt, I think, would be out women's-libbing. I don't know what my mother would be doing. I think she would be behind the scenes smiling with pleasure, even laughing with glee, glad to see them doing it but keeping her mouth shut. She might have apprehensions that they might be "doing themselves in" and jeopardizing past gains by strategy that is not well thought out.

I think I have a pretty clear idea of what my father's views were. I think that my father was actually in awe of women and felt that one of the things that any intelligent man did in self-defense was to protect himself against intelligent women. After my mother died, he mentioned her one day in the car and said, "That was the smartest woman I ever knew." Then, he stopped a minute, and he said, "I think maybe the smartest human being." I had thought he felt his own mother was the smartest woman he ever knew. She was what he would have called a "humdinger." I asked him, "*Who* do you mean?" And he said, "Your mother!" I wish Mama could hear this because he had never shown her those feelings. I think that he maintained all his life an armed defense against this dangerous species called woman, thinking: "You have to keep them continually subjugated, because—oh, God! If they ever knew their power."

Our family was a matriarchy with perpetual patriarchal fight, so most decisions became a contest. It usually ended up that my mother was right and he knew she was right, but he couldn't let her get away with anything easily. It was always like a bulldog with somebody pulling at the shoe in his jaw. You know who is going to win. The shoe may get wrecked, but the master is going to triumph. I don't know who triumphs in a case like that. But anyway, my mother and he wrangled on practically every kind of decision. It's hard to tell whether her triumphs were because she was the leader or because she hung on and endured, especially for her children.

My parents must have had enormous love to have lived with such hellfire and damnation. Really, I just cannot describe it to you. It was like living in the whirlpool at Niagara Falls. I couldn't imagine a marriage that was not a chronic fight. I think it had an effect on my view of marriage.

I wanted to get out and away to help my little brother get out. It was not just a matter of career aspirations; it was a matter of wanting to get out and survive. You knew that it could be the death knell to stay there. The whole home situation gave me enormous concern. I don't see how that place held together except in that era people stayed together. The children hung on until they freed themselves by getting out and going to work. From the time I was about fifteen I was out.

On my seventh Christmas I received a set of Louisa May Alcott books. I'd discovered one Alcott book in the family bookcase and told my mother, "This is the best book in the house." My mother acted upon that, and at Christmastime, I received a whole set. I started out and read *Little Women* and was interested. Then came *Little Men*, and the girl named Nan. I rushed to my mother, and I said, "Mama, you know this girl Nan? She is going to be a doctor." My mother said, "Yes, I remember the book." "Well," I asked, "Mama, are girls ever doctors?" "Yes," she said, "certainly." "Oh, for goodness sake," I said, "well, then, that's what I'm going to be." She said, "When did you decide that?" I said, "Now, right now. I didn't know before that girls could be doctors." My mother went on and told me, "Why, yes, we have two women doctors in our community." One was Jane Lincoln Greeley, a wonderful woman, highly esteemed by everybody in the community—by patients, by the community in general, and by physicians. In fact, she was called the Doyenne, the Dean, of physicians in Chautauqua County. I heard that she was Horace Greeley's cousin. I don't know, but certainly he had been editor of the paper in Fredonia at the other end of the county.

I recall that Grandma Stitt went a few times to Dr. Jane Greeley when she had what she regarded as "female problems." She had some kind of a breast tumor one time and was alert enough to know it required attention, but she was also careful enough of delicacy to think, "Well, with a personal matter like this, I'd better have that woman look at me." As long as Dr. Jane Greeley was at their sides, matrons who were careful of propriety could accept other care, too, because Dr. Greeley's recommendation conferred respectability on referral. She could send a patient to another doctor, and he would be acceptable. If a referral was needed Dr. Greeley was alert to arrange it, and she stood by her patients literally and symbolically. Her patients proclaimed, "There's nothing wrong in going to Dr. Whosit; Dr. Jane Lincoln Greeley sent me there." She not only wrote referral notes, she even accompanied patients on some visits. Everything was done with dignity, and a woman patient could make that clear to her husband, too.

We had polio, but even before that, we had a close call with death. My brother and I went to Tennessee with our mother. She was pregnant and was advised to get away from the northern winter. She took us to her sister's home in Jackson, Tennessee. We children proceeded to get severe measles and then became desperately ill with pneumonia.

The doctor, a Dr. Duckworth, looked like *The Doctor* in the Luke Fildes' painting of that name. I saw him as a dear old man. He was probably all of thirty-five. The nurse was a marvel named Kelly. Their care inspired me for a lifetime. I kept thinking, "Children need people like this. When I grow up, I am going to stand by little children who are sick in strange places and have sick brothers and mothers who are having babies." By the time we got over pneumonia, I was pretty well persuaded that if I wanted to do anything worthwhile in this world, I had "better get into that outfit."

We had polio when I was nine and William was eight—he was just short of his eighth birthday—and Austin was a year and a half. Two little cousins were there in the household, and they were William's and my age. We all had polio, but William and I were the only ones that developed paralysis. We had already had our experiences with severe illness, but now we were really knocked out and lay absolutely still in bed for several months. We had polio in August, and on Thanksgiving Day I moved about half an inch and took it to be a sign. I called to my brother, "It's a sign!—something to be thankful about."

At that time, our diagnosis was rheumatic fever. We came from a family ridden by that disease, and my brother had already had attacks. We were almost entirely in bed until spring, though at Christmas we began to try crutches. There was no other progress.

Dr. Hubbard from a New York State Department of Health traveling clinic told our parents that we had residual paralysis from polio. Then, he and a nurse applied plaster casts to correct the contractures we had developed in bed and taught our father how to wedge the casts to straighten our legs. Then the doctor said, "Now, when their legs are straight they must go for orthopedic care, either to New York or Boston." My mother asked which was better, and Dr. Hubbard said, "They're equally good—Royal Whitman in New York and Robert W. Lovett in Boston." "In that case," Mama said, "we'll go to Boston. It will be better for their minds." Off we went.

We started physical therapy immediately when we reached Boston. That experience had enormous influence on my life. We landed in Boston at the end of World War I, when the United States was collaborating with Britain and Italy in the first big program for rehabilitation of war wounded, the first such in the history of the world. The doctors who worked on us children were collaborating in order to work on the warriors. This gave us self-respect and a whole new outlook. We were part of historic happenings, and we knew it. Dr. Robert W.

Lovett, who was Professor of Orthopedic Surgery at Harvard Medical School, was uniting his efforts with Sir Robert Jones, England's principal orthopedist, and they were working with Vittorio Putti, an Italian military officer and orthopedic surgeon from Rome. We were enchanted to see how they helped wounded soldiers get around and about again. We saw that disasters happen but that you pick up, get fixed up the best you can, and go on. We saw that clearly. We understood that we would never recover completely from polio, but we intended to get fixed up the best we could. I knew I had to, for I wanted to be able to join doctors and work for other patients.

Dr. Lovett's office had two physical therapists, Miss Laura Henrich and Miss Wilhelmina Wright, pioneers in physical therapy in this country. I worshipped Miss Henrich. She thought it perfectly sensible that I should become a doctor. My mother said, "Pauline has this idea, and you can't get it out of her head." Miss Henrich said, "Well, you wouldn't try to, would you?" My mother said, "But it's so preposterous." "Oh, no," Miss Henrich told her and said to me, "Keep right on with ideas like that. Those are the things that grown-up doctors are made from. You have to have ideas like that and have to have them early." I thought, "Now, listen to that!"

In Boston, I used to go to Trinity Church, where my mother would keep praying that her children would get better. I joined in with her but told myself, "We're doing all right in that line. Don't waste any more time on that. You have other things to pray for. We really have to get underway about getting to be a doctor." So while Mama prayed for us to get over polio, I was praying heart and soul to be a doctor and come back to Boston and take care of children.

I was walking with leg braces, a back-brace, and crutches from about the time I was ten, but when I was twelve I went to summer camp and learned to swim. Around thirteen, I got off crutches and on a cane. My brother reached cane walking first, and I struggled to get so I could do that, too; but in general, my condition was so vigorous compared to his that I felt like a "Band-Aid" case. My whole attitude was, "Well, this is an inconvenience but nothing that should stop a person." I only needed to look at my little brother with advancing scoliosis and heart disease to see someone who was really stopped. His whole body was collapsing and his heart failing so rapidly that my mother could not stand to watch him die.

She would say, "Pauline, you're the one that wants to be a doctor. You find out what the doctor wants, and you take care of it." I would carry out Dr. McCulla's orders and keep the sad little downhill records. It was very bad in many ways. Until a few years ago, I had a recurrent nightmare in which I could see bedspreads with stripes that said UNIVERSITY HOSPITAL and recognized that I was a medical student on internal medicine, looking for the patient assigned to me. Down at the end of the ward I would see a patient propped up, leaning on a "cardiac stand" and struggling to breathe. Suddenly, I would recognize him as my brother William and hurry to him. He would say, "Oh, Pauline, I knew you would come." And I would tell him, "William, oh, William, I'll take good care of you this time. I don't know how I got the idea that you were dead. But I've gone to medical school. I've learned how to take care of sick people and won't let you die."

I felt that it was my fault—that if I had given him better care, surely he would not have died. I felt I had to hurry to medical school because it is a very dangerous world if you're responsible for the care of people who get sick around you and they "die on you," as they say nowadays—isn't that a dreadful expression?

I didn't want to be measured and found wanting in taking care of people. Growing up in my era, it wasn't a matter of *choosing* to take care of the sick. They existed, and you existed, and you'd better learn how to provide care. The same was true of social problems. If your eyes were unscaled enough to see the suffering in the world around you, you had a responsibility to take care of those within your purview—literally, "for God's sake," you must get equipped!

Actually, my childhood was not as totally dreary as it sounds. I was a ringleader, the initiator of all kinds of fun. Over there on the table is a picture of four of us on an outing. That's my close friend Onnolee Hallock in the big hat. Next is our little brother, Austin, age three. I am age eleven, and William, age ten. We're holding a cardboard fish. I had told them of a place in Celoron, New York's amusement park, where you could get your picture taken and appear to be coming home from a fishing trip. I had many good friends in our village.

Of all the periods of my life, I do not think on the whole I would care to tackle high school again—that was the all-time low. It was a real struggle for every kind of reason. In the first place, it was ushered in with William dying, and the whole atmosphere at home—my mother was in a chronic reactive depression. Then, my father went broke, and I was in real anxiety about what I was going to do to get an education, knowing that my father wanted me to get through, get out, and get to work. From my mother it was, "Oh, my children, you should have something better than this; I had such hopes, but they're all gone. There's nothing."

And then, I did not like my looks. For one thing, I knew that people thought it was hopeless to fix me up. My mother tried, but she made some unfortunate clothing choices. When you try to dress a child who wears a back brace and leg brace, a fancy garment just doesn't go too well. But I had good friends in high school, boys and girls. I did real well academically. We were all friends enough that nobody noticed it. We all knew enough dumb things about each other that we couldn't take anyone's grades too seriously. If a high grade turned up, the rest could say, "Well, don't worry about her." They could remind themselves how you had burned a hole in this or that or made some other bungle. They knew your boners too well to be jealous, which sounds funny, but it's true. I certainly didn't have to worry.

The high-school principal was my great ally. Years later, when I was in practice, he said, "I'll tell you a secret. I never enjoyed a student more. You were so *interested.*" I baby-sat for him and his wife. Each time they'd pay me twenty-five cents an hour and put the money in a teapot. The principal said, "I think it best that you just leave this money in our teapot because we're going to get you out of this village. I'm thinking about the University of Michigan. That's my school, and I know you. If I can get you there, there will be scholarships and other help."

In the meantime, at the end of the senior year, I won about three literary prizes—small amounts of maybe ten or fifteen dollars each, but they looked big to me. Then, the morning after graduation, the school principal came to our house, sat down in the dining room, and said to my father, "I want to extract a promise before I leave this house, a promise that Pauline is to get out and go to college." My father said, "Professor, we respect you highly in this family, but there are some things that are impossibilities. It is not going to be possible for Pauline to have a college education." The principal said, "I'm just sitting right here until you promise that you will not stand in her way. You tell me you cannot help her. That's what I'm here for. I'm asking that you stand back and keep from hindering her." My father said, "Well, my God, how can she do it?" The man brought out the teapot money and laid it on the dining table along with envelopes with the prizes, and said, "Don't let anybody touch these. They will be for her going away to school." Tuition at the University of Michigan at that point was sixty-eight dollars a year. So by the time I pooled the baby-care money and the prizes and some graduation presents, I could say, "Now, I'm only a few dollars short of tuition." My mother and little brother pitched in, and we took in tourists and saved the money for clothes for college, and before summer ended, my father went down to a bank in Youngsville, Pennsylvania, and borrowed enough to pay for my room and board for that first semester. That is the last money I ever had from my family.

College and Medical School

It was unbelievable to me that there was anything as wonderful as the university. I would stand on the campus and look at those buildings and think, "Everything happens in this place; there's music, there's everything." And I got into the Choral Union. I can't sing. I don't know how I ever made it, but I got in, and that gave me tickets to the university's concerts plus our own practicing and participation in one Mass, one opera, and a couple of chorales each year.

Then, I'd iron shirts in interesting faculty homes, especially homes where they let you play the victrola while you ironed. You'd really learn in Ann Arbor, and I'd say, "Oh, this is the life!" I'd stand on the campus and think, "In that building they're working on embryology. This building—look at that— philosophy!" I really liked engineering and enjoyed the engineering "open house."

All my jobs were domestic up until I was a junior in medical school. Oh, I never had any cash, but I worked in the kitchen, and that gave me board. My outside work was more to get money to buy part of the things that you need—your lab fees and so on. From the time I entered medical school I had help from New York State's Office of Vocational Rehabilitation for tuition and books. Oh, what a blessing! The support they provided me in medical school was an experiment. They doubted that it was ever intended that vocational rehabilitation should prepare anybody for a profession, but they experimented on me, and they told me later that they regarded it as an investment that "paid off."

I took almost too much premedical science. When the Dean of the medical school, Dr. Hugh Cabot, interviewed me for possible admission, he recognized that at once, and I think he almost turned me down. He said, "I'm not sure that it would be wise to take you. You are too young, and you have concentrated too much on science"—I was nineteen at the time of the interview. I said, "I have done *what?* I thought that's what you were supposed to do to prepare for medical school." "No," he said, "you'll never get a chance to get the enrichment of a broader point of. view. You've over-restricted in chemistry, physics, and biology." "Oh, dear," I said, "I wish I'd known that. I thought that other subjects would have been luxuries and self-indulgences."

That took us into a conversation that has affected my entire life in medicine. Dr. Cabot's interview was an eye-opener. I said, "How would I use these courses?" He said, "You're going to be dealing with human beings. Part of the person is sick, but the person himself has more to do with his life than to be taking pills and suffering. His illness is interrupting something interesting. If you don't know enough about how interesting life is, you're not even going to be aware that this man has been interrupted by his illness." I felt, "Oh, how deficient I am!"

Now they take quotas in order to give access. Then they had quotas to exclude—for instance, taking no more than 10 percent of some group. This applied to other than women. At Buffalo City Hospital, they had quotas on ethnic groups that could be represented in the internships and residencies. It was not, "We shall be certain that we have so many." It was, "We will not, no matter how many come, have any more than one-third Catholics, one-third Jews, and one-third Protestants. You don't need to come because we don't intend to disturb our quota." So a quota was not something that scooped you in, it was grillwork that kept you out, so never did I expect to get in. Dr. Cabot said during the interview, "You are aware that there are very few chances when people come here for interviews that they are going to get admitted. There are something like 1,600 applications, and 160 people get in." And within that number women knew their quota was way down low—I forget what it was.

In the meantime, I was in love and engaged, and I really was holding out against myself. I couldn't possibly go to the interview and not do my level best. I hadn't reached such a state of depravity that I would actually act out my misgivings. But I honestly did not expect to get in and thought what a relief that would be when it was all over, and I had tried but got turned down and could go ahead and get married.

I had met this really nice boy, and we thought a lot of each other—so much that we were talking about getting married. He reminded me of my brother William—comfortable, kind, and sweet. Now, he, too, had had polio in childhood; it was very common then. I think that was one reason I felt a lot toward him as I had toward William. Neither of us felt that we had had polio severely, but we certainly had had it, and I felt very protective of him. I think that meant something to him.

But then he met someone else, a nurse. She was absolutely beautiful—I think she's one of the most beautiful women I ever knew—and had good sense and was a very nice person. He had a lot of male chauvinism, and nurses were in a different category in his mind from women doctors. He didn't think he had to compete with them, and besides, they were a comfort to have around; whereas his attitude toward a woman doctor was more, "Who wants one?"

The idea was that she'll only give you trouble plus humiliation. Also, there was a feeling in those days that girls who went into medicine were some kind of nuts. Families did not want to say they had a girl in medical school. I know my father was embarrassed. My brother studied hotel management, and my father said, "My God, who can face the world with such kids? The girl's a doctor, and the boy's a cook."

I was crushed, just crushed, after the broken engagement. How in God's name I kept going, I don't know because I had been going with him for seven years. I felt it was better to have loved and lost than never to have loved at all but that I'd never love anybody else. That's what I thought. It didn't turn out that way, but I concluded that I had my chance, and I had certainly learned I wasn't worth a damn. I figured that if I could manage to do something in a professional career, I should by all means do it because I was obviously nobody anybody would want. I thought, "Given a second choice, nobody's going to be fool enough to waste his time with you." I had no sensation that there was anything better in store in that line. That was the end of that.

Incidentally, my former boyfriend's wife and I later became good friends. The way life worked out, I stood by her during a time of terrible trouble when they lost a child. They lost it from such damnably poor obstetric care that the tragedy may have had something to do with my later concerns for maternal health. I was stricken by what that girl was subjected to. She nearly died, was never able to have another child, and to this day has health problems of the gravest nature, all as a result of this induced delivery. It is still so upsetting to me that I stumble over the words. The obstetrician induced her in order to go on his vacation. It was a beautiful baby. A big, healthy, boy baby was killed.

I began medical school September 1929, the week the stock market crashed. We were up in anatomy lab when that happened, and you can believe that the part

uck us the most was news of people jumping out windows, suicides, and
)dies. There was some overt discrimination from faculty members, but it
really didn't bother me very much because I knew that the University of Michigan was proud to be one of the first universities in this country to have women in
medical school. So though they might talk in a rough way and have a variety of
feelings, they still had some pride. The man who talked the worst was actually
married to a woman physician. That was Professor Aldred Scott Warthin. He
would say that medicine was no place for a woman and add that he had the
highest esteem for his wife but on other bases than her being a physician. Then,
one of his favorite former students was Dr. Alice Hamilton, a pioneer in the
study of occupational diseases. He was so proud of Alice Hamilton that as I
listened to him, I thought, "This man's bark is worse than his bite. He never
misses a chance to run women down, but his face just glows when he tells about
Alice Hamilton. And Mrs. Warthin is no slouch, and he knows it." I had so
many genuine problems to worry about, especially financial, and worries about
my family back home that I couldn't get all in a lather about the antiwomen
angle, though it existed.

I was one of the only girls—I guess I might have been the only girl—that
landed with the men at the dissection table. I was with another girl and two men,
but the other girl was not a medical student. She was working on a Ph.D. The
other girls were practically all in a medical sorority. I wasn't asked to be in it.
But I'm not sure that I can pretend to myself or to you that if I had money, they
would have welcomed me. They thought me insufficiently dedicated to
medicine. Oh, yes, because they knew I really enjoyed the boys and other
interests they regarded as trivial. They could not view such a person as one you
could count on. You'd better show yourself to be a determined, grim person, and
if you didn't feel very grim, at least determined. Otherwise, they expected that
any minute you would go off to a home and family and other "trivia." I just
personified things that they were fighting in themselves. "We are not trivial
people. We are forthright, up-and-coming women working for our careers. We
do not associate with the flibbertigibbet over there who puts ruffles on her
blouses and laughs." The men were the in-group, and those women were outside, so they were cutting their hair more like the men and doing all kinds of
things to join the "in-group." The classic cliché about women doctors in those
days was that they were very masculine. We were called "hen medics."

All my dissection table partners stayed away when the day came to dissect the
male genitalia, and I was the solitary dissector at the table. Apparently, the whole
class was waiting to see what would happen. The only thing that happened was
that I was there all alone, and I went through with it. I look back now—I didn't
see anything odd about any of it that day. I thought it was most unfortunate that
they all got sick that day, but I certainly wasn't going to quit. I had the same old
notion that has always stood me in good stead: "I may have need for this
experience someday!" I had every reason to think that the time would come

when I darn well better know the male genitalia if I were going to be on a big service. It turned out to be true when I was assistant medical superintendent at the Meyer Memorial Hospital in Buffalo and had to make decisions about male urologic patients in admissions. But I remember that that day in anatomy class wasn't the pleasantest afternoon of my life.

Internship

When I was a senior in medical school, I couldn't get a place for an internship. Students applied individually in those days, and I collected a pile of rejections. Every place said that I wasn't physically of a caliber that could cope. They thought that with the polio I just couldn't manage. They'd say, "Oh, no, we couldn't risk that." I finally got accepted in California but then received word that they had reconsidered the polio part and had withdrawn their acceptance.

Then the Vocational Rehabilitation Office said, "Where are you interning?" I said, "I misinformed you. I told you I was going to San Francisco, but it's fallen through." "On what basis?" they asked. So I sent them a copy of the letter. They said, "Come right to Buffalo. We'll see to it that you get on at Buffalo City Hospital."

When I arrived in Buffalo, I went to the Vocational Rehabilitation Office, and the director, Mr. Jarnagin, took me over to Buffalo City Hospital and introduced me to Dr. Walter S. Goodale, the superintendent and a man years ahead of his time. He said, "We'll take you, but there are only two places open where we will take a woman." "Oh?" I said. "Oh, yes," he said, "we will take a woman on either psychiatry or pediatrics; take your choice." He was talking about openings for interns or junior house officers. I said "Pediatrics." I thought, "I don't want pediatrics but it is the 'lesser of two evils,' for I don't want to go on right now in psychiatry. I want a broader background."

I wanted a general type of internship. It was not that I had views like Gloria Steinem's when she is alleged to have said, "Oh, women in medicine! They put them in pathology or pediatrics, where they're working just with the dead or babies." When I heard that, I felt like saying, "Now, Gloria Steinem, let me just tell you a thing or two. The foundation of enlightened medicine is pathology, and at the same time, anybody without a notion of the juvenile *anlage* of the adult is on thin ice. Put that in your pipe and smoke it!" Anyway, even that day in Buffalo, I already reasoned that you could never go too far astray learning something about puppies before you started working with dogs. If you get so you can repair watches, you won't be too bad with clocks. But I did not think I would be staying in pediatrics.

Then, I got on that pediatric service, and what a service! In those days it was absolutely cracking medicine. It covered not only pediatrics per se but communicable disease—some chronic communicable disease and several floors of acute communicable disease, in an era when people with diphtheria were clawing for breath, when you'd have whole floors of typhoid fever, streptococcal infections—erysipelas, scarlet fever—and, for instance, a woman with puerperal sepsis would be transferred from obstetrics. It was the part of the hospital where red-hot infectious diseases landed. So you had every age, from a newborn with an omphalitis on up through old age with such infections as Ludwig's angina and erysipelas—both invariably fatal at that time.

Then, one day when I was in the basement standing by an elevator, a fine looking woman came along with a stethoscope in her pocket. She said, "Wait a minute! Are you the new doctor on pediatrics?" "Yes," I said. She told me that she was Helen Toskov Wolfson, and she said, "Welcome! We've been dying to meet you. Come on up to the women's quarters. I want you to meet the bunch." I went with her and met the women on duty at the time, and that opened a new chapter in my career and a whole new outlook on life. They were absolutely outstanding—among the best physicians I have ever known and fine people.

I soon discovered that in every service where they worked, they were not just "as good as the men"—they were the best in the place! When the going was tough, they could count on those women. For example, if a complication arose on TB, they might say to each other, "Get hold of Helen Walker. She will stand by when somebody's in trouble."

Well, we talked with each other. We'd sit there in the quarters talking and blowing our noses. When I would come in from a high mortality pediatric floor, they would say, "Oh, here comes Stitt, emoting. What are we going to have to watch today?" For when I reached the rooms I often would say, "Now, sit down, somebody, anybody! I just have to tell you what has been happening on the ward." And I would go on and say things like, "Now, he was lying on his back, cyanotic and with his *alae nasi* dilating like this. . . ." They would say, "Don't bother to tell us the diagnosis; one look at this performance and we can figure out what he had. It's great to have this with our fruit salad"—in shared escape from the hospital cafeteria, we used to make ourselves an occasional lunch. They joked; we all joked with each other, but we understood what we were all going through from the impact of human sorrows. It was truly a mutually supportive group.

The other women got involved with the patients, but you see, they were a little older and much more experienced. They figured that it was all right for us to get involved, providing that when we went to the floor we did not squall or anything like that. If you have to vomit or cry, that's what toilets are for, or quarters. But self-control does not mean that you have to tune out. Oh, you never tune out!

Often I have not fully recognized that I was in new territory. I just went along and went to work, and I have been *so* lucky. When I worked at the Ypsilanti State Hospital in medical school, part of my job was doing spinal taps and syphilis treatments. I was at home doing spinal taps—not in the sense of doing them casually but doing them competently and recognizing the risks involved.

Boy, I really used to be afraid that somebody was going to drop dead in the process.

When I got to Buffalo, they sent me to do a tap on a baby about as big as a pint of ice cream. I was used to big, hulking patients, and I said to the nurse, "A spinal tap on this little baby?" She said, "Yes. Have you never done a spinal tap?" I said, "For two years I did them all the while, but there was never anybody much under 175 or 185 pounds. I've never done anything like this." But the chief on the Pediatrics and Communicable Disease Services had made it clear that in all communicable disease treatment techniques the supervising nurse was queen. No doctor was to contradict a supervising nurse about established procedures, and when we were in doubt, we were to ask them to guide us in the techniques of that service and were to follow those procedures to the letter. "Oh, yes, sir!" I said, because I had already worked happily with capable nurses at the Ypsilanti State Hospital. They were superb, and I knew it. So I now said to this nurse, "I don't think I can do this. But the chief says if we get into a situation where we don't know what to do, you can tell us." She looked at me and grinned, and then she did the nicest thing. She said, "How would you like to use *that* needle?" and pointed to the right size needle on the tray. In other words, she just told me.

Well, she didn't say, "Any fool knows that you can't take the kind of needle you're used to." I said, "You mean, that little needle can be used as a spinal needle?" and she nodded. I said, "Even that little needle looks so big with this little baby." I felt like I was going to vomit. She said, "I think you'll be all right." I said, "Stay here, stay here." "Oh," she said, "I'm right with you." I said, "Thank you very much." Isn't it funny; I'd forgotten all this, but now I can remember the very feeling of my gloved thumb going down the spine, and I relive the whole process of placing the needle. I made the skin marks and looked up, and she was quietly smiling away. I was so surprised and relieved to find that at least the baby's anatomy was comparable to an adult's. Then, I put the needle in cautiously, and sure enough, I could feel when it went through the covering of the cord. I said to her, "We're in."

They had found somebody to do spinal taps on a service with meningitis— "Oh, hurrah, hurrah!" But I was working happily into the service, and I liked that chief. He was rigid as anything. There must have been something in my nature that wanted law and order at that time. I liked to know what was expected of me and what was good quality care. So anyway, I worked on in that service, and at the end of the year— I really have to tell you this, because this is one of the best compliments I ever had in my life—the first thing was, he asked me to stay on. The next thing, I went up to the quarters, and I said, "What do you think—the most remarkable thing has happened. They want me in pediatric service. But you'll never guess—Gus, the chief, you know what he said today? He said, 'Let's have a cup of coffee this morning. We can tell you now, since it is the end of your year here, that before you came, we had never had a woman on this service, and we took you on only because Goodale made us. But we want you to know that from now on we are never going to be without a woman on this service!' " I was so dumbfounded I could hardly respond. But I finally said, "Why is that?" And their reply—in keeping with the times—was, "Well, you have brought a womanly humanity to your work."

I was so happy that I rushed up to the quarters and said, "Oh, you are going to be bowled over. You are just going to be bowled over." I told them about the morning's adventures, and they said, "Yes." "No, no," I said, "I don't think you're listening. Do you realize they never had a woman on that service until I was on?" They said, "Yes." I said, "Have you girls known this right along?" They said, "Yes." "Well, why didn't you tell me?" They said, "Don't you think it's a lot better that you found out this way?" How wise they had been! How wise and kind! If they had told me I was the first woman, I would have been scared to death. I would have been self-conscious. Oh, I assumed that women were often floating through that service.

Career

It became clear to me one exhausting night in Buffalo City Hospital when I had been working with both psychiatric and pediatric patients: I said to myself, "It is really too sad to work only after the damage is done. The main need is to work with the young. I'll work with the young." I had begun to see that much adult medicine is too little and too late. So I was becoming genuinely interested in pediatrics.

I left Buffalo to go into private practice in Jamestown, New York. There, I was on the visiting staff of the two hospitals, the WCA Hospital—Women's Christian Association Hospital—and Jamestown General; that is, they were where I hospitalized my patients.

Home pressure made me return. "You've goofed off enough now. You must come back. We're all in need of help now." Long drawn-out educational programs were distrusted in those days. Their plea was, "Get down here where you belong." But what turned the tables was that the leading group of doctors in Jamestown invited me to join them. Well, you can't both deny opportunity and defy your family in the same breath, so off I went.

It was a group in the sense that you shared a building, "curbstone consultations," and a lab and had great mutual support from each other. But it was not structured like groups are today. You were each alone; and yet spiritually you weren't alone because you could go and say, "If you have a minute, there's something here." I can remember only a few times when I asked any of them to come right in my office to see a patient with me. But over and over again we discussed patients. But I soon discovered that I was pretty much on my own because pediatrics is different from adult medicine, and when I needed help I usually needed it from somebody well grounded in pediatrics.

My practice took right off. There were three, maybe four pediatricians in the area, but we covered a large geographic territory and a big population. The pediatricians were so busy that a new one was welcome. The leading pediatrician of the place was subject to psychotic disturbances which compelled him to go away frequently, and one of the first things that happened was that he kept choosing me to carry on his practice in his absence. That was a mixed blessing. I was scared to death to have the responsibility. On the other hand, it showed me that he had confidence, and it also showed the community.

In 1940, I left private practice because I had to go to a TB sanatorium. In those days it was hardly news. The highest mortality and highest incidence and prevalence of TB was among medical and nursing personnel. So it was not, "Will it happen?" It was almost, "Oh, God, *when* will it hit?" So when they finally said, "You'd better go over to Cassadaga for a while," I replied, "What do you mean, 'a while?' You mean to go over and get some x-rays, maybe?" "No, Pauline, you must move in and stay." My reaction was, "No!"—but I went.

While I was there, I kept saying, "Well, when I go back to practice...." They said, "No, that is over. You cannot go back to practice." I said, "Why not?" They said, "You cannot withstand the irregular hours. You can't 'hitch up early and plow late,' and maybe work all night or even forty-two hours at a stretch. You have to be able, when the evening sun goes down, to read and stay home, or if you work nights, to do it on a reliable schedule—say, every third night." When you have finite means, you cannot meet infinite demands. If you try it with money, you go broke; if you strain your energies, you can get sick, go mad, or drop dead.

When I got up there, I was in the best health of any physician there. The other doctors were very sick with tuberculosis and made no bones about it. Then, our head doctor became so ill that he had to go to the Trudeau Sanatorium at Saranac Lake. When he went to Trudeau, I was put in charge in his absence. That was excellent experience because I really had responsibility for that hospital. I was actually running the place and also, at his request, looking out for his family. I even took care of his little granddaughter, who came down with typhoid fever. I became much interested in tuberculosis control and worked with all age groups. Many were desperately ill or dying. It left a lifelong impression on a person going into public health.

After that, I went back to Buffalo. I became an Assistant Medical Superintendent, which simply meant that every third night, every third weekend, and every third holiday, I was in charge of that 1,350-bed city and county hospital—one of the most instructive experiences of my life.

But then, bombs fell on Hawaii. My brother was in the Philippines on Clark Field when it was bombed. When he came up missing, I decided I must get into the service. I felt that I should be serving my country. I felt, "Oh, you should be an upright, helpful woman, serving your nation and trying to take the place of your brother." It turned out that he was all right. He's now alive, well, and in Texas, but at that time he was missing, and I was inconsolable. I had to pitch in.

I got in touch with the Children's Bureau in Washington, D.C., and as a result was commissioned in the U.S. Public Health Service. I was commissioned as a Passed Assistant Surgeon—equal to a captain in the army and a lieutenant in the navy—then sent to Hawaii on a troop ship. On arrival in Honolulu I was assigned to the Territorial Board of Health.

I worked in maternal and child health and the program for crippled children. I became an itinerant pediatrician going from island to island. When I arrived, Hawaii was in the midst of a severe polio epidemic, and I was assigned to the polio wards which had been set up in the Shriners' Hospital for Crippled Children. It was a natural transition for me, since I had come directly from an acute infectious disease service. I had never had any public health experience that was designated as such, although saying that is like Molière's character who was so astonished when he discovered he had been "speaking prose all his life." No one could have been in practice in those years in acute infectious disease or tuberculosis control or psychiatry and not have been involved in public health. I had been a straight clinician, so I started out going from island to island and worked with the practicing doctors, especially on differential diagnosis of fevers and rashes. It was most interesting.

Again, I was usually blessed by being with terribly sick patients in places where there were well-informed nurses. When you're with well-informed people, relationships get off to a good start. I have worked with so many nurses that I could not lump the whole profession as "those blessed creatures," or "oh, that crowd." There was great diversity among them, but I would not be alive physically if I hadn't been a recipient of good nursing care in my life, and I wouldn't be alive professionally if I hadn't known and worked with the most remarkable bunch of fine nurses. They have been fine—actually, each in her own way. Not one of them could have substituted for one of the others. I think of those who showed me the ropes at Ypsilanti State Hospital, and I wouldn't have been worth a hoot on Wende, Buffalo City's acute communicable service, without those Wende nurses. Then, there have been a host of fine public health nurses, a whole new set of experiences in a new day and age. Each time in my life that I have needed the help and guidance of competent and friendly nursing colleagues, lo and behold, they have been there!

I went to Hawaii in 1943. In 1945, Washington invited me to join the U.S. Children's Bureau, and so I left and went to D.C. I was assigned as the Regional Medical Consultant and Regional Officer for the U.S. Children's Bureau in the southeastern states, working in and out of the Atlanta office. I stayed in that post in the southern states the rest of 1945 and 1946.

The U.S. Children's Bureau was one of the most remarkable organisms I have

ever seen. In the early years it was in the Department of Labor, where it emerged
to protect working women and children—the child laborer whose plight wasn't
too different from Charles Dickens' bottle-factory and blacking-mill experiences,
and women whose working conditions were equally deplorable. The bureau had
come into existence in 1912 when Theodore Roosevelt was President. He had
lost his first wife when she gave birth to their daughter Alice, the present Alice
Roosevelt Longworth, and he was receptive when socially alert citizens proposed
the idea of a children's bureau.

It was strongly shaped by women. But the woman physician part was only one
of the shaping forces. The early staff were mostly social work people. As for Dr.
Martha May Eliot [Associate Chief of the Children's Bureau, first woman president of the American Public Health Association, advocate of government support
for health services and first cousin of T. S. Eliot], she started out, even in her
medical student days, working with Miss Ida Cannon, a pioneer social worker
who was at Massachusetts General Hospital, so Dr. Eliot was imbued with the
importance of social work. She worked closely with social workers throughout
her career and was alert to signals from the sister profession of social work.

When I first went with the Children's Bureau, the Chief was Miss Katharine
Lenroot, daughter of Senator Lenroot of Wisconsin and a woman of statesmanlike ability. It was still an era when people thought it a compliment to say of her,
"She thinks like a man." But the real truth was that she knew government skills
and thought and felt in a fine, human way that would do credit to either a man or
woman. I don't think that women have a monopoly on a decent orientation to
life. Let's not reverse sex bias and claim that a person has to have breasts to
produce the milk of human kindness. That is not true. But surely Miss Lenroot
may have learned much of her orientation and skill from her father.

My situation was delicate in those southern states, for first of all, they would
see me as a "damn Yankee." As for being a woman physician, those southern
gentlemen knew chapter and verse how to treat a lady. They may have questioned
whether a woman could go through medicine and still be a lady, but they never
showed a flicker of doubt. I think I felt more uneasy with them because of being a
Yankee than I did being a woman. I didn't have really very much trouble on either
score. Gentlemanly behavior always brings out the best in a lady. I don't know
anything that helps you more to be a lady than to be with a gentleman.

I had reached a point in the South where I was so homesick for Hawaii that I
couldn't stand it. An anthropologist could very well explain why. I had intense
cultural shock going to the South directly from the multiethnicity of Hawaii and
the joys of living in a place that is hundreds of years ahead of its time in such
matters. So after a while I told Dr. Eliot that I just had to go back to Hawaii. Dr.
Eliot had a true New England conscience, inclined to doubt that worthy effort can
be conducted in a pleasant setting. She may have thought, "Well, a woman of
sterner stuff wouldn't give in and go to palm-bedecked islands," or "You cannot
serve humanity unless you are in a blizzard or an agony area." She never said

ng like that, but I felt guilty. I didn't delude myself that I could save the world all by myself, but I was tormented by the thought that I was walking out on the migrants and the fine people who were trying to help them. Aside from that ambivalence, I wholeheartedly wanted to go back to Hawaii. How I missed it!

So I went back to Hawaii and worked several more years in the Maternal and Child Health and Crippled Children programs. Here in Hawaii, many mothers and children had been moved to the mainland, but new babies were being produced. After Pearl Harbor, there was an unbelievable concentration of the military here and lovely, lovely local girls. In short order, we had what I believe was the nation's only Emergency Maternal and Infant Care (EMIC) Program for out-of-wedlock women and their children. That program became one of my assignments. It was strenuous administratively and an intensely emotional experience. I still like the music of Puccini's *Madame Butterfly,* but the betrayal and desertion of Butterfly and her little boy are too much for me after working in our EMIC program.

Then, I came to realize that I had no right to go further in public health without learning something about it. I knew that there comes a limit to learning to play the violin by ear; I had to have formal training. Another thing was that I was having complications of serious surgery and wasn't getting over them well. It even looked as though I might not be around much longer, so I wanted to get out and see some of the world. Really, I felt that I had been living a somewhat constricting existence and thought, "I've got to get out. If I am going to live, I want to see Europe and I want some education. If I am not going to live, I want to tackle those same things anyway while there is still time."

So I went to an American Public Health Association meeting in San Francisco to get a line on a job and on training opportunities—an APHA meeting is a good place for such a search. While I was there, I ran into my friend Dr. Jessie Bierman, then Professor of Maternal and Child Health at the University of California at Berkeley, and she said, "Come with us. We need a senior pediatrician at our child development center at Children's Hospital of the East Bay in Oakland." I did just that. My post was Lecturer in Pediatrics at the University of California's School of Public Health, and the teaching was done in the clinical setting of the hospital now known as Children's Medical Center of Northern California.

Well, after I worked there about a year, I said to myself, "I have time on my hands. I think I'll go to school." So I started working on a master's program in maternal and child health in Dr. Bierman's department. When I completed the M.P.H. course at Berkeley, I went directly to the Harvard School of Public Health to teach.

Harvard does not have a great reputation for equitable treatment of women in medicine. I heard, even as late as 1974, when Mary Ellen Avery was made Chief Medical Officer in Children's Hospital, that some people were still protesting, "But she is a woman"—that kind of thing. But I can testify wholeheartedly that women worked happily and effectively in Dr. Stuart's department where I was. I don't know a lot about the rest of the university, but I was busy and happy there. I loved it.

Let me just tell you this: in my own experience at Harvard, I really don't think that I fared any less well than I would have if I had been a man. But I saw women around me in some other departments who were mainstays of the departments, where men were in leadership roles but were buoyed, sustained, and held aloft by capable women. Their attitude to those women was such as sailors might have had for life preservers. "Oh, you wouldn't want to be without one, but let's not lose our heads and promote a life preserver or make one the head of the department. *I'm* still skipper of this ship."

In the meantime, Dr. Harold Stuart retired, and when he retired, Dr. Martha Eliot came, so I had two or three years when I was assistant professor to Dr. Eliot. They were very interesting years. Her successor was Dr. William Schmidt. Now, this is so absurd that I can scarcely allow myself to tell you—but when he came on board, I assumed that he would want to start out fresh with new staff and would not want me, so I resigned. Later, I learned that he had intended to have me stay on but had not told me so. In the meantime, I was appointed to be an associate to Dr. Henry Bakst, Professor of Preventive Medicine at Boston University Medical School. Just before all changes were finalized, I myself was almost "finalized," for I landed in the Peter Bent Brigham Hospital for an emergency bowel resection to relieve a sudden obstruction, probably related to that intussusception I had when I was twelve years old.

I am proud of my students, and some say I influenced them. Among them is Dr. Roberta Savitz, who was one of my students at Boston University and worked with me later in the Children's Bureau's Research Division in Washington. She is a practicing psychiatrist in the Boston area. And there is Dr. Joan Babbott, the first student I met when I went to Boston, a friend ever since, and now outstanding in social pediatrics and maternal and child health in Vermont.

A former Harvard medical student who brings special joy to my life is Dr. Donald Yamagucki of Gardena, California, a hand surgeon, who has for several years honored me by giving an annual "Pauline Stitt Award" to an outstanding student in the University of Hawaii School of Public Health. Incidentally, Donald Yamagucki was also a patient of mine as a boy on the island of Maui.

In 1962 I went to Washington, D.C., to be Chief of Child Health Studies within the old Children's Bureau Research Division. I directed the rapid research—so-called "quick and dirty"—studies to pull together the essential data the Children's Bureau took to the Congress. It provided facts for the subsequent establishment and funding for the Children and Youth and Maternal and Infant Care programs—C & Y and M & I projects.

The process of locating, assembling, and analyzing data of that sort is an eye-opening experience, especially when it has to be done rapidly. It was really exciting, for once you have worked in the field, you do not see data as numerical abstractions or decimal points. You are working with real lives.

The Children's Bureau was suffering onslaughts from governmental reorganization influences. Maternal and child health work per se is always uphill work because, despite pious protestations to the contrary, public officials see children as little people with little problems, and women's problems are equally invisible.

At Boston University Medical School, I had been in charge of the home-care service, so before long Dr. Claire Ryder, head of Home Care in the Public Health Service, asked me to join them. I was glad to go over and work setting up home-care programs, for I was sure that any such basic community resource as home care should be developed with long-range concern for children and "mothers and others" and not be solely focused on the geriatric Medicare population. I wanted to be in there and help make home care as useful as possible to those programs and to whole communities because home care was perceived in such constricted fashion in different parts of the country. The medical profession rarely got the drift at all. They thought everybody who was sick ought to be in the hospital. Well, you know that that just isn't true at all. Innumerable people are ill at home, ill with conditions which would be inappropriate to hospitalize, but they still need sorts of care which can be provided at home.

I was detailed from Home Care to do staff work on the Secretary's Advisory Committee on Health Protection and Disease Prevention. This was an advisory committee to the Secretary of HEW chaired by Arthur Fleming. Secretary Wilbur Cohen set it up just before he left HEW. It served Secretary Finch briefly, then vanished, and I was invited to move over and carry some of the committee's impulses into the preparations for the 1970 White House Conference on Children and Youth.

I was in charge of health forums, five—finally four—forums and several thousand delegates. The work took all of 1969 and 1970. After the conference, when we processed the recommendations, I was given the task of following through on all health and law recommendations and getting them in shape to go to Secretary Elliott Richardson for action. It turned out to be ever so interesting, one of the best assignments I ever had.

When the assignment was completed, I was to go back out to Rockville to the Parklawn Building and reconnect with health-care delivery portions of the Public Health Service. The programs appealed to me, but I could hardly stand the thought of the way the winds and blizzards sweep around that building. I felt tired and inadequate. As Dr. Edith Sappington, former Children's Bureau Regional Consultant, who inspired me every inch of the way in my first years in Hawaii and ever after, says, "There are just so many jumps in a frog."

While I was being interviewed by a really fine public health officer and for an interesting post, Dr. Roy Smith, acting Professor of Maternal and Child Health at the University of Hawaii, was waiting in an outer office to see if I would come to Hawaii as Professor of Maternal and Child Health. I was honored·by the PHS offer. But I thought of the physical struggles I would have in the ice and snow, and I knew I must choose Hawaii.

I took early retirement from the Public Health Service and came to Hawaii to teach for three years. I expected to go back to Washington, where I had a choice apartment all set for retirement. But despite asthma, pneumonia, and a few other physical upsets, I found Hawaii the place to stay.

On Women In Medicine

Well, now, they're going great guns, and I think on the whole that they're a fine crowd, and I am all for them. I am concerned about a small fringe of women today who jeopardize all fields of women's progress by being hellishly hostile. It seems to me they are saying, "By God, we are going to wreck the joint." On the other side, there are some other women pussyfooting along in ways that were outmoded in 1926. I feel like shouting at them, "Yoo-hoo, yoo-hoo! Awake from your slumbers!" In between, I think there is a broad area of truly fine medical women—the best I have ever seen. An international view of medical women is inspiring. Think of the pediatric contributions of the late Cornelia de Lange of Holland and of Doctora Fé del Mundo of the Philippines, of Ida Mann, the British ophthalmologist, Viktoria Winnecka of the World Health Organization, and Maternal and Child Health Professor Dr. J. Harfouche of Beirut, and the Chief Health Officer and Director of Social Security for France, Dr. Simone Veil. Also, Dr. Genevieve Massé and the late Nathalie Massé of the International Children's Centre in Paris—what physicians and what women! All girl medical students and women physicians can take heart from such women. Their kind are now found scattered over the whole globe.

On the Health of Women

I think that many of us feel that women must keep their history straight. Many don't comprehend what realities earlier women were up against. I read a medical article where the writers were saying, "What a put-down! Women were regarded as physically inferior." They seemed unaware of the physical problems women had contended with—the number who had dragged around with pulmonary tuberculosis or hearts ruined by rheumatic fever—and appeared oblivious to the gynecologic wreckage of pathologic childbearing, puerperal sepsis, and pelvic inflammatory disease. All that and no penicillin or other modern measures! When contemporary writers judge without valid data and dismiss those disabilities as poppycock, they are unfair to women.

On Abortion

My mother had abortions, and they constituted desolate chapters of her life. She thought that's what birth control was. They were, as in so many localities, done by a good physician who had met with personal misfortune. This one had developed a paraplegia but could still work from a wheelchair, and everybody knew that Dr. X., "dear blessed man," had "kept his family going and sent sons away to school and lived a life of great shame" because of "what he had to do." Apparently my mother and father went to that doctor repeatedly, and they had nothing but affectionate sorrow that the man had been reduced to such a grisly way of practicing the profession for which he had prepared with such care. Ultimately, my mother had complications that nearly caused her death, a perforation of the uterus. She reminded me in our conversations, and I began to recall a time when she had nearly died. I had not understood the nature of her illness but knew she gave me heartrending instructions about mothering my brothers if we "lost" her.

I could, in total harmony with my conscience, work in a birth control clinic, but if I noticed that there was an overrepresentation of minorities, or if I heard the people in charge calling them "these people" or some patronizing term like that, I would wash my hands in more than green soap! That's the best I can tell you.

On Men

All through my life I have had important relationships with men. I think I have known some of the finest men that any woman ever had the good luck to know. Even the heels have been interesting, and I don't think they meant to be heels; I think it just came naturally!

On Never Having Had Children

I don't know when I finally reached that point of being glad that I have no children. I think that the sixties and the plight of youth in wartime affected me. My own brother came to Washington on a visit. Ben Spock stood over in front of the HEW building holding a youth rally, an anti-Vietnam War protest, and I said to my brother, "We must get over there—with them." My brother and his wife left town! I went over and stood with the youth. I saw how Spock had aged and how desperate he looked, like a man whose heart was broken but who was going down fighting to the finish! I thought, "Ben Spock, I know how you are feeling. If you are going to go mad, so am I and for the same reason. To think we have poured our hearts and souls into these children, only to see them swept away to destruction. By God, if you are crazy, I am crazy, too. This is too much."

On the American Medical Women's Association

I've belonged to the association, and I was part of New York State Medical Women. I've always enjoyed them, but I've never been a tub-thumper. I was on the Editorial Board of the *Journal of the American Medical Women's Association* for a while. I worked with them for two or three years and enjoyed them very much. But I do not care to be a segregationalist in this. Now, Alice Chenoweth and Claire Ryder, oh, are dedicated members, and I respect their enthusiasm. They found me a little pallid as a professional partner in these lines. We are friends, but they must feel that I have a little aplasia of those parts of my development.

On Her Life Choices

Well, I often ask myself, and I do not know the answer. I have had many times brief passing moments, lasting from minutes to days, when I have wondered, "How did I ever get into subject areas confined by renal tubules and cerumen and pus, when I really like the theater and art and music and social history? How did I get into this?" Then, I tell myself, "Well, that doesn't mean that I wanted those fields instead of medicine." I think my interests are "medicine plus."

On the Future of Medicine

We agree that there have been great changes during my lifetime—and now, what do I expect? Oh, I expect it is going, as it has gone, like a Ravel *Bolero*—a continually accelerating tempo—and I would like to see the score. The pages of the score are glued together for me, but I would like to know what others are going to experience. I have an idea that good things are coming.

Honolulu, Hawaii
December 9, 1977

DISCUSSION: PART I

For a woman born in the first decade of the twentieth century, the choice of medicine as a career was unlikely in the extreme. All the practical problems that face women seeking medical training today existed then and were compounded by widespread public prejudice, rejection by colleagues, severe institutional restrictions, and lingering doubts about the mental and physical capacities of women for such work. Clearly, it took an unusually strong-minded woman to surmount the obstacles to such a commitment. Indeed, the most immediately striking thing about Katharine Boucot Sturgis, Alma Dea Morani, and Pauline Stitt—even among women physicians, individualists almost by definition—is their forceful, colorful personalities. So highly differentiated are they that one might despair of making any generalizations at all. On closer inspection, however, it is possible to detect certain common elements in their stories.

Like most women physicians, all three reached their decisions to pursue medical careers rather early in life. Predictably enough, all encountered some opposition from their parents, particularly their fathers. Yet despite their traditional beliefs about woman's place, one senses that Morani's and Stitt's fathers, at least, tolerated and to some extent encouraged their daughters' feistiness. Their mothers may have been somewhat more sympathetic to their daughters' medical ambitions, but they provided little support either by precept or by example for the kind of aggressiveness required to reach such goals. Morani's mother felt that motherhood was a woman's highest calling and deplored what she saw as her daughter's tomboyishness—an attitude shared by Sturgis's mother-surrogate, the nurse Katie. Stitt's mother, while willing to stand up to her husband in matters of principle, tended to advocate a more "behind the scenes" approach in pursuing one's objectives.

Although their early backgrounds differed radically from one another, all three women found in their childhood experiences sources of strength and determination to overcome parental objections. Morani, the oldest child in a family of ambitious and energetic Italians living in New York City, may have been influenced by the familiar immigrant conviction of that era that anything was possible in America; telling her she couldn't do something simply spurred her to prove that she could. Stitt, also a first child, suffered many childhood illnesses, including a bout with polio that necessitated long-term rehabilitative therapy and left her permanently crippled. Despite her impoverished, rural, somewhat anti-intellectual environment, her extensive interactions with doctors convinced her beyond a doubt that medicine was "the outfit to get into." Sturgis, although not a firstborn child, also enjoyed a great deal of parental attention and perceived herself as the favorite among eight children. Coming from a wealthy, privileged background where everyone seemed a little larger than life, she was strongly imbued with a sense of her own specialness as well as with a tradition of service to the less fortunate.

World War I was a fact of their childhoods, but although it must have tempered their view of the world, it occurred too early to have exerted a direct effect on the course of their careers. The Depression, which occurred just as these women were embarking on their adult lives, had an impact on all three and sorely tested the strength of their commitment to medicine. Morani recalls pooling her limited resources with an equally penurious friend during medical school. Stitt began her medical studies the week the stock market crashed in 1929 and worked as a domestic until she was a junior. For Sturgis the Depression actually precipitated her medical career: when her husband and her father suffered substantial business reverses, she took a secretarial post at the University of Pennsylvania School of Medicine, which rekindled her youthful dream of becoming a doctor.

World War II also played a part—perhaps an unexpected one—in the lives of Morani and Stitt, prompting what might now be thought of as a midlife career change. Major advances in plastic surgery in response to the needs of the war-wounded piqued Morani's interest; she subsequently became one of the first women to qualify in that field. Stitt, when her brother was reported missing in the Pacific, developed a strong conviction that she too should be contributing to the war effort, which led her to join the Public Health Service. Sturgis, of course, had recently made her own career change, entering medical school in 1935 at the age of thirty-two.

As an interesting sidelight, the stories of Stitt and Sturgis, both of whom contracted tuberculosis, provide a grim reminder of what was, until quite recently, a fact of medical life for all physicians, men as well as women. Until the advent of effective pharmacological treatment, TB was fairly common among medical personnel, even after improved sanitation had reduced the incidence in the general population.

Sturgis, Morani, and Stitt belong to perhaps the last generation of heirs to the nineteenth-century tradition of medicine as a calling that required of women an uncompromising dedication and sometimes great personal sacrifice. They are less likely than those who follow to think explicitly in terms of having to make a living. They see medicine rather as a useful and appropriate channel for woman's finer instincts. Sturgis sees "giving, caring" as the essence of medicine and likens it to breast-feeding. Although Morani was acutely aware of the feast-or-famine quality of her father's life and wished to avoid such an existence, she also speaks feelingly of the "need for a woman to express her womanliness, her motherliness" that can be filled by a medical career.

Despite the theoretical link between women physicians and the maternal instinct, however, medicine and marriage were not seen as particularly compatible pursuits for women. Medicine, on the contrary, was viewed as a substitute for family life rather than as an adjunct to it. Indeed, few institutions would have considered accepting an older woman with children, as Woman's Medical College did Sturgis. Some women physicians did marry, of course, but for them medicine was supposed to be relegated almost to the status of a hobby, certainly subordinate to the needs of husband and children. Such women were considered—by some of their female colleagues as well as their male—less committed, less serious, less truly devoted to their calling. Stitt was thought to be frivolous and "insufficiently dedicated to medicine" by her fellow female medical students because of her interest in men.

Thus, we see all three of the women presented here adjusting their expectations in one way or another. Morani decided early in life that marriage was excessively risky and never seems to have wavered, even momentarily, in that position. Rather, she sought a community of women, as evidenced by her active involvement in the American Medical Women's Association, which provided her with social as well as professional outlets. Stitt was interested in marriage and was briefly engaged to a man ultimately unable to accept her vocational commitment; over the years she has not found it possible to reconcile the demands of her profession with the needs of the men with whom she has associated. Sturgis, once she married, abandoned her plans for continuing her education. Not until she was divorced did she again address herself to her original goals. When she remarried, it was to an atypical man who was content to "live in her life." Interestingly, once she did resume her education, she seems to have been amazingly free of the guilt that so often plagues employed mothers today, perhaps because she came from a background where it was perfectly acceptable for children to be reared by housekeepers.

During the formative years of these women, analysts had not yet begun to examine critically the assumption that the practical problems facing women physicians were rooted in eternal verities about the nature of women and their role. It is, therefore, perhaps not surprising to find a certain amount of ambivalence in their attitudes toward other women. All three women have observed some discrimination against women and sympathize with its victims up to a point. Yet, all are careful to differentiate themselves from other women physicians in one way or another and to dissociate themselves from what they regard as extremist positions. Quotas, after all, were simply a fact of life, something to be gotten around. One senses here a deep-seated conviction that if a woman is good enough, she will be able to achieve success in a man's world, on male terms, whatever barriers are thrown in her way. In the end, rising above discrimination commands more respect than attacking it head-on. Such a position, whatever its merits, clearly places a greater burden on women than on men and demands more sacrifices. In the context of the nineteenth-century model of medicine as a quasi-religious calling for women, the burdens and the sacrifices could be justified. As that model broke down, the situation for women in medicine became even more complicated than it already was. The problems remained, the obstructions remained, but as the stories in the next section illustrate, women physicians were beginning to experience a growing restlessness with traditional solutions.

PART II
BEARING FRUIT

4

Beryl Michaelson

INDIAN HEALTH SERVICE DOC

*Born in 1918, Beryl Michaelson grew up on a farm in Humboldt, Iowa,
and taught in rural schools in Iowa and Alaska to earn money for medical
training. She subsequently returned to Alaska as a physician for the Indian
Health Service, where one of her proudest achievements was the initiation
of a successful program of ambulatory chemotherapy for tuberculosis.
After five years, a bout of infectious hepatitis forced her to leave Alaska,
and at her mother's urging, she decided to enter general practice in her
hometown. She remained there for seventeen years, until mounting paperwork and rising malpractice insurance rates drove her out of private
practice. Retirement quickly palled, and at the time of this interview, she
had returned to the Indian Health Service as a staff physician at the United
States Public Health Service Hospital in Eagle Butte, South Dakota.*

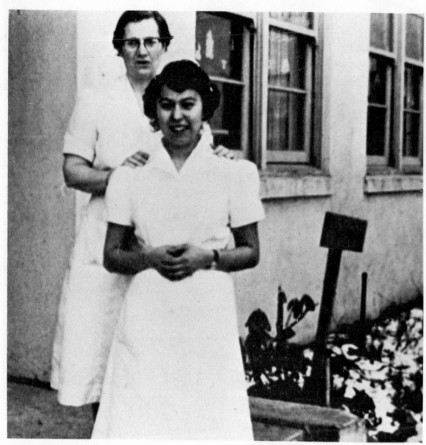

Beryl Michaelson (rear) in 1954 in front of clinic at Mt. Edgecumbe, Alaska, with a nurse.

Childhood

My father bought a farm when I was a year old, and it was the only place that I ever knew as home base. My father was beautiful. He very seldom ever got angry. He had a real good sense of humor. And oh, he was a very jolly person and had a lot of feeling for independence.

Well, like he used to say, he was a king in his own right. He didn't have to answer to anybody. He got up when he wanted to, and he went to bed when he wanted to; he did what he wanted to. He wouldn't have done anything else but farm because that was the only type of a business where he felt that the only thing he had to answer to was Mother Nature and the Lord. So he used to tell his children the same thing. He said, "Okay, you can do whatever you want to do. You can be at the head of the line, or you can follow along like the old cow's tail." He would mention this several times, especially when we'd be sitting on a load of corn following the cattle home from the field. He would introduce his philosophies in this fashion.

I was the apple of his eye. I could do anything. It made the boys kind of mad once in a while, because I always was the favorite. But as such, I became quite a tomboy, too. Well, I would milk cows, and I would go out cornhusking. I even, at one time, drove a horse team on a horse-drawn cultivator—and I couldn't have been more than eight or nine years old at the time, either. But, I do remember it. That would make my dad so proud—that I would do most anything; he did show his pride.

He and Mom were really, truly partners. It was rather strange because she came from city life. She didn't have any farm background or anything. He wanted her with him in all activities. He even took her to farm sales to buy cattle and horses when she was the only woman on the lot, and stuff like this. It didn't bother him in the least. They did things together. They did things together even on the farm. She learned to go out and husk corn and whatnot right along beside him.

And anytime that—oh, say that she wasn't feeling good, he would fix breakfast, get our school kids' lunches ready, and this type of thing. It was strictly a partnership. They were practically inseparable, even to the point of the things they liked to do. They loved to fish, and all of us children learned how to fish, too. But it was a family affair, and there was nothing that we loved better than going fishing. I can still remember when we wanted to go, or we were going to go on a certain weekend, and he was disappointed; he said, no, the weather wasn't holding up just right—he'd better get his cultivating done before it was too big for him to finish—and he felt he had to work over the weekend. But he finished in the middle of the week, and he finished in the middle of the morning. He came in, and he said, "Okay, we're done with the field. How about going fishing?" And we were gone in thirty minutes.

My mother hated school. She said she couldn't wait until she finished the eighth grade, and she wouldn't go on to high school. She did take a musical conservatory course for a couple of years. But she always said, "If you don't want to go to school, stay home. You're welcome to stay right here. We like to have you kids around. If you want to go, okay. Fine. We won't stop you. If you want to stay home, you can." I had a warm relationship with my mother. She believed that women should be individuals, too.

My mother was a card, a character right up to the moment she died. The day before the night before she died—she would have been eighty-two a month after she died—there was, oh, a group of us there together. So she was singing, and they were all singing together, and of course, I was kind of choked up and got off key, and she said, "Well, it would sound a little better if everybody was in the same key."

I had one older brother and two younger brothers. Well, I don't remember that my brothers had more privileges. We were expected to be home at a certain time, but most of our recreation, again, was family recreation. My folks played for dances four and five nights a week through the Depression years, which kept bread and butter in the house, and we would go to those same dances. They were family dances—so, the nights we were out late, coming in at two, three, four o'clock in the morning, they were, too! So, it didn't seem to make that much difference.

We had this fire. I remember my brother . . . I can still remember him looking down on me. It had to be a crib with side rails on it because he was hanging up over the top looking down, trying to tell me to get out of bed, there was a fire, and I thought he was trying to con me into getting up with a tall tale. I wouldn't believe him at first, but then . . . I also remember this teacher dressing me out in the barn, and seeing the house burn, and standing alongside of my mother when they were carrying the stove and all this stuff out of that fire. It was one of the early tragedies of childhood.

There was one severe illness. I don't remember the illness, but I remember coming out of it. I asked my mother about it later on. I told her one time, "You know, I have a recollection of getting out of a crib and being on the floor and seeing a baby bottle on the end of a dresser and trying to get to it—and I couldn't walk. Did I ever actually learn how to walk over?" She looked at me kind of funny, and she said, "Well, yes, but you surely don't remember that, do you?" I said, "Well, I sure do"—because there was a fear that I could remember and recall when I couldn't get up and walk to what I wanted to walk to. And she said I was only about nine, ten months old, but I could walk between eight and nine months. Then, they got this 1918 flu, or 1919 flu, and we were all sick. They expected my father to die. She and my brother were all in bed, and I was, too. They finally got a practical nurse to come and stay with us. Dad was sick for over six weeks. We were sick for about two weeks. She said when we were finally coming out of it and they put me out of the crib on the floor, I couldn't walk. I crawled and then learned how to walk over again.

I knew I was going to be a physician at thirteen. My freshman/sophomore year in high school decided that, and it was Leone Arent that influenced me primarily. She was the niece of one of the physicians in town and a daughter of a pharmacist in an adjoining town. She was a history teacher; she taught medieval history and American history. But one of the things she brought in, in one of those classes, was a series of talks on careers. Well, as an individual teacher I used to just worship this woman. She really was somebody that I idolized.

She had an outlook of . . . well, everything was a joy, and you looked for the good things. That, again, was reemphasizing more or less what my folks always said—that life was something to enjoy, and work should be a joy as much as vacation and play and so on; that everything could be fun. She made school fun. I mean, her teaching, her classes were fun. I suppose this is one reason I took to her, because she was patterned more or less after the principles my folks used to have. She began to explain all these different types of careers. She started out more or less with a hierarchy, and she put medicine at the top. I had always been taught, well, you head for the top. You don't go for the lower ones. It's like this bit of following along like the old cow's tail. You could either be out in front or you could be behind.

She said that medicine required the highest IQ and highest grade point average. At that time, I was very conscious of grade point average. I guess when I first entered school I became conscious of grade point because they had an honor roll, and I know I was very proud—because, I guess, my dad was so proud—that I was on the honor roll. So this was one of the things; I was vying for the top of the class from the time I entered as a freshman and was within one-tenth of a percent of being valedictorian. I could fit the criteria that Miss Arent was setting up, and I thought, "Well, now, the way she puts that, I am a candidate." It never occurred to me there would be that much difficulty. Never occurred to me that there was preference for men and not for women in medical school.

I know that I was very resentful when I mentioned that I was going to be a doctor and somebody laughed and asked me, "Well, you mean a nurse?" I said, "By no means do I mean a nurse. A nurse has to take orders from the doctor. I'm going to be the one to give the orders."

And, the idea of helping other people was very attractive. I feel that the height of anyone's career is to be of service to other people. I think that's actually the only goal anybody should ever have—how much can you do for your neighbor.

College and Teaching

When I graduated from high school I had a four-year scholarship to Iowa State Teachers College. I thought it was mine outright, and so did the folks; nobody explained to me that you used it that year or it went to somebody else. I had just turned sixteen before graduating, and granted, that was a little young to go away to college; my folks thought it was just a little bit too young. And though they were very delicate about presenting it as such—they never made me really feel bad about staying home that year—they asked me to stay home a year because they thought that I would benefit more by the college work if I waited a year. They felt that I would be more with my own age group and could compete with the social requirements of college and so on if I were a year older. Besides, it was going to be a rough year at home.

Well, the next year started, and we found there was no scholarship. It was a blow. My folks were just more than upset. I think I felt more sorry for them than the fact that I had lost the scholarship. They were just crushed because they knew how much I wanted to go. So they had a family conference, and they said, "Well, we've got the other three kids to think about, too, but we also promised that you could go." So they had to borrow money to let me go to school that year, and I think they sent me five dollars a week to live on besides paying my tuition and dormitory and so on.

I looked over the courses—they said they'd pay for one year, and from then on I'd have to do it on my own. The only thing I could see in any of the college curricula was a one-year rural teaching course, and I thought, "Well, that's a way of getting started"—not a very good motivation to be a teacher, but at least I could get some working capital to go on. So I did take the one-year rural teaching course and started teaching school the next year when I was eighteen. I got a total of seventy-five dollars a month for nine months, which was top wages in those days, and out of that, I went to school summers and took correspondence courses during the year. Then, after five years I accumulated enough so that I could take off and stay in school the year of 1941 through 1942 and got my bachelor of arts degree from Iowa State Teachers College.

I had one boyfriend. We had some good times together, but it was never too romantic. We were more or less having good-time dates—going skiing, going dancing, this sort of thing. I was afraid of getting too serious with him because I thought it would interfere with my career, and that was more important to me than romance. I felt I wouldn't do justice to a family. I loved kids; I loved the idea of a home and family; and there were times when I'd look at it and think maybe I was missing part of it. But I'd think, well, really, if I was going to do what I wanted to do, it wouldn't be fair to kids or to a husband. I couldn't do justice to both, and I didn't feel that I should get involved with both. Then, I didn't have too much opportunity to develop anything else because I was so involved with teaching full-time, taking correspondence courses, going to school full time in the summer . . . then what additional time I had, I had to be working part-time to get the money to stay in school, and so what time did I have for social life?

After finishing at Iowa State Teachers College, I spent two years in Alaska. Money was the objective. Outside the Placement Bureau in the university, there were all these little signs about jobs available. I went by there one day and saw a sign from Civil Service asking for teachers for the Indian Health Service, which at that time was under the Department of Interior and Bureau of Indian Affairs. They wanted teachers, and the requirements were five years rural teaching experience and a bachelor of arts degree; and I thought, "Boy, I just meet it." Well, base pay was $1,800 with a 25 percent differential for outside the continental United States living allowance, which made a $2,200 salary. At the time, I had signed a contract to teach in a small school, south of Waterloo. I was the next to highest paid graduate of the class, and my contract was $1,100 a year. But anyway, I decided to go to Alaska. Your way was paid up if you stayed a year, and it was paid out if you stayed two years. I thought, "Well, it'll take me two years to get what I want anyway." So money was the sole motivation, but I thoroughly enjoyed it.

Selawik was the first place I went to. It was a little, isolated Eskimo village six miles above the Arctic Circle, a hundred miles inland from Kotzebue, which was the northern point of the Bering Strait. It was a very fascinating experience.

At the time, we had so many other things to do besides teach school. One of them was to hold a medical clinic after school hours. The teacher was the only source of medical help that these people had, and the school had a certain number of pills—I remember we had sulfacetamide and sulfathizole and aspirin and APCs and all this sort of stuff; we had kaopectate and some ergot and all. But we also had a little recipe book, you might say, telling things that you used these medicines for. After school, they would bring a whole bunch of things in, whether it was taking out a sliver or putting on a Band-Aid or . . . there was a good deal of gonorrhea, and we had a ten-day treatment at that time with sulfathizole. We'd hand out the pills. Now, we never took an examination or a smear or anything like that.

Medical School

In transferring the credits from State Teachers to the University of Iowa, there were quarter hours transferred into semester hours, and it ended up I was two-thirds of an hour short in chemistry and physics. So I had to take a year over; I had to take these whole courses over at the University of Iowa before I could start medical school.

During the spring of that year, when the acceptances were being made for medical school, that was the only time that I ever had any doubts of whether I was going to make it or not. The acceptances were being given out on an alphabetical system. Well, I didn't think anything about it until all of a sudden Munson and Opfell were getting theirs, and I hadn't gotten mine. This physics instructor, Dr. Eldrich, kept asking me every day about whether I got it, and I said, "No." So this one time he said, "Well, it looks to me like I'm going to have to go over and talk to those people," and the next day I got my acceptance. So he was, I'm sure, the one that was very influential, somehow or another, in getting me past the Dean—because when I had my personal interview with the

Dean, even though I knew I had one of the highest aptitude tests, which I had taken as a senior at Iowa State Teachers College in 1942, the Dean told me, "Well, you know you've got three strikes against you." I said no, that I wasn't aware of the fact that I had three strikes against me; what was he talking about? "Well," he said, "you're approaching the deadline on age." This was during 1944, when we had our application in. We entered in 1945, so that would make me twenty-six, I guess. And he said . . . that was the time that he brought up that I was a woman; that was the second thing. He said, "And you're a woman. And the third thing is, you're too goddamn fat." I almost said, "You s.o.b.," but I thought, well, that wasn't safe under the circumstances; I was still trying to get by this guy. But that was the first inkling I had that there might be any discrimination in admitting women to the class.

"Well," I said, "I don't think any of those three would bother me too much." Then, he wanted to know what my motivation was, and I said, "Well, right now, my motivation is to go back to Alaska—because having been there in the past two years as a teacher, I realize that their greatest need is for physicians rather than teachers, and I'd rather go back there as a physician." Somehow or another I got the idea—I don't know how he conveyed that idea—that as long as I wasn't competing with physicians in the state of Iowa, this might be acceptable.

There were thirteen women in my class. There was a Dr. Scheldrup whom we could have tarred and feathered and crucified. He was so against women—it stood out like a sore thumb. He was the only teacher who really made an issue of it. He was a devil on wheels. I almost got thrown out, I think, in my freshman year. There were six of us around this cadaver, and we were having oral examination. Well, here's a guy that's about six feet two, so by the time he held something up to his chest like this, I was looking up at it. He was sitting there with his big hand around the heart with a pointer, pointing to all these different things, asking me what this, that, and everything was. I said, "Now, if you expect me to answer those questions, you're going to have to at least put it down where I can see what you're doing." He went, "Hmf!" like that and tossed the heart on the table and wrote a zero down for my mark. As he turned around to walk away, I picked up that heart, and I had it like this, and the whole class went, "Ooooh." Their reaction made me drop it, or I'd have hit him right in the back of the head with that thing—knowing that if I had, that would have been the end of things; but at the same time, I almost let him have it.

Half the class, at the time when we entered as freshmen, were what we called V-12 or ASTP [Army Specialized Training Program]. They were military programs to produce physicians for the navy and the army, and I thought that some of them were there as part of their military training and might have been motivated more by the educational benefits offered by the military. There were some, I felt, that were motivated possibly by money; others because they had physicians in the family. The bulk of them, I felt, were there for the same reason I was—to be able to help humanity. There were only three out of our whole class that ended up saying they wanted to be GPs, though there were quite a few in our freshman group that wanted to be GPs. I don't know what the percentage was—I think it may have been 25, 40 percent who wanted to be GPs as freshmen, and their attitudes changed by the time they were seniors. I always wanted to be a GP because I felt that total family practice would be more gratifying than doing a specialty.

We had sympathy for each other because we didn't know who was going to be weeded out. The Dean also came in the first day of the medical class and said, ''Look to the right of you and look to the left of you. At the end of this year, one of you is going to be gone.'' They figured that they had to weed out at least a third of the students the freshman year. So we never knew who was going to be dropped or why. We knew there would be some on behavior, some on ethics, but most of them on a grade point average—so there was competition as far as trying to master the subject matter.

Yet, we would exchange study questions, review past examinations, and so on. Like every medical school, I think, people came out of an examination and tried to record the questions that had been asked, and these were kept for the next class so they'd get an idea of what was being asked—and we shared answers back and forth to these questions. In a sense, we were helping each other in that way, though we knew ultimately that we would be dropped if we didn't attain a certain grade level.

I was working nights from eleven to seven at the psychiatric ward as an aide. I was supposed to be just relief, but it got so that relief meant six days a week. We weren't supposed to be working more than two nights a week, but nobody ever checked up on us, so I was actually working, oh, on the average of five nights a week, anyway—sometimes more. But this more or less kept me in school—with the assistance of my brother, who was in the service at that time; he sent me some money. He was married, and he loved to play poker. He'd keep out seventy-five dollars of his pay to play poker, and the rest of his paycheck went to his wife. Then out of the poker winnings, he'd send half to his wife and the other half to me. That half just more or less kept me in medical school for about two years.

In my senior year, I took a preceptorship at Saint Monica's Hospital in Phoenix. There was a Father Emmett McLaughlin who was in charge of the hospital, and at first he wasn't even going to see me; the secretary wasn't going to let me in to see him. I said I had come some distance, and I at least would like to talk to him. So he came out when he heard my persistence, and he wanted to know who I was and where I came from. And he said, ''Well, you're from the University of Iowa—I don't want anything to do with you.'' I said, ''Hold on a minute. You've got to explain that one.'' He said, ''Well, do you know this fellow?''—and he held up the name of a fellow who had graduated the year before and had all sorts of recommendations and had accepted an internship there. Well, he spent one day in the emergency room, and he had gotten involved with a syphilitic mother who had come in and precipped [precipitated delivery] in the emergency room, and it turned his stomach. He said that was enough; he had walked out. I looked at him and said, "Well, I'd be a poor substitute for an intern, but I think you're stuck with me, because you can't be left with that impression of the University of Iowa." He said, "Do you mean for free— gratis?" And I said, "Well, I've got to get back to the university, and I've got to live while I'm here." So he ended up giving me seventy-five dollars a month and board and room and laundry, and I stayed as a preceptee. He let me do anything. I had forty-nine deliveries that year.

I was functioning as an intern those three months that I was down there in the summer. It was kind of funny; I was given the first gruesome, bloody mess that they got in—an alcoholic that had gotten into a fight and was half stoned, and his scalp was cut open and blood all over everything. Father McLaughlin insisted that I take this case in the emergency room. I caught him watching me out of the corner of my eye. Looking sideways, I could see he had the door open and he was watching me; and I thought, "You son of a gun, you're not going to see me squeamish in this situation. I'll get through it one way or the other," and I hadn't even had ahold of a needle holder! So I sort of winked at the nurse; I said, "You help me through this thing." She was handing me the instruments, and, of course, I was identifying them quick enough to know what to do with them. I went ahead and sutured that scalp up, not ever having done one before. So the minute I passed, I was in like Flynn.

Internship

Father McLaughlin had me signed up beforehand for my internship, which was illegal, but he wanted to make sure I was coming back; and I had had such a thoroughly enjoyable experience that I felt it was worth coming back, so I signed up a year ahead of time.

We were taught we should know when to back off. We were either sure of what we were doing, or we asked for consultation, and we had a good background in that. I mean, what I knew, I knew; and I knew what I didn't know. So when we'd run into a situation, if I had time to look it up and then go ahead on my own, fine; I did this. But if not, I wasn't the least bit hesitant about calling in a consultant.

One time in OB, I called in this consultant five or six times during the night. I thought he was going to cut my head off, but nevertheless, I'd call him back. We had a toxemia of pregnancy, and it was really acute. He came out and saw the patient initially, and then he gave me standing orders: "You give 100 milligrams of Demerol on the hour and a grain and one half of phenobarb on the half hour, and you keep that up until the woman is sedated to the point that she doesn't rouse when you come into the room but you can shake her and get some response. But she's supposed to be down to that degree." Well, I did this for twelve hours, and she never did get down to that degree—and that's enough medication to kill a horse, let alone a human. I'd get a little bit squeamish after awhile, and I'd call him back up and say, "Are you sure I'm supposed to keep going with this?" Oh, he got hostile; he said, "I don't want to be bothered again with it." Well, I didn't hesitate to call him again. I called him four or five times during that night because I thought that was a huge amount of medication to give, and I wanted to make sure he'd back me up, because even the nurses were leery of giving it. Yet, that baby came out of there screaming; I delivered that kid, and the kid wasn't even narcotized. And she did fine. But I just couldn't believe that a person could absorb that kind of medication.

The nurses had problems taking orders from any intern. I mean, you'll find that all nurses seem to feel that they've got to mother the interns and buffer them through. I think they feel that they really educate the interns into the practice of medicine, which maybe they do. I think there are a lot of benefits from the nurses, too, to the intern who's starting out. I don't think it's so much on the basis of being a woman, though I do know that I resented a few times when they refused to accept my orders.

One of these times was again on the OB floor. The University of Iowa was one of the foremost in the obstetrical field; we were the university that started getting women on their feet immediately—the same day—after delivery and not keeping them in bed for ten days. I went to Phoenix and ordered this—up the first day and so on—and they just thought this was rank heresy. They wanted to call the Chief of Staff and countermand my orders. This was the first realization I had that nurses could do this in the first place. I respected their belief that they had the right to check because I realized then that there were physicians who could order things that weren't just exactly according to the general accepted method—and if they did, who was to check on them but the nurse? So anyway, the year that I was an extern, I found I had to kowtow to what the nurse said. The next year, when I came back, this new practice of getting patients up immediately after delivery had been propagated, and that same nurse was on. She said, "We didn't realize when you were here last year that you were a year ahead of us."

Indian Health Service in Alaska

I went initially to Mount Edgecumbe, and there they had a 400-bed hospital with twelve physicians on the staff. I was there from July until the end of November. But on Thanksgiving Day, the hospital at Bethel had burned, and the patients were scattered in all directions. Then, the doctor at Kanakanak, which was the nearest hospital to Bethel, was going on vacation, and I was sent up there to relieve him while he was gone; he was gone for three months. Then, I was sent from there over to Bethel to open up a first aid station, clean up this fire rubble, and try to keep some type of medical facilities going. At Mount Edgecumbe, I didn't know what it was to be in charge; I was just a staff physician. At Kanakanak, I had to be the Medical Officer in Charge, being the only physician there, and at that time, the Medical Officer was also the Service Unit Director in charge of all departments. This was rather strange, because it was the first time that I realized I covered maintenance, I covered nursing, and I covered all aspects of running an institution.

When I was sent into Bethel, which was in March of 1951, we had been held up by a blizzard, a seven-day blizzard, and it had covered everything with drifts of snow. They couldn't get planes in and out of Anchorage or any other airstrip. You could fly the bush because you landed on skis in a bush plane and you could land anywhere. So I was flown going from Kanakanak into Bethel, and as I got off the plane at Bethel the manager of the roadhouse was there and said, "I understand we've got a doctor coming in on this flight. I've got two patients for you." I said, "Well, I don't know as we're prepared to accept a patient." He said, "They're your responsibility. No roadhouse can take care of two bed patients. One of them has blood poisoning, and the other one has frozen feet and hands from being caught out in this blizzard."

So I proceeded out to what had been the hospital grounds to observe the fire rubble from the hospital, and there was a residential house, a one-story frame building that had been the previous doctor's residence, and there were three quonset huts. One of the quonset huts was the residence of the maintenance foreman and his wife, and the other two quonset huts were for medical use—one with medical beds for patients, and one with an examining room that was finally equipped with x-ray and a lab. At the time I got there, there was just an examining room with an examining table. In the quonset hut for the patients, they were in the process of trying to move in some beds for the nurses' quarters—regular sleeping beds; they weren't the beds you could crank up and down. They later put some gas pipe on the legs to elevate the beds to a level where the nurses wouldn't break their backs taking care of the patients. The maintenance men built the bedside tables. There was no running water in this facility when I got there; they had heat in the building, but the plumbing wasn't accomplished yet. They had the head nurse who had been there from the hospital that had burned, and she had two of her staff nurses. Then, there was the public health nurse from an office downtown. She had a little different function; she visited all the villages. We went down and borrowed thermometers and dressings from her.

But the maintenance foreman met me when I arrived, and I said, "You know, if you've got an ambulance, you'd better send it down to the roadhouse and pick up two patients. They tell me that we've got two patients down there." He just looked at me and said, "You're a little premature, aren't you?" I said, "Well, can it be done?" He said, "Well, if you say so, I guess it can be done." So he went down and got the patients. We talked to this head nurse, and she said, "Well, we've got bedding; I'll bring that over from the nurses' quarters. We'll put two beds up and carry bed pans, and we'll have to carry water and food from the . . ."—they had converted this previous doctor's residence into a kind of mess hall for the general staff, and they had used the stoves and household equipment in there for cooking food for everybody. It was just start from scratch. I stayed there for three years. After the new hospital was built, I was transferred back to Mount Edgecumbe—and that was a story in itself.

During my stay at Bethel, with these seven beds and three cribs we ran an average census, I think, of something like twelve, fifteen, which, you may see, meant that we had patients on the floor and everywhere else because that quonset hut wasn't going to take care of the amount of people that a sixty-bed hospital had serviced. The same number of people and the same number of medical problems had been there all the way along, and I was supposed to keep things running as a first aid station. Well, I saw as high as 160 some people a day in an outpatient clinic.

But one of the things that got started was we had these TB patients—20 percent of the population had active TB—and some of them had waited as long as ten years for a hospital bed—no beds available. The government's attitude toward TB had vacillated. One time, it was taking in the serious ones—let them come in to die. Then, they thought they would refuse these admissions and take those they felt that surgery or hospitalization could cure. So there were a lot of terminal cases that were left out there to contaminate everybody else. There was no consistent attitude. But at this time, Fitzsimmons had released an article on outpatient chemotherapy that he was trying. I had read that article, and I was so fascinated by it. I thought maybe this was the answer to what we were facing, and we started in medicating the patients that came for whatever—if they had TB, they were treated this way, partly because if everybody was in the same room, how could you isolate them? They were going to contaminate everybody else. It was much better to put them under therapy, try to control the contagion. All of a sudden it began to work, and these people, once they were discharged, would ask about continuing the shots and continuing the medication. Well, we would give it to them. Then, word began to spread, and it began to be a problem. People were moving in from the out villages, setting up camp at Bethel, because the word was out that they were getting better. I didn't realize that this was being propagated so much among the natives themselves until the thing began to mushroom, and I thought, "Well, golly, what have we got started here?" I got almost more than what I could handle, so I went down to the area office and was going to ask for help. I started asking the Area Medical Director about outpatient chemotherapy, and he turned me off before I even got started; he said, "Absolutely not." And the Territorial U.S. Commissioner of Health for the territory—well, absolutely thumbs down. How can you go on? I got something started I couldn't stop. No way was I going back up there and let those people down. I couldn't carry them all that way and then go up and face them and say, "Sorry, we can't do it any more." So I thought, "Well, you're getting your neck stuck out here, you know." Well, I thought at that time again, "Okay, you stuck your neck out, you're going to have to take the consequences," which is actually what happened.

It ended up that I had—oh, I've forgotten the exact number—160, 170 patients who had improved so much that they no longer needed hospitalization. This Surgeon General, Thomas Parran, who had been the previous Surgeon General of the Public Health Service, had been sent in by the University of Pittsburgh, and he had a crew with him that had been given a grant by Congress to review the health facilities in Alaska. He came to Bethel—we only expected him to stay a half day and then go on—and he said to one of the schoolteachers, "And I suppose TB is one of your biggest problems?" She said, "Well, it used to be, but it isn't any longer." He said, "What?" "Well, not since Dr. Michaelson was giving them this therapy." He said, "Hey, what's going on here?" He started to investigate, and he ended up staying a week. He took pictures; he took copies of all the records and photostated all the x-rays and left his statistician there for another week. He wanted to take the records, but I said, "No way"—they were government records; he couldn't take those. But he took copies of them all. Then, he went down to my supervisor, who was the Area Medical Director, and said, "Hey, why isn't this being done in all the service units in your area?" Of course, this took my supervisor by surprise; he wasn't even aware of the fact that it was going on. It embarrassed him; he was in an embarrassing position. Well, he came out there, and he was madder than a hornet, and he said, "It looks like you're getting too big for your shoes. You better come back to Mount Edgecumbe and learn how to take orders again before you can be a field physician." I knew at the time that he would just as soon I resigned, and I wouldn't just because—well, it was a matter of pride, I suppose. I stayed one more year.

Private Practice in Iowa

My mother probably decided *where* I was going back into private practice. I really wasn't sure what I wanted to do, and I hadn't had a good vacation for a long time, so I said, "Well, I'm not carrying too much. I'm going to take off and have a vacation." I went down to visit one of the nurses who had been with me in Alaska and who was married, and I had delivered her child; she was living in Avon Park, Florida. And I said, "I'm going down to see part of Florida. I've never been there before, and I love to travel." So Mom had said something about, "Well, would you consider going into private practice here at home?" "Oh," I said, "I might if I had a place to practice" and hadn't given it any more thought than that. Well, I hadn't any more gotten to this nurse's home when the phone rang. Mom was on the phone, and she said, "Well, you better come back home. We got you an office." I said, "What?" She said, "Yes. You know that building on the corner of Such-and-Such Street in Dakota City? We bought it. Please come home to remodel it."

All of a sudden when she called, I realized how much it meant to them for me to do it. At the same time, I also noticed something else that had occurred. Just prior to that, in 1954, my folks had gone to California. They were beginning to sound old. My brother had gone away to school, and they were by themselves, and they just didn't know what to do. My mother, who had been driving all over the United States, all of a sudden couldn't drive from Humboldt to Fort Dodge, which was only a matter of eighteen miles, let alone go to further places. Then, she had a new lease on life. Why, she could drive anywhere, all of a sudden just overnight; it was no problem.

She was my receptionist to start with—first job she'd ever had. She was thrilled to death; I think she was going to frame her first check. But she was a delight in the office. In the first place, she knew everybody, and then, she was such a card. They'd come out with a bunch of pills, and she'd say, "What do you want those for? Throw them away." She just tickled the patients. She'd have them out there laughing so that by the time they came in to see me, they didn't need anything anyway.

I was snowed right off the bat. Like I said, my folks had lived in that county long enough to be known by everybody. My father, my grandfather, whatnot—all well-known. So whether they were friends or relatives or just people I had known when I was in school . . . people remembered me as having been an honor roll student when I was there.

More children, I would say, came at first. I have a natural knack with children, and the kids enjoyed coming. Then, the mothers and especially the OBs; I did—oh, something like 3,500 deliveries. But I loved OB work and the pediatrics. Then, the husbands just naturally came along because most of them didn't want to have more than one physician—though we did have a very good working relationship in Humboldt. Just like when I was a child—Dr. Coddington's father delivered all of us. My dad used to go to Dr. Arent's father. And here were young Dr. Arent and young Dr. Coddington and I, all working in the same area and having known each other from school days. We had a mutual respect, I think, even before we ever went to school. So there was never any question of competition. I think it was Dr. Coddington who got me into the American Academy of Family Practice. So we had a good working relationship and switching back and forth made no difference.

If I had to go somewhere, I'd put a sign on my door: "I have been called out of town"; and they would go see somebody else. When I got back, they'd come back. I mean, there was nothing like this bit of having to notify all your clientele for all the legal responsibilities and so on. It was an understood, accepted thing that if one doctor was gone, you saw the other one in town. You were never left without anybody. The rewards—I mean prestige and the amount of service I could do and so on—were great, but it got *too* great. I couldn't get somebody to come in and relieve me because a small town doesn't attract physicians too easily.

The prospect of facing any more of it was horrendous—seven days a week, twenty-four hours a day, just couldn't go on anymore. I was exhausted. My mother had become too ill to stay by herself. She had tried to be independent as long as she could at the lake cottage, but it became obvious at Eastertime that year that she was going to have to have help. So I brought her home, and I had somebody twenty-four hours, so she was never alone, and took care of her at home until she died, the third of August in 1972. Of course, that was an extra strain which didn't go too well with the physical stuff that was going on with the practice itself.

Then, there were always outside things that were intervening. I became very leery of what was happening with Medicare. The hospital was going in the red because Medicare would disallow 10 percent across the board. We had this stupid group in Sioux Falls City that reviewed Medicare claims, that felt that they were obligated to disallow 10 percent regardless of whether the patient was eligible or not. I found that that was just a local thing. They didn't do that in Minnesota. I don't know why the Iowa group felt that they had to keep down the Medicare payments to that extent. We had several that we protested. One of them we fought all the way to Baltimore and back and . . . they ended up paying the bill.

So here the patients were left maybe with the remainder, you see, to pay themselves, and maybe they didn't have anything to cover it. So then, the hospital was getting involved with a lot of debts that they couldn't collect. So all of a sudden, they were talking about making the physicians responsible for this. The idea was that if you didn't get patients out of the hospital at the time when Medicare was no longer going to pay the bill, then maybe the physicians were at fault.

So here we were being told by an outside agency *when* we had to discharge the patients, which burned me to a crisp in the first place. If you can't take care of the patient for the patient's good, then where do we stand? Why should we be involved with people who don't even understand what's going on saying when to discharge the patient? So I was rebelling against this.

Then, I heard that in Cleveland there was a physician who was negligent— there was no question about his negligence. He had a patient with a fractured leg that he put in a cast. He left on a Friday night; he didn't make any arrangements to have this patient seen; he returned on Monday. When the doctor got back and took the cast off, the leg was gangrenous. The guy loses his leg, and he sues the hospital. He doesn't only sue the hospital, he sues the doctor, the hospital, the Board of Trustees, and the whole medical staff, each one individually and totally—won on all counts. Each one of the physicians who were on the staff was held personally responsible on the basis that the hospital okayed the physician's credentials, accepted him into the staff, and this obligated them to monitor his work, and since they didn't they were equally guilty. I said, "My gosh and hemlock! If we're going to be responsible for all our colleagues. . . ."

All these things sort of snowballed at the same time as far as a reason for getting out. I said it was just too much third party interference, too much exhaustion. The emotional aspect of my family being gone in Humboldt was a part of it, too. I had nobody at home anymore, and so this was an element that was involved, too; I can't deny that.

Indian Health Service in South Dakota

I left private practice in October of 1972. I had surgery myself, and then I recuperated. Then, I went to the lake cottage, oh, about Christmastime, and stayed there for awhile. Then, I took these various trips—I went to Mexico, to California a couple of times, and so on, and I got tired of traveling. I would go back to hang up my hat, and I found I was getting just a little bit bored.

Actually, there was a good spiritual side of that thing, too. I went to church one morning, and here was Father Gall talking about not hiding your talents under a bushel; if you were prepared to do something, you should be doing it. I listened to the sermon he was giving, and I thought, "Gee, I almost fit that category, too." Here I was—I had the qualifications, I had the ability, and I still could do it; and I wasn't using it.

I went home that day and was going through the mail and found a newsletter, *Family Practice News,* and right on the front page: "Indian Service Desperate for Physicians." Then, the article went on to say how all these positions had been filled by the Public Health Corps, which completed the obligation for military service; young physicians could go into public health and not have to put their two years in the military. So, there had been no problem filling these positions. All of a sudden the draft had ended, and those who had been there, their service was up. The places were empty, and nobody was filling them, and they were in danger of having to close the hospitals—there are several of them in the Aberdeen area. They were asking for help from the American academy—anybody who was willing to come, even for a week or two weeks or a month at a time. Initially, I set out for two weeks, and I liked it, so I said, "Okay, I'll come back for another two weeks." I was there from October 1973—hit or miss that year—and then I went back the first of September in 1974 to stay permanently.

I liked the freedom from Medicare, Medicaid, outside interference, to take care of patients with no paperwork. That's all that was needed—I mean, there was desperate need for medical care for the patients, and there still is a great deal of work that needs doing there. I also liked the satisfaction of being able to help out where I was really needed. Of course, my hometown would object to that because they said, "The need is here, too, and you left us."

I'm Clinical Director of the hospital and, as such, Chief of Staff—an appointed position here because of the fact we are not totally commission corps [commissioned officers in the public health service]. Where all of them are commission corps and on the same status, they will elect. As it was, I was the only one. I got the position partly because I was the oldest in the Indian Service, having had ten years of government service—seven years when I got here and three years since.

I come in about eight, and leave, well, supposedly at five, but that's never really true. There's always something to do afterwards, especially since I go out in the field—because when I get back from the field, there's more stuff to do than I get done between that time and five o'clock. Like last night, it was about 8 P.M. when I went home. I imagine we spend fifty-five to sixty hours a week.

There is not so much tuberculosis anymore; that seems to be the one problem that has been fairly eradicated. Since the advent of chemotherapy for tuberculosis, they're closing TB sanitariums and converting them to regular hospitals rather than just using them as sanitariums any more—very few strictly sanitariums left. Number one problem here is alcohol and related conditions.

That talk about involuntary sterilizations is a bunch of bunk. That isn't so. I don't know who started it, but that has never occurred. The Indian women themselves come in asking for sterilizations, and the government makes it very difficult for them to get sterilized. They have to go through a whole book of all the ramifications of sterilization—the fact that it's irreversible; the fact that they might lose their children or might lose their husbands and then want more children with another husband; the fact that it's one of those things that can't be undone—that it's a myth that the tubes can be tied and untied. They have to read this thing and wait seventy-two hours to think it over before, so that they're given every opportunity to change their minds. If they don't do this, it won't be paid for. That is the government requirement. The government makes it very difficult for them to get sterilized because it wants to make sure that they really want sterilization. If they insist on having it all the way through, then they're accommodated. But, this bit of saying that it's forced upon them is a bunch of bananas.

Well, we're constantly frustrated by the lack of facilities and lack of funding. But at the same time, considering the overall aspect, I think our patients get much better care than the average American nationwide, because in some respects we're not limited in our referrals. We refer all the time to Creighton and to Omaha and to the University of Minnesota, and we go for CAT scans and tomograms and this type of sophisticated medicine on a referral basis under contract care all the time. We have a large expenditure in contract care that isn't available at the local level, but it is available to these people. There are many times at home that there is no way the people could afford such type of sophisticated care.

Once in a while we'll run into somebody who will come in and say, "Well, you're not going to touch me. I want you to send me to a specialist; there's no one around here knows anything." We get a little of this once in awhile. We were getting a lot of it when we were first here, which I accepted as a challenge. I thought, "Well, I've never been anywhere I wasn't accepted." In fact, my being a woman doctor may be of some benefit, because there was a Doctor Molly here at one time that they liked quite well. She stayed a little longer than the average, so they got to know her. Same thing happened with me—since I have been here the longest, they will come to me, and they will open up to me, and they are friendly with me, and so on, just because they know me. They have been very rude to some of the top specialists who we've had in here who came and donated their services for a couple of weeks.

On Women in Medicine

I don't think there's been too much change in the status of women in medicine. I think that attitude is one that has been generated by the public more than by the individual woman physician. I think she was comfortable going into medicine in the first place; she's still comfortable in medicine, or she wouldn't be staying there. I have found that colleagues accept colleagues on an equal basis, and there hasn't been any distinction, woman or male.

I haven't known any women physicians to be, say, president of the medical association in Iowa. I was president of our local one because a rule was adopted that each one take his turn. The presidency just rotated, so we've all had that experience. The same way with the secretaryship of the staff at the Lutheran and Mercy hospitals in Fort Dodge—the new additions to the staff are usually sec- retaries the second year so they can get acquainted with the process. We took our turn at doing that, but it was a matter of taking our turn, not a matter of being elected to the position. Not having had or having seen a woman elected as president of the state society and so on—I never thought of that too much one way or the other, because there weren't that many women in the society to make a political bloc. I don't think any of them were interested in the politics of it.

Women bring special ability to medicine. I would say more sympathy, more empathy with the patient's condition, probably more of a gentleness. I know I resent it when I'm watching some physicians that I think have been too rough. I think men tend to be a little rougher than women, and I don't think they sense this. Patients came to me specifically because I was a woman, especially for certain things. If they had a boil or an abscess or something similar that was really hurting them, they would come to me and say, "No way I would let a man touch this." And for Paps and pelvic exams and so on, they would prefer me.

On Friendship

I like people, and I have a lot of friends. We have, oh, about 150 Christmas cards go out every year to people that I hear from every year. And these are varied; they go from—as I said—this girl that I knew when I was seven or eight years old; I'm still corresponding with her.

On Hobbies

I love to fish. I like to have somebody go fishing with me, but that isn't a requirement; I can go and enjoy fishing by myself, too. I like to sew a little bit;

I've got a sewing machine, and I like all different kinds of fabrics. I enjoy a certain amount of art work. I used to do an awful lot more than I do now. I like to draw scenery pictures with chalk. I did that when I was in Alaska; that was one of the things I took with me that I enjoy doing. I did a little ceramics when I was at Mount Edgecumbe. I haven't been able to keep up with that, but I do have a kiln. I think some day I may get back into it, you know. This rat race that I'm into prohibits me from doing many of these things, but I still have the interest. I'm going to get to that soon.

On Feminism

I don't think women need advancement any more. They've got that already, if they want to exercise it. I mean, they've had the opportunity; they've always had the opportunity. I think it's a lot of baloney, the women's lib bit; I think they're destroying their women's image rather than improving it. I think we've always had the right to be a woman, which has got a kind of special category of its own; why destroy it? I'm very much against the women's lib movement, because I think it's destroying the image women had.

On Her Life

I've enjoyed every bit of it. I wouldn't have missed any of it.

Eagle Butte, South Dakota
July 27, 1977

5

Marjorie Sirridge

LATECOMER TO ACADEMIC MEDICINE

Though she graduated at the top of her medical school class, Marjorie Spurrier Sirridge experienced great difficulty in establishing her career. She found society offered little support to women determined to balance the demands of a family with those of medicine. Becoming pregnant at the beginning of her residency, she interrupted her medical training for five years to raise her four children and to keep house for her husband, a physician who was struggling to establish a practice. When she returned to medicine, she entered nonapproved programs in pathology and hematology because part-time residencies were not available in any of the accredited teaching hospitals in Kansas City. Her unorthodox training was held against her when she sought full-time faculty status at the University of Kansas Medical Center, although they did not question her expertise when they needed her services on a part-time basis. In 1971, after many years in private practice with her husband, she welcomed the opportunity to become involved with the innovative, six-year medical school being set up by the University of Missouri at Kansas City. She is very conscious of serving as a role model for the students, 50 percent of whom are female.

Marjorie S. Sirridge (1976), Senior Docent and Professor of Medicine, in her office at the University of Missouri, Kansas City School of Medicine.

Childhood

I was born in a small town of about 3,000, Kingman, Kansas, in the year 1921. There is a lot of wheat farming in that general area. I went to school with children from all the families in the community—all the way through grade school and high school.

My father was the superintendent of the light and power plant. He was an extremely bright man who had dropped out of high school to help support his family, so most of his education in engineering was self-taught. He was a very good mechanic, and he served as a mechanic in World War I with the air force. He was able to handle machines of great intricacy, and he was very good at math and physics. All self-taught. He really knew more than my teachers in high school. If we had trouble with problems in math or physics, we used to take them to my father because he knew how to do all these sorts of things. He was very important to the town in many ways because he did run the light and power plant throughout his entire life and was superintendent there. But he also could repair musical instruments; he could repair guns; he was a good electrician. So he was essentially the town repair-person, and for that reason, I think, he had a different place in the community than he might otherwise have had. He was known throughout the community as kind of an eccentric but also as a person who would help anybody in trouble, or try to help, by being able to do the things that he could do. He was bright, a tremendous individualist, a nonconformist.

I liked him as a person. I was aware of the fact that he was different, and there were problems. In my adolescent years, I think I tried to change him; or at least, I think I tried to feel that perhaps I might have some impact on his behavior.

In many ways, I was close to my mother in that she was a warm, quite happy person and easy to be around, not demanding. And yet, intellectually I suspect I was closer to my father, and I always felt something sort of special when he took time to go over things with me. I can remember once lying out on the grass looking up at the stars. He knew a lot about the stars, and we'd lie out there and pick out stars. Well, it's funny that I'd remember that because that's a little, isolated thing; and yet, obviously that must have meant something to me. I think the main thing is that my father never really treated me as a woman—or he never implied that a woman was any different than a man with respect to what she might want to do. I don't think there was ever anything that I said I would like to do that he ever implied that I couldn't do. So as I look back on it, I think this must have been terribly influential. I went hunting with him, and he never treated me as if I were any different. If I wanted to go and carry a gun, that was fine. Of any of the things that I wanted to do, there was never any thought, "Well, girls don't do that," or, "You should do this because you're a girl."

I think my mother was much more interested in my feminine development, dancing lessons, and my social success, for which my dad had absolutely no concern. Nor do I think he ever at any time commented on my appearance. If he cared how I looked, he never said so. So I never did get any positive strokes for looking one way, or negative strokes either. All that came from my mother. My father had a lot of respect for my mother. I think he had a lot of respect for women in general. I believe he had a lot of respect for his own mother, and I think he perceived in his own mother a strong person, a person that he probably had related well to, although I don't know this because I never knew her.

My mother was a very capable woman and very much an individual in her own right. I don't think that people often even thought of them as a couple because they sort of went their own ways. She was a schoolteacher and did a lot of substitute teaching. In fact, I think I probably went to school to her at least once every year while I was in school; and frequently she would finish terms for people during the school teaching year. During the war, when they were short of teachers, she actually went back and taught in a one-room country school. And she taught herself to type after the war and became a newspaper writer.

So in a way, it was not the usual kind of family relationship. They were kind of two independent people, my parents, and they interacted with a lot of people in the community. There was a sort of expanded family for me. I was an only child and had no brothers and sisters and really didn't have very many relatives in the community, but there was a lot of expansion; there were women I called aunts who weren't aunts to me at all but were friends of the family. And there was a lot of communal activity—Sunday dinners when everybody took things, and quilts that were made for the children of the different families. So it was a different way of growing up, really.

I think my mother's attitude was that women should be independent, that they should have the capability of doing things, and she had always demonstrated this. One of the things I know I did acquire from my mother is a feeling about homemaking and housekeeping in the sense that my mother was a reluctant housekeeper. She would much prefer to teach school and hire somebody to clean her house. And I learned to do housework very early and was pretty good at it partly because she didn't like to do it. I always liked things to be neater than she did. It wasn't exactly conflict; it was just that we didn't do things the same way—I'd clean the cupboards and she wouldn't. It was just a difference in the way we approached housekeeping.

One teacher I remember in particular was my Latin teacher in high school, who was a very ladylike, prim, precise person whom I had a lot of admiration for. I think it was her independence and the fact that she taught well; she did her job extremely well. There was never anybody who didn't think that she was really top-notch.

And then I remember another teacher that we had that I was terribly impressed with because she was so glamorous. She was really the only glamorous teacher we had, and I was quite impressed with her for that reason.

I do have certain feelings from high school in that I don't think I considered myself strongly physically attractive. I think I thought I was okay, but that there were a lot of girls who were more attractive. And I think there was in myself a certain envy of girls who were little and graceful and much more feminine than I was. But it was not a terribly big problem. I think I probably always felt like it wasn't *the* most important thing. It was certainly important. I think the most important thing to me was really doing well . . . I was always at the top of the class. That's not exactly a comfortable place to be, particularly when there are boys in your class; and I always did better than the boys in the class. And I'm sure this was not really comfortable. I was valedictorian of my high school class, and I earned it; I felt that I earned it.

I was not an unpopular girl; I did get asked to most of the things that one needed to be asked to, like the proms, but I never really felt that the most attractive boys were interested in me. I guess one would like to think it's mostly because they didn't want to go out with a smart girl. I don't know whether that was true or not, but I guess one likes to use that in a way.

I never really wanted to be a man—that I know. The fact is, I don't ever think I thought that it was bad to be a woman. I think I thought it was kind of a challenge and sort of liked the idea of doing things that women hadn't done before. It never occurred to me that women couldn't. But I certainly don't ever remember really envying boys. And of course, maybe I didn't really know much about what boys did, because I didn't have a brother and I didn't have any close men; and my dad was a lot different from lots of men. I think I liked being the kind of girl that I was—a little bit different. I still like this. I mean, I like being a woman doctor because I think it's something kind of special. And I like the role. I've liked it from the day I said I wanted to do it, and I think I liked saying something which was just a little bit different. I think that gave me a certain feeling of satisfaction, saying, "Well, I will do that."

I just felt sure I wanted to do something different; so when I enrolled in college, I enrolled as a premedical student. And I remember my first advisor was almost unwilling to advise me. He said, "Well, you'll never last. There's no way that you'll ever make it." I told him, "You know, that's really silly. I will make it. If I decide that's what I'm going to do, I will. And I want to be enrolled in premedicine." I finally ended up having a course from him, my third year in school. He was a physiological chemist. It really gave me a feeling of satisfaction to do very well in this course and say, "Well, look, I really am still here, and I'm still in premedicine, and I am going to go to medical school."

I don't think my parents believed that I would do it either. I think they thought, "Well, it's okay. She can do lots of other things if she starts out this way, and this doesn't really mean that she'll. . . ." My dad used to say, "Well, you'll just get married; you'll never make it clear through. That's eight years, and you'll never do it"—even though he thought it was okay. He said, "If you want to try it, it's fine; I just don't think you'll ever get there, that's all." And I don't think mother ever said much one way or another about it, as I recall. Other members of the family, I think, thought it was all right but that I wouldn't finish. I think that was how it went.

College

When I got to college, there were a lot of people that I met who were in premedicine. There was one girl, who was a very good friend of mine, who was a year ahead of me, and she did start medical school the year before I did. However, she didn't make it past the first year, so that was kind of a worry to me. She was bright enough to have done it, but I think there were a lot of other pressures on her.

Then, there were at least two boys that I was very friendly with in college who were both in premedicine. We knew each other well, took the premedical exams together, and were interviewed together. They both are physicians, as a matter of fact, in Kansas. One of them had to drop out and go in the service because of the war; he came back, then, and went to medical school later. The other one went on to medical school at the same time I did. He went to Washington U. So there were people I knew in premed, but there were no other girls from Kansas State who went on to medical school the year I did.

I did finally meet two women doctors in college. One had just come to Kansas State as a student health physician; I didn't know that. I had no idea how young and inexperienced she was. But she, in fact, did my first physical examination when I entered college, and I was very impressed with her professional manner and the fact that she was a doctor. And so whenever I had health problems of any kind, I always went to her; and she's the one who helped me fill out my applications for medical school and encouraged me regularly during that time. She went to medical school at the University of Kansas. She is now an ear, nose, and throat physician at Halstead Clinic in Halstead, Kansas. The other one was an older woman physician, who actually was retired and lived in Manhattan, Kansas. I found out about her, and she invited me to come over and visit her in her home. It was just grand to know somebody who had practiced medicine for many years. I remember being very pleased that I had a chance to know someone who had actually done this thing that I thought I would like to do.

I was really active at Kansas State. I was active in YWCA and in a church group there, and I was a class officer and on the student council. I belonged to the honor society for people in general science and later was elected to Mortar Board and Phi Kappa Phi. I joined a sorority in my sophomore year. I did a moderate amount of dating weekends, but nobody steady really. I went with a lot of different people and people who did a lot of different things—really some kind of interesting people, as a matter of fact. I think I felt the pressures to marry and have a family quite strongly, and I think that I might have succumbed to such pressures had I happened, during that period of time, to meet somebody that I really wanted to marry. I didn't, and that's very lucky in a way. And I do think maybe bright girls are protected to some degree in the sense that they're busy, they are involved in what they're doing, they usually like going to school, and they tend not to be as involved socially. And I think they tend not to be asked out a lot, too. You sort of get the reputation of being a scholar and a studier. But the pressure was there; there's no question about it. I think maybe if I hadn't had a goal set, I could have been unhappy. Maybe this is one reason I clung so to the goal—because the goal always gave me an out. If you weren't getting married, you were going to do something else. I've always said that I think one of the reasons we have so many girls in this school [University of Missouri, Kansas City, Missouri] is because they have not yet had that kind of pressure put on them at a high-school level. It's much easier to commit yourself to medicine at a high-school level than it is later on.

Medical School

When I came to medical school, I lived in a cooperative house where we did all of our own housework. Later on, another woman medical student and I took over the school bookstore, which was, in those days, run by medical students; and we were able to make money and get our textbooks at a reduced rate. So we did that for about a year—we two women did this together. And then, I decided that I wasn't getting ahead doing that, and I got a chance to be an extern at Saint Mary's Hospital. So I worked there for the last eighteen months I was in medical school; I worked every other night, as soon as I finished classes—I got off at four o'clock and worked until about ten or eleven for thirty dollars a month.

The boys in our class were all in the service, because that was during the war, and they were not allowed to work, so women were very much in demand as externs. One other girl and myself were the only externs at Saint Mary's. The availability of that job for us women was directly related to the war.

I didn't have any trouble being accepted by the University of Kansas Medical School. I graduated with high honors from college and had an extremely high score on the MCAT examinations. I did have some unfortunate interviews when I was interviewed by people who were really kind of discouraging, suggesting that maybe I ought to rethink this. They'd keep saying, "You know, this isn't really—you don't really think this is a field for women, do you?" And I'd say, "Well, yes, I really do." One of the men, who later was my teacher, said to me, "I don't know why you women want to keep coming to medical school; then the men can't tell all the jokes and dirty stories they want to." I became one of his prize pupils, and he never really told such stories, which was what was so strange—that he would have said this to me during an interview. I suspect he felt he was expected to say something about the inappropriateness of women in medical school.

I thought, "That is really silly." You know, it seemed to me like a very silly reason to try to talk a girl out of coming to medical school. I did have the real feeling that people were discouraging me when I was interviewed. I worried a lot that if this is the way people felt, maybe it was going to be worse than I thought it was going to be—because, frankly, I just really hadn't thought much about the fact that it was going to be bad. After all, I'd been going to school with men in college, and in high school, I had been the only girl in my physics class. And being the only girl in the class didn't trouble me because that had been true in many of my classes in college. And I figured, "Well, there are certainly going to be some other girls in this class." And I wasn't really worried about that aspect of it. I mean, what I was worried about was, "Well, if they're going to be unpleasant, or if they really don't want women, I'm not sure I would look forward to that." I guess it had never occurred to me that they wouldn't want women.

I think in my first year in school I was just so concerned with making it that I paid very little attention to the way I was treated. I eventually perceived, toward the end of the year, that the men didn't much like it that I was getting the best grades, and I did accomplish that my first year in school. But still, they were fairly friendly, and it wasn't that bad.

I was in medical school at a strange time. It was during the war, when most of the regular Faculty was off to the war. There was a sense of fluidity; women were moving out of their roles very rapidly. Most of the people who were back teaching were people who were in private practice, and they did not have the stereotyped feeling about medical students. And in fact, we had three women on the Faculty who would not regularly have even been on the Faculty because there weren't regularly any women on the Faculty. In fact, one of the women was pregnant when she came back. I can remember thinking, "Well, now, this is really interesting that she can come back and teach while she's pregnant." But there were less men to teach. None of these three women were particularly inspiring role models, but just the fact that they were willing to come and teach us, to take time off from their private practices, which all of them had at that time, made us all have considerable respect for them.

I think there was much more male chauvinism after the war. As I think back on it, I don't remember feeling that the men were unhappy about our being there, particularly, and I think in general, the women in my class were moderately successful. None of them did badly—some of them did better than others, but they all graduated. So there were no real problems. Also, I think everybody was sort of concerned with getting these doctors through on this hurry-up program, and I think that made a difference.

We women did group together by necessity—particularly, I would say, in the first two years. And this was because there were three fraternities for men, which allowed men social activities together. They also had quiz files for all the exams, and the women did not have much in the way of quiz files.

I really don't think we women talked much about the psychological problems of being in medical school. We talked a fair amount about just problems, such as not having quiz files when other people did and being economically strapped, not having automobiles, not having wives to type our pathology notebooks. But we talked very little about getting married and how we were eventually going to juggle a career and marriage. And another thing, I think we were all fiercely kind of independent, and I think we almost hated to admit that we didn't really have these things worked out. I don't think we ever talked much about how we felt about what we were doing. We were very concerned with doing it and doing it well.

As I think about it, I believe I set more limited goals for myself in medicine because I was a woman. For example, I never really seriously considered doing surgery. I'm quite sure of that—even though I realized that there was no reason why I wasn't technically as good as anybody else, because I soon learned that. I always considered OB-GYN, but I dropped out, and I know when I did it: it was when I was married and decided I was going to have to make some commitments that had to do with marriage.

I met my husband in medical school. We were in the same class. I remember seeing him my first year in school. He remembers when he first saw me, because he thought I was kind of an aggressive girl. He had been at Saint Louis University where aggressive women were not around, I guess; and he said that he remembered seeing me and thinking, "Well, that gal had better be smart"— because he thought I was "biophilic"—I was bubbly, I was there to get on with being a doctor—and he just hoped I was smart because I was certainly not going to make it if I wasn't. Apparently, he was more attracted to me early. I did not date very many people in my class in medical school—didn't date very much, period. But I did go with a man who was later Bill's roommate. And he knew— found out—a lot about me, I guess, through this relationship. But we really didn't start dating until—I would say, maybe, almost till the last year we were in medical school, though we had been good friends. And then, he asked me out just before Christmas, and sort of very quickly we decided that maybe we really did like each other a lot. And within two or three months, we had decided that we would get married. So it was a quick decision, but I think we grew to know each other really quite well during that period of time.

I think by that time he felt very comfortable with women in medicine. I don't think he ever didn't. He had a very good relationship with his mother, and his sister, at the time that I first knew him, was getting a Ph.D. at Saint Louis University. So as far as he was concerned, he had good feelings about women in higher education. I don't think he'd ever known any women doctors. But I think in general, he thought the women in our class were appropriately there. And he had never had any real problems about my excellence. I did a lot better in school than he did. This I do not believe bothered him; he's one of the few people about whom I can say this. If I could do well he'd say, "Fine; go ahead and do just as well as you can do." He's not really strongly competitive except in sports.

Internship

I had no problem getting an internship; I was accepted at Cook County in Chicago, in Portland, at Barnes in Saint Louis, at KU, and in New Orleans. I chose New Orleans because I wanted to see another part of the United States. I thought I shouldn't stay at KU because I had already seen what went on there. I wanted to do something different, that nobody else had done—I'm still sure that this entered into the whole thing. It was romantic in the sense that I'd read a little bit about the history of New Orleans and it was kind of rich in history and color. It just seemed like it would be a fun thing to do. And, as I say, I wanted a big hospital, and I thought I wanted a charity hospital. And I thought I wanted a hospital that had university affiliations.

We were married the day before we graduated from medical school, but because internships had been finalized before we decided to get married, we were separated the first year. My husband interned in Cleveland. I thought about postponing internship, but Bill encouraged me to stay on. Once the decision was made it was a good year.

We wrote daily to each other—we even sent special delivery letters to arrive on Sundays! Each one of us wrote a letter every day, and the mails were such that I got letters in about two days. And I was so challenged by my learning experience. And there were a lot of people there that I liked; I had very good women friends among the house staff and men friends, too. I sometimes was lonesome and homesick. Bill was called into the army, and I did ask for a month's leave of absence; and I went up to Cleveland and spent one month—I was there when V-J Day came, and then he didn't have to go. I spent the month there and then went back down and finished my internship.

They had a good group of women residents and interns at Charity, and the experience itself was so challenging. And the city was so interesting—I mean, life was just plain interesting at Charity. As women we had no particular problems. We worked harder, maybe, than the men did mainly because we were so afraid somebody'd say, "She's a slough-off," or something like that. And we all had reputations for being very good house staff people. First of all, almost none were married, though a few were; there was one girl who was married and had a baby during her internship here. But in general, very few were married. I was married, but my husband wasn't there, so I was essentially unmarried while I was there. So we didn't have responsibilities at home. A lot of the men were married and did have, so we would be much more likely to take call, sleep in, take somebody's call when they had to leave. So we essentially were, in a way, better house staff officers.

Fellowship in Hematology

My decision to go into hematology is a complicated story. It was essentially influenced by two separate things. One of the things was that when my husband started his internship at Cleveland, one important man who was there was Dr.

Russell Haden, who was really one of the pioneer people in hematology. He had been at Kansas originally, and this is why a lot of people went to Cleveland from Kansas; he left the University of Kansas and went as the Chairman of the Department of Medicine at Cleveland Clinic. He was one of the few people who was really doing hematology at that time. So during my first visit there, I met him, and I became kind of interested in what he was doing; I'd never known him before. I had some time to spend in the library, so I read some of the things about hematology, and I thought, "You know, I believe I could do hematology, and it's exciting to me." So when I was finishing my internship, I applied for a fellowship in medicine with the idea of doing hematology at Cleveland Clinic, because Bill was going to stay on there if he didn't have to go in the army. It looked like something I might be good at; I was attracted to Dr. Haden. Well, as it turned out, it proved to be very fortuitous because by the time I got back there to start my fellowship, I was pregnant, and in those days, pregnancy was not very much condoned for house officers.

I have four children, and none of them were planned.

But anyway, when I got back there, I went to Dr. Haden and said, "Dr. Haden, I didn't know when I applied for this fellowship that I would be pregnant, but I am. And I would like to go with the fellowship, but I realize that you have certain rules and regulations about who works on the wards and in the clinic"— because in those days pregnant women just weren't accepted very much—and I said, "But I'd still like to go ahead." And he said, "Well, that's not bad. If you really want to do hematology like you told me you did, why don't you start in hematology? That way, you can minimize your ward work, and you can work in the laboratory, which is what you need to do for six months anyway." So that's how I started in hematology. And I think in many ways it was extremely fortuitous because I got unusually good basic training, which I probably would not have gotten if I had started a regular residency in medicine. I would have let the basic training slide, and if I had found time to do it, I would have done it. This way, I did it at a very good time, and I spent a lot longer at it than I would otherwise have done. So I spent six months essentially in basic hematology, and then my first child was born, and I did not go back, though I did go on writing. I wrote one article after that, but I never really went back to finish my fellowship at Cleveland because they really—well, it's partly my own fault. I didn't have any imagination. We didn't have any money; I had no one to leave my child with. We had no family there, and I basically thought I shouldn't leave my child—I had guilt feelings. And I didn't have enough imagination to figure out some way I could leave her. I wound up staying home for five years—from 1946 to 1951.

Five-Year Hiatus from Medicine: Family Life and Private Practice

When my first child was born, it was right after the war, and it was at the time when many physicians were returning from the war. At that particular moment, there were really probably plenty of doctors in most settings, and the ones who returned from the war were very eager. It was not a good time to be starting in the practice of medicine. Competition was very, very strong, and there were very few part-time positions; nobody wanted somebody who wanted to work half time. And also, at that time, household help was not particularly easy to get. It certainly was almost impossible—or I thought it was impossible—in Cleveland. Probably this is my own psyche that said it was impossible. We lived in kind of a poor section of the city. We had a very, very small income, and I would really have had to have made a substantial salary to afford household help. I couldn't have taken a residency because residencies paid, at the very most, $75 or $100 a month and I had no backlog of money. So the only alternative for me to have continued to do something professionally in Cleveland would have been for me to have worked in somebody's office, and I don't think I even had enough imagination to work that through. I simply don't think I even knew enough about the practice of medicine. I didn't even inquire, which is really kind of silly as I think about it now, because I think if I had gone to the medical society, I could have said, "Are there people who would like someone to work a couple of afternoons a week in their offices?" But I didn't do this. I think it was partly a lack of experience; it was partly not really knowing for sure that I would be wanted or needed in a setting like this and being a little afraid to get out in the real world and try to practice medicine.

I was very anxious to have a child; I was very delighted with the child; I enjoyed the care of the child. It was a good experience for me. I'd liked being pregnant; I liked having the baby. This was positive. I had always looked forward to the time when I would be able to have this experience. It seemed to me like the sort of experience that I didn't think my life would be complete without, so it was a welcome experience in that sense, even though it was a real struggle economically.

But I didn't seem to be able to get involved with moving ahead in medicine, and I know my husband at that time felt really kind of stressed that I wasn't—knowing that I'd been a really good student, why wasn't I really pushing to be a better doctor, to learn more? I now know, as I look back on it, that when your main concern is keeping house and taking care of a child, when you have no medical stimuli coming directly into you, you really can't drive yourself to keep up. Had I even been going to the clinic as a volunteer twice a week, it would have been easier. I'd never do this again; I mean, I would insist on doing volunteer work, doing something so that the stimulus would be fed into me, and then I would read. But I was getting no direct medical stimuli. I learned to knit and crochet—a lot of the things that I really hadn't had time to do that were kind of the homemaking sort of thing. And I was a really good manager. I could cook, and even though we lived in just a little apartment, I developed a lot of homemaking skills during that time.

Then, I found I was pregnant a second time. And even though this seemed bad, it didn't seem terribly bad because I was already stuck at home; and if I decided that I wanted to have more than one child, I could convince myself, certainly, that this was probably a good thing. I never felt this was permanent. It was always a matter of waiting until we could economically afford some kind of reliable help and until there was something for me to do that I thought I could successfully do. I think this was the feeling. But I just didn't see solutions. I didn't even seek solutions, which is probably what I would do now with the information I now have. But I really didn't seek solutions.

In 1948, we moved back to Kansas City, and my husband started private practice. We came back with the two children and found an apartment to live in on the second floor over a grocery store and, again, had substantially no income. We had to borrow the money to buy the first car. And he had a terrible time getting started. It was hard for a young internist to arrive in town even if it was his hometown, as he had not maintained any contact with physicians. From the time he left to go off to medical school, he broke all contact, so he essentially had no contact. He started practicing alone—in a building with other doctors but essentially a solo practice. It was really, really stressful economically because the first year he couldn't even pay office expenses. So again, this remained kind of a challenge . . . in order to make ends meet and to move into the medical community; there were a lot of things about that that were challenging to some degree.

But I do think that after the second child was born, I had begun to feel like, "Well, as soon as this one's a little older, and Bill gets started. . . ." I was beginning to make plans. In fact, I'd arranged to go one day a week as a volunteer in the clinic at KU. So I'd begun to think, then, that I was ready. And then, I was pregnant again.

We were Catholic, and we were very anxious to do just the right thing. And so we were using rhythm—and I thought, using it extremely intelligently. I thought that I understood this thing and that I could do everything correctly. Every time I became pregnant, it was after a move, so it was obvious that moving changed my menstrual cycles. So each time, even though we were still deciding not to have children, it was really due to some change which we couldn't foretell in these particular instances. I felt quite badly about the third pregnancy. That was really a low point because I had just begun to make the decision that I could get back into medicine. I began to think, "Now I can get somebody to take care of these two children." My husband had gotten a job with the VA part-time in addition to his practice. Well, with the third child, I then sort of gave up again. I really gave up the ghost that time because here I was with three little children.

I don't think we talked a lot about it. My husband was having such a hard time making a go of it in practice that he was feeling kind of desperate. We were struggling in so many ways. But the kids were really pretty rewarding in the sense that they were fun children; they were healthy children. There were a lot of good things about this. I had never had siblings, so there were many rewards in watching these children grow up. I sort of went through doing all the things that I liked doing, like reading children's literature again and learning things that kids did and remembering the things that were important to me in my childhood and trying to make these available to the kids. So it was not bad from that standpoint. It really wasn't. But it was just hard work, and I was depressed in that I felt, "Where am I going? Will I ever go anywhere?" I think the hope level was low at that particular time.

And then, we finally decided to buy a house. And again, this takes a lot of energy. You buy a house; you have to move into it; you have to furnish it; you have to do all this. And it was the first time we really had had enough money to do this. But it was when we moved into the house that with the house we also bought household help, because the lady who had helped the previous owner wanted to go on working. And so for the first time I had a good household helper who could also help care for children. And it was on the basis of that that I was able, then, to start casting about for some way in which I could get back into medicine. So really the move into the house was fortuitous in that, for the first time, here was somebody who wanted to work five days a week; and I had never found anybody who wanted to do that before.

Part-Time Residency

So with that economic feasibility and my youngest child being two, I then started trying to find out if there was any such thing as a part-time residency, or would they take somebody who couldn't work full time?—because I didn't think I could take night call. My husband was on call at night, and I didn't see any way I could do this. There wasn't any such thing. Nobody had ever heard of any such thing. The university had no such program. So finally, I went to one of the private hospitals, which didn't have an approved residency program, and I talked to the pathologist there and said, "Would there be any chance that I could essentially take on the role of a resident in pathology"—even though the hospital was not approved for a residency—and could I work five days a week, days only?" And he was delighted to have me because he didn't know any hematology and he needed somebody in hematology in a bad way. So he said, "I'll take you on if you'll supervise the hematology, and then I'll try to teach you what I can teach you about the rest of the pathology." So it was a very good arrangement. He was an excellent teacher, a very kind man, and I will be eternally grateful to him for giving me the opportunity. I apparently did well enough that he even would go off on a two week vacation and leave me in charge.

The only way I could get to the hospital was to ride the bus from my house and then transfer, and then I had to walk about five blocks in order to get there to do this residency. And then, if I was late in the afternoon, I'd have to call a taxi and come home in a taxi. I did this for a whole year. It really meant a lot of organization. I had to get up; get the kids taken care of; the lady had to get there; I had to get on the bus; I had to get to the hospital. It was a struggle; it was really a struggle, and I think if I hadn't had such a pleasant working setting over there—in the sense that they wanted me, I felt needed, I was learning, I was reading again, I was stimulated to do things again—I think it would have been hard because it was really a struggle to do this.

I don't even remember feeling deprived that I didn't have a car of my own. It was at the end of this year that we decided that there wasn't much point in my staying another year there—that if I was going to do hematology, I'd better see if I could get some more hematology training. And there was no way I could do that without a car—we had gone over bus schedules. So this precipitated our buying a second car then. I then went back to the University of Kansas to see if they would let me come back on a similar program, where again I would not be getting official credit but would be spending five days a week and not be on night call. And they said, "Okay." It was Dr. Sloan Wilson who was the Chairman of Hematology there at that time.

In those days, residencies and fellowships were not nearly as tightly organized, and there were no fellows in hematology. So having a resident or a person who was going to be full time the year round in hematology was really kind of an asset, because they had not yet gotten to the fellowship stage. They just had rotating residents through hematology, so to have somebody who would be there for a year looked like a pretty good thing, I think. And I think I was very useful; and I learned a lot during that period, because there had been quite a lot of changes—the chemotherapeutic drugs were just coming in—and so I needed desperately to learn about them. People were using the chemotherapeutic drugs, and I knew I'd never be able to go into practice if I didn't understand them.

Private Practice

Then, there was one time during that year—it seems to me like it was toward the end of that year, in May of that year, a physician who practiced in the same building with my husband desperately needed to get away for two weeks, so he asked me if I'd come and take his practice for two weeks. I hadn't had any vacation, so I took that time. I thought, "Well, I'll just find out whether I can practice medicine. I've never really tried." And so I went over and worked for two weeks and actually got along pretty well, which gave me confidence that I probably could manage.

So my plan was then that I would go into practice in the same building with my husband, starting on sort of a small scale, and begin to do hematology, even though I was not, in the conventional sense, trained the way most people were. But I felt that by working with him as an internist, if there were problems that were above and beyond what I would do, I could refer them to him.

I just had made arrangements to do that when he was called into the service—that was when they were calling everybody back during the Korean War—and then I was pregnant again. They decided not to send my husband overseas but to

Fort Riley, which is in Kansas. So when we got that information I decided to join him there. We postponed the opening of a joint practice until he was released. But while I was there, I decided that I wanted to keep up. In fact, I remember when I was in the hospital at the time my son was born, I read a whole year's issues of the journal, *Blood*. I checked them out of the medical library on the post there, and I read twelve monthly issues while I was lying in the hospital. And I knew then I wasn't really going to be content not to do something. Fort Riley is close to Manhattan where I'd gone to school at K-State, so I went over to Manhattan and asked, "Do you need any help in student health?" And they said, "We desperately need help in student health." So I worked about four days a week in student health on the campus there while we were at Fort Riley.

We moved back to Kansas City in February 1955 and opened a joint practice. I fully intended to do primarily hematology because I really had not been well trained in internal medicine. There was room in the office for me, and I knew a lot about the laboratory, and since we were going to have our own laboratory in the office, this gave me the chance to see that that went well. And since there were no hematologists in Kansas City, Kansas, except for Dr. Wilson who was at the university, there was a real need for this kind of skill. So it really didn't take long for me to start picking up practice.

The Chairman of Hematology at KU never made any effort to help me. Fact is, I tried desperately to do a lot at the university, and he really did not want me to do anything. I really had bad feelings about that because I would have really liked to have been part time—it would have been much better for me than to be in private practice. He knew this, but he simply did not choose to ask me, even though I really let it be known that this would have been better for me, because I would have found it easier to practice. Maybe it was because my training was not exactly orthodox. I don't know whether that was it. Part of it might have been that I was a woman, a woman who really was kind of a pusher. So I felt badly about that—partly because I eventually developed some skills in coagulation, self-taught totally, and they had nobody who knew anything about it at KU. They definitely could have used me, but they didn't—except whenever they needed teaching done. I did the teaching in coagulation all through the years. I taught in postgraduate courses over there regularly, and I taught almost all the students in the sophomore year. Then, later on, as I became better in medicine, I began to teach in medicine in the junior year. Then, I became very well acquainted with Dr. Alan Thal, who was in surgery, and he wanted to have some teaching done in coagulation in surgery in the senior year, so then I worked with him on some research projects and taught in the senior year. So all through those years, I was sort of teaching continually at KU.

I found the university much more competitive than private practice. I was just a little bit pushy because I sort of intended to stay; and I remember going to conferences over there and really being put down by my male colleagues in hematology. I would make a statement, and they would deliberately get up and imply that I had no background for making it—even though I had had experience, too, but in a different setting. This made me insecure and made me say, "Well, maybe as a woman—because my training is different, and my whole story is different—the whole way I've gotten where I am makes me feel maybe I'm not as good." These feelings of insecurity made me work harder, try harder to be better. For example, I wrote a successful textbook in hematology on my own and published a number of scientific articles. KU offered no help with these efforts. That's the only way one knows how to fight back, really; that's the way I've been taught to fight back. But I wanted academic medicine and probably would never have chosen private practice. As it worked out, it was not a bad choice, but it was not really a voluntary choice.

When I started practice I essentially was working maybe about three-fourths time. I also managed the laboratory, the finances, and the office. I took a lot of that kind of responsibility because it fit into my schedule. I could do it at odd times.

I feel pretty good about the mothering I gave my children. First of all, I wanted to be a mother—I think that's probably number one at the top of the list. I really and truly enjoyed my children, and I enjoyed the things I did with them. They were things that were fun for me. I liked children's literature. I liked going to the zoo. I liked children's movies. I liked children's music. I still do; I still read children's things, even though I don't have children to read them to now. So for me, the chance to have a reason to do a lot of those things was kind of important. And I really felt I was a good mother to children. Many people would argue that if you're going to be a professional woman and a mother, you wind up being second-rate in both fields. They say you can't really be a successful professional and you can't really be a good mother. I really don't think that's true. For one thing, I think I always tried to separate those two roles; most of the time, I tried to. In other words, I didn't usually bring work home while the kids were at home. I take work home now, but I didn't do it then. When I walked in the door at home, I became Mother. But I always told them a lot about what I did. They knew I was a doctor—I talked a lot about what I was doing; but I still didn't work at home.

I think you really have to be committed to both jobs. So I think that basically, if I had to say, the things that have made a difference for me are first, a strong commitment to two kinds of jobs. Right now, I'm not as committed to homemaking as I was earlier. And I was as strongly committed to medicine—I think my commitments were strong both ways. And second, I always was a good organizer, even as a little child. When I was a student, even in grade school, I did things in kind of an organized fashion, and I didn't waste time. My children used to complain about Saturdays. They used to say, "Oh, Mother will be home again, and we'll have another one of those organized Saturdays"—because I would think of all the things that everybody needed to get done on Saturday and would get up and get everybody up, and we would start getting all the things done that I hadn't been there to supervise during the week and hadn't gotten done. And I realize Saturdays were kind of rough and rugged, as a matter of fact, because it was for everybody to get done all the things that I thought should get done every week. But again, it was my pushing . . . and really none of the children are as organized as I am. I think this is probably because they didn't like that.

Faculty Member at University of Missouri-Kansas City Medical School

My first interest in this school came from the publicity in the newspapers, and it was very appealing to me because I had gotten where I was in medicine by working alone, by getting there on my own steam. In other words, every step of the way had been a way in which I'd had to work it out myself, and I had a lot of feelings that the system that was operational had not been very helpful to me in getting somewhere in medicine. I didn't think it had been very helpful to women in general; and it sounded to me like the chances of a system like this new one being more helpful to students was pretty good. It certainly appeared to me that what we really needed in medicine was to try to get people involved in health care; and I had the very strong feeling that the institution that I was teaching in [KU] was not really concerning itself with health care. It looked to me like if you could get an institution like UMKC, which started out saying, "What medicine is all about is taking care of patients"—and if you said this from day one, and when you took biochemistry you learned biochemistry so that you could deliver health care, not so that you could end up in a research laboratory—then your chances of providing health care were probably going to be better.

And this is an interesting thing which came out of some of my teaching at KU. When I was teaching medicine in the junior year, I used to have four or five students whom I would teach for six weeks, and what I found out was that these students were coming to me and asking me to write their recommendations. So I would say to them, "Well, certainly you know somebody at KU better than you know me." And they'd say, "Well, you really know more about me"—and I would have been with them two mornings a week for six weeks! And I thought, "If the educational system is such that there's nobody over there who knows those students as well as I know them in that length of time, then there's something radically wrong with what's going on."

I also feel that the program we offer is more attractive to women. A lot more women are going to come to medical school here because they're going to have the option to come earlier in their lives. And I think one of the reasons that a lot of women who might have become very good and happy physicians have not come to medical school is because they've started as premeds. They've been discouraged in the system, and they've found other alternatives.*

*UMKC Medical School is a six-year program.

On Women in Medicine

When I chose medicine, I don't think I had any sense that I could help other women. Now, I see this more at this point in my life. All of a sudden my experience has led me to believe that as a woman I have been able to do certain things in a different way, and that certain patients that I have had, have benefited from my being a woman. And I have encouraged many of my women students to consider particularly areas of obstetrics and gynecology because I think these are very underserved by women. I think they're underserved in the sense that there are not nearly enough women in these areas, and I think women have been discouraged from going into the areas because of the hours and the demands— and because men don't want them. And so I really would like to see more and more women go into them.

Women have certain kinds of needs that they simply know that men are not going to understand and with a woman patient—if she's having certain problems, a woman is going to be able to feel with her about certain of her problems, is going to be able to relate. If she has menstrual cramps, a woman will know what she's talking about. It may be harder for a woman to be professional about certain things that she has experienced. If a woman is having a baby, and you've had one, you're going to feel a lot differently about this. I think I feel totally different about the problem of breast cancer than most men do. I think that very few men are able to comprehend the psychological impact of this, and I think that in general they give very poor advice. I don't think they even ever talk to a woman long enough to know how she is going to deal with the problem.

On Feminism

Well, I certainly know when I read Betty Friedan's book that I felt very much at one with it. In fact, for Christmas one year, my kids gave me Kate Millett's book with a badge that said "Women's Rights Now"; and that's been—oh, ten years ago, I guess. So I'm sure they sensed this in me—though, as I say, I've never been one to carry placards or run up and down the street. If there was a chance for me to do something and to say—in a personal way—that I thought a woman ought to do this, then I would always be glad to go and do those kinds of things. So I really think I've had a strong feeling. And I guess maybe I've been turned off a little bit by some of the things.

On Working with Men

I have been given positions working with men, and it's very interesting—you can almost figure before you start whether you're going to be asked to do nothing; and there are a certain group of men that will never ask you to do anything. Now, there's another group of men that'll ask you to do all the things they don't want to do, and they will do the things that they want to do. I've seen this on almost every committee that I have dealt with at the medical school, and I think it's extremely real. I think other women have felt the same thing.

I also know that as a woman, I have some problems—oh, I suppose you might consider it a little bit of a different way of dealing emotionally with situations. If things really go—if I really feel badly about something, I may tend to weep just a little bit. And if I do this, I just immediately get the negative—totally negative— response, you know, "Oh, a weak woman. Who wants a weak woman around?" And yet, in many instances, you know, it seems right to me to do that. If I feel that this has been an inappropriate way to deal with someone, then it's quite all right to weep.

On Her Life

Well, I think I would have gone to medical school. I mean, that choice was a good one. I have never regretted that choice in any way. In fact, I'm very glad that I made that choice. I'm not sure that I would feel quite the same about making it now. In other words, the way medicine is now is not as attractive to me as the way it was, say, twenty years ago. The complications of medicine; the problems of the ethics of practice; the governmental controls—not that I believe that government can't do a certain number of things and do them well; the lack of free enterprise, which has been one of the things which I've enjoyed; I see this. In fact, as I look at my own son, who's going to be starting before long, I don't envision his life in medicine as being as exciting as mine was, because I think there was enough pioneering during my time. I think just the whole discovery of antibiotics and steroids and things like this really made it a great time to be in medicine.

So for me the choice was a great one. Now, I'm sure that if I had it—or I *think* if I had it—to do over, there'd be two or three things I'd do differently. One is that I would really try to get my residency training before I started my family; or I would have hoped that I could have combined the two more effectively than I did. I feel sure that that's something that if I were advising a young woman, I would advise her to do. And I would never stay out five years totally like I did; I simply wouldn't. I think it was possible then, but even then, it wasn't very good. I would have done something on a voluntary basis, rather than just some of the community things that I did. I did do a lot of things in community health in those years, but I still would do something where I really had a professional job that I had to do. That's something I'd do.

I suspect that maybe something a lot of women ought to think about is how hard it is to combine marriage and medicine. It's so easy when you start out; when I started out, it never occurred to me that it was going to be a problem. Of course, I think a lot of people that married at the time didn't really worry much about the problems. They just sort of believed that everything would be happy ever after. But I think that there are a lot of problems. Of course, I'm sure that any marriage has problems, but I think a marriage that involves a professional woman has a lot of difficulties. There are difficulties between the spouses which are not easily solved, and I think there just continue to be problems. I don't think they go away; I think they're there.

And then I found it very hard to be accepted in the medical community as a woman. In other words, our social life among couples has never been very easy. It's been easier with couples who were not medical at all because there are many wives of physicians that really resent wives of physicians who are doctors. I have really been insulted by women—at times, really badly—because of the thought that I thought I was better than the wives. And I don't ever remember thinking that. I always thought I was different in the sense that I did different things and I didn't have time for this committee or that committee; I might not work in the Women's Auxiliary and do these kinds of things. If I did anything at all, it was almost always something that was just about the limit of what I could do. And that was not easy.

Another thing is there are certain problems that have to do with dealing with male physicians within the profession that come up. This can make for some seemingly real problems, even though they're really not there. I'm sure that if you do a lot of consultations for somebody, then this can be the subject of some kind of gossip. Then the next thing you know, there are those kinds of explanations that have to be made. And your life is not really terribly free. You are not free in the sense that you have responsibilities to patients. You're not free in the sense that you have a responsibility to the physician image. And I think as a woman that physician image is even much greater, because I think the community accepts a renegade male physician—I mean, he can be a drunk, he can be a drug addict, as long as he does the things that are expected of him. But the community doesn't accept eccentric women very well and certainly not loose women at all. Now, maybe that's not going to be quite so true as more women come into the profession, and one doesn't stand out quite so much. It's just that if you're the only woman on a hospital staff, or one of the few, then it's very obvious when you're there. And I definitely think there are some problems with children. In fact, I had quite a long conversation with my son on Saturday, and I think it all sort of came out of the problems that I had been bringing to the surface. I simply came right out and asked him, "You know, if somebody were to ask you a question about how you feel about having your mother be a doctor . . .?" And my youngest son, the one whom I think is probably best adjusted to that, said that he always kind of liked it because it was different; he could tell people, and he liked to tell people different things. But now for the oldest son, who is more of a conformist—I think for him it was not always easy; I get the feeling that it wasn't. So I guess maybe I don't know how much different my life would have been. I haven't the faintest idea. And I never really thought much about, "What if it were different?"

Kansas City, Missouri
February 18 and 25, 1977 and March 1, 1977

6

Marjorie Wilson
CAREER ADMINISTRATOR

Dr. Marjorie Price Wilson has enjoyed a long and effective career as one of the few women in the upper echelons of medical administration in this country. After completing her medical training she expected to become involved in patient care and research. Instead, almost by chance, she fell into a position with the Veterans Administration at a transitional point in the organization's history. She has parlayed that position into a series of increasingly responsible posts with the Veterans Administration, the National Institutes of Health, and the National Library of Medicine. Since 1970, she has served as Director of the Department of Institutional Development of the Association of American Medical Colleges, where, as the only woman member of the senior staff, she has overseen the accreditation of medical schools and supervised the development of a management training program for medical school deans and other executives. She and her husband postponed having children until her career was well established, a decision that has worked well for her.

Marjorie Price Wilson (1979), Director, Department of Institutional Development, Association of American Medical Colleges, Washington, D.C.

Childhood

I was born in 1924 in Pittsburgh, Pennsylvania, and lived there until I married and moved away from the city. I was an only child.

My father was a 1915 graduate of what was then Carnegie Institute of Technology, now Carnegie-Mellon University. His grandfather established a glass manufacturing business near Pittsburgh and in Saint Louis and was a very successful businessman, well-liked and well-admired. My father became an engineer and also went into the glass business.

I would consider my father a reserved individual, but a very warm, generous person in his close relationships. He enjoyed beautiful things and had good taste. He was always immaculate in his appearance. He encouraged my wearing good-looking clothes, light, beautiful things.

My father had high expectations for me and of me. He was very approving of my pursuing a career. What I did not appreciate so much when I was younger—I came to appreciate it as I matured—was that what my father really wanted most was for me to be happy and to be satisfied with what I was doing. Even if I had not pursued a career, if he had been able to feel that I was doing what I wanted to do and that I was a happy individual, he would have been satisfied. I would have been closer to him had I understood that.

My mother came from a large family of nine children, which must have been a marvelous family. Her father was in the steel business in Pittsburgh. My grandfather's house was a lovely house in a neighborhood that enjoyed a nice community. I can remember the basement of the house with many pairs of ice skates of all sizes hanging up and with canoes stored in the rafters. It was a family that enjoyed good times together.

I saw my mother as probably the stronger of the two parents. She did not have a career and had not been educated formally, but she had tremendous energy and talent and intelligence. Much of this was focused on me, and I'm quite sure that that was one of the strong influences that propelled me toward the kind of career that I pursued. She thought it was important that I complete my education, for example, before I married. I think she wanted very much for me to be a physician. She admired the medical profession. She never expressed it openly, but I think she had regrets that she hadn't pursued a career, that she had married at eighteen. She would have liked to have been a nurse, as a matter of fact, but her father did not want her to do that.

My relationship with my mother was close. I felt that she was clearly someone that I could depend on, who would defend me and protect me. But I also felt that she was a strict taskmaster, that I had to maintain standards, that there were tremendous expectations. I wanted to meet them, and I feared disappointing my mother if I did not meet her expectations.

I had a great deal of confidence in my parents. I had respect for them—and, I felt, with good reason. I admired both of them and wanted their approval. I think one would cite this as a characteristic of me as a person. I sought approval from people who were figures of authority, beginning with my parents.

We attended church regularly. We all were touched and moved by religious ceremony and religious experience. We really believed, my mother always said, in the power of prayer—not in an emotional, excessive, evangelistic way, but as a deeply personal experience.

I decided quite early that I wanted to be a doctor, and there's a story connected with that. I spent an extended period of daily visits to Johns Hopkins, where my cousin had been taken for neurosurgery by Dr. Walter Dandy. I decided after that experience that I would like to be part of medicine someday. I was then six years old, and I never changed my mind.

Also, we lived next door to our family physician from the time I was born until I was about six years of age, and we continued to be fairly close to him. He was greatly admired in the community, and I'm quite sure he influenced me also. I had a fair amount of illness, and I saw it as a positive experience for someone to be so helping and caring.

No one ever tried to tell me that women could not be doctors. They would tell me that it was going to be difficult, but no one ever said to me, "Women cannot be doctors." I was nearly always encouraged. It never occurred to me that my ambition was an unusual one.

I was generally interested in everything, and through high school I had a straight "A" average in all subjects. Chemistry and physics I did not find as fascinating as biology. I really liked biology. I was not good athletically; I could not hit a home run if my life depended on it, but I was always picked to be on teams in school, and people were somehow willing to carry me in spite of my poor athletic abilities. I was elected to the girls' athletic leadership club. I must have been a good sport or something!

I would not describe myself as outgoing. I do not see myself as a gregarious individual, but rather as a more conservative, reserved individual. But I think I would have considered myself as a leader. I usually had class offices, and I was usually elected to leadership clubs.

I went to two different high schools—a large public high school and a small private girls' school in Pittsburgh. I transferred primarily for educational reasons. My family was somewhat concerned that I might not be getting the kind of preparation I needed to go to the college of my choice, and they wanted me to be able to go to whatever college I wanted to. I got a great deal academically from the private school and was able to do well on College Boards. Perhaps I could have done as well from the other school, but I would not have had the same preparation. I guess what I learned was that I could get along with a different group of individuals, in a different economic group, in a different social group. I felt equally comfortable with either group, and I found an equal acceptance in either group. I'm glad that I had both experiences.

I never thought much about having children, but I was very much oriented toward marriage. There was a fair amount of social life at the public school, and I thoroughly enjoyed it.

College

The headmistress of the private school, who was a strong British woman, very traditional, very academically oriented, encouraged and supported me. She was the one who suggested that I go to Bryn Mawr, which I had not considered until then. In that school, we thought very much in terms of the "seven sisters." So I looked at Bryn Mawr, Mount Holyoke, Smith, and Radcliffe, but I applied only to Bryn Mawr. Can you imagine what would have happened if I had not been accepted? It was certainly different in those days from the way it is now.

My experience at Bryn Mawr was something that was very different than I had ever experienced before. I came from a conservative, traditional, structured educational environment and from a solid middle-class social background. I was suddenly with a group of individuals many of whom came from academic families, diplomatic families; it was during the war. I was thrown in with a different kind of individual who was prepared for college in a different way than I had been—in many instances, a much more sophisticated individual. So there were intellectual experiences that were quite new to me. I suddenly wasn't making a straight "A" average anymore, I was making 70's and 75's. I was shocked, but I wasn't dismayed or disheartened by it. When I worked a little harder, I did better, and when I didn't work a little harder, I didn't do better. I was not particularly oriented toward grades. I was really not aware that they were particularly important.

The attitude at Bryn Mawr was one of expectation that their graduates would do whatever they wanted to do. If they wanted to go to graduate school, they would. There was a good graduate school at Bryn Mawr, so we were used to women graduate students. The undergraduate student body then was about 550, and the graduate student body about 150.

I also had a good time socially in college. I enjoyed being able to travel to Philadelphia and New York. I'd been away at camp as a child, but this was the first time I had felt independent and away from the family. This is the time when I began to appreciate how strong my mother was in influencing me and in making sure that I continued to pursue my career and did not succumb to social pressure to get married early. Without my mother's support, I think that would have been hard to do.

I did not realize the extent to which my family sacrificed financially for me to go to college. I was not on scholarship. I did work some, but it was mostly just to earn spending money. I did things like baby-sitting, typing papers for graduate students, selling magazine subscriptions. In the summers, I worked at jobs in Pittsburgh—in a bank, in a department store.

I always assumed that I would have to earn my living. It was not a burning issue, just something I accepted. I'm more interested in economic rewards now than I was when I was younger. I used to say, "If after medical school I make $5,000 a year for the rest of my life, I'll really be satisfied." And I really meant that. However, from the standpoint of being able to make that $5,000 a year, I felt that medicine as a career could assure me that, whereas in another career that I was tempted to pursue, which was art—painting and sculpturing—I felt that I could probably not earn a living. In Pittsburgh, the public school stytem has a marvelous program of Saturday morning art classes for children. I started in that in the fifth grade, and I pursued it all through high school and was offered a scholarship to Carnegie Tech Fine Arts School. I enjoyed sculpturing, and I think I had some talent for it—at least the school felt I did and Carnegie felt I did. I have not done any painting or sculpturing since then, unfortunately.

I also wanted to do something that contributed. I wanted to feel that I had done something here on earth, and I felt that medicine was a natural career for a woman because of the caring, serving function it represented. I sensed that intuitively.

I had no decent counseling about medical school—where to apply, how to apply, what courses to take, any of that. I had no guidance, no advice, no anything. The medical school thing I did completely blind, you might say. The reason I feel I was badly advised at Bryn Mawr was that I carried a double major. I took as much chemistry in that institution as I took biology—unfortunately to the exclusion of some of the humanities and other subjects that I could have really profited from in that setting. Also, it gave me a very hard curriculum to pursue in a very difficult school, which probably contributed to the fact that I did not make terribly good grades then. I thought I needed to take all those things to go to medical school, and no one told me otherwise.

Medical School

I settled on the University of Pittsburgh Medical School quite by happenstance. I had taken a physics course there during the summer to meet the requirements. I did that partly because I thought I could probably pass it easily there, which was true, and also because it would not take a whole year out of the curriculum at Bryn Mawr—because I carried so many chemistry and biology courses that I did not know how I was going to get physics in. That summer one of the young men in my class was applying for medical school at the University of Pittsburgh, and he said, "If you want to go to medical school, why not come and apply with me?" So, I did.

Now, I really did not want to go to Pittsburgh for medical school. I wanted to go to Yale. Harvard was not accepting women at that time. I did not seriously consider the Medical College of Pennsylvania. My father thought that would be a nice place for me to go. I did not want to go to a woman's medical school because I felt that I would be pursuing a career in a man's world, literally, and that having gone to a women's college, I ought to go to a coeducational medical school. That was something I was very clear about.

When I was interviewed at Pittsburgh, they asked what I would do if they did not accept me in the next class, and I told them I would apply to Yale. So they did accept me. Then, there was a dilemma. My family said that if I went to Pittsburgh, they could afford to send me, whereas if I went to Yale or to another school, they really could not meet the cost. Financial considerations really became major for me for the first time. My father said that if I wanted to go to medical school, I would have to live at home and go to Pittsburgh. That was, I might say, a very difficult decision.

When I got to Pittsburgh, there were six women in a class of, I believe, eighty-six or eighty-nine. There was a higher percentage of women than usual because of the war. This was the last class with men in what they called the Army Specialized Training Program and the V-12 Program, which were the subsidized military service programs. Those men were discharged halfway through that year, as World War II had ended the previous summer.

I suffered another culture shock when I went to medical school, after the kind of educational program I had at Bryn Mawr—going back to the medical curriculum on the one hand and to a school like the University of Pittsburgh on the other. It was like going back to high school—the learning by rote, the didactic approach. So medical school was relatively easy for me. How well I did was directly proportional to the time I spent memorizing, etc.

Some of my professors encouraged me considerably. Occasionally, when I would, as my children say, "goof off," they would let me know that I ought not to do that. My anatomy professor, for example, had been on the Admissions Committee, and he let me know that he had spoken for me and that I damn well better not let him down. In keeping with my usual reaction to figures of authority, I got myself into shape, at least in anatomy. In retrospect, I suppose this was my first awakening to the fact that grades might be important. My attitude was that you went to school to learn about things, and what followed more or less took care of itself!

The Chairman of the Department of Medicine, Dr. James Heard, was really negative about women in medicine. He felt they had no business being there. He played a game with me which turned out to help me learn a great deal. I was assigned to the hospital where he was chief of the service, and week after week, I was assigned to present the case. It became a game as to what questions he could ask that were tough; it became a game for me to be sure that I was able to answer them. The class was aware that this went on. At the end of the year, they gave a prize for the four people who had the highest grades in medicine, and he had to give me the one for his service. We had a talk about that, and he seemed pleased, actually, with the outcome after all.

The Chairman of Pediatrics in medical school took a particular interest in me. He was someone I admired tremendously. He reminded me of my father, incidentally. He wanted me to go into pediatrics and when I finished my internship asked me to take a residency at Children's Hospital in Pittsburgh.

You asked about women physicians who might have influenced me. There was one woman on the Faculty who stands out, who made a positive impression, although not from the standpoint of someone that I wanted to emulate personally. She specialized in physical medicine and rehabilitation. She was a very competent woman, and I admired her competence. I felt she did exceptional work. She was a very stocky woman who dressed in tailored suits and four-in-hand ties and flat shoes! She always arrived on the scene in full sail!

Then, there was a woman neurosurgeon in Pittsburgh who became a friend of mine—Dorothy Nash. She had her training at Columbia University College of Physicians and Surgeons. She was one of the first women neurosurgeons in the country—in fact, practically the only one. She came to Pittsburgh—her husband was an executive in one of the companies there—and gave up medicine to raise her family. Then, during the war, her husband died, and she had to go back to work. Also, they needed her desperately in neurosurgery. She and I talked about what it was like to go back to neurosurgery after five years away from it. It was not easy, but she managed it.

During those four years I came to appreciate more what medicine really meant and what it was about from the standpoint of practicing it. It was less romantic than I had thought. I really did not appreciate the demands nor the hardships. I came to realize the dimensions of the profession.

I did not find much in common with the other women students in my class. No one had gone to the kind of college I had gone to. University of Pittsburgh drew its student body almost exclusively from western Pennsylvania, except for those students in our class who were subsidized by the federal government in the special navy and army programs. So most of the women were from Pittsburgh. I really did not spend much time with them.

I *was* willing to join the women's fraternity. At first, I was very negative about it. I had no need for a support group. My social group was elsewhere. However, I decided that since I was in the medical school, I should try to be part of it. If I did not join the fraternity, I would be the only woman in the school who did not. I felt an obligation to join. After I joined the organization, I felt it was a poor organization, and if I were going to be part of it, then I wanted to do something to make it better. So I accepted an office and worked with it to try to make it something, but it was not one of my brilliant successes.

I had a fair number of men friends in the class. It varied from year to year. Some of my friends transferred out of Pittsburgh, and more left the second year after losing their government support when the war ended. I had tended to become friends with that group because they were a more cosmopolitan group. So every year I seemed to end up with a different group of friends.

I was rather shocked to learn that a number of male students really looked at medicine as a way to change their social status and to enhance their income. Many of them were second generation, and the expectation of their family was, "My son is in medical school, and it's going to change the status of the family." That was important to them. That was a new thought to me.

I did not feel competitive with the men. I felt I was in a different place than they were because I was a woman, and therefore I was not competing with them. They competed against each other, and I competed against myself. I was two years into medical school before I realized that many of the men students studied from what we called archives—old sets of examinations and all of the things that fraternities handed around. I did not know anything like that existed. That was really amusing. They had all this stuff, and I had been killing myself for two years doing it strictly straight.

I think that people were conscious of the fact that I was a woman, but I do not think I experienced any unusual kind of treatment. One of the things that I became conscious of and aware of—and this stays with me today—was that my behavior was observed very carefully because I was a woman. This is something that happened to me during medical school. I know that I became much more conservative as I matured in medical school. I felt that I needed to maintain a very conservative standard of behavior—much more so than some of the men and much more so than I maintained when I first entered medical school. That became an important issue, because I did have the sense that people observed me, that I was always noticed, that I stood out in the crowd.

One of the things that happened to me as a person, as an individual, was that I became much more conforming, much more limited. The behavioral thing that I just described—I would say that happened to me almost across the board. The college years, in the kind of educational setting I had been in, were an expanding, liberating experience, and this was a constraining experience, putting me into a mold. I became resigned, conforming, and accepting. It was not hard to wear me down, really, I suppose, because of my early childhood and the very structured environment. It was not hard to push me back into that mold.

Internship

University of Pittsburgh students were educated to practice medicine in western Pennsylvania. There was very little research going on, very little full-time academic faculty. When you were a senior in medical school and you talked about where you applied for internship, it was Saint Francis or University Hospitals or Mercy Hospital, or one of the nonaffiliated, small, community hospitals, but you were going to be in Pittsburgh. It was rare for someone to go away for an internship. So I applied to University Hospitals because to me that was the most prestigious group of hospitals in the Pittsburgh setting. I just took the straight rotating internship because that was required in Pennsylvania in those days.

I had one funny experience when I was an intern. We rotated through several hospitals; one of the hospitals was Magee Hospital, which was the OB-GYN service of the medical center. The women interns had to live in the nurses' quarters; to take call we had to walk either through the parking lot or through what they called the archives, the dungeon which was down underground under the parking lot, through narrow corridors in a basement where they kept all the records on endless shelves and there were only bare lightbulbs for illumination. Well, I was much more willing to take my chances running like hell through the parking lot than to go through those corridors, but I was resentful of this. I really reacted powerfully against it. I don't know how I managed it now—I block it out—but I got my roommate and we moved to a room at the end of the corridor where the male residents' quarters were located. Our furniture and all our belongings were moved over there, and we used that room during our time there, for a month or two. My roommate helped me move the furniture, but she did not take part in the ruckus I caused to get us over there. Subsequently, no other women interns in our group were allowed to use that room. Nobody else wanted to fight the issue.

The following year, a woman who was a friend of mine, and still is, and whose father happened to be on the Board of Trustees, did the same thing, and she was able to make it stick. I did not have that kind of power, but I was becoming aware then of things like that; I was rebellious about different living conditions and different requirements for women.

I found that the male residents and interns were very supportive of me and helpful. For example, the women interns were required to catheterize male patients. Often when I would meet a male intern or resident in the hall, they would see me with the tray and would say, "If you will go to see Mrs. Whatchamacallit, I will go and do that chore for you." I accepted things like that and was glad. Made it easier on the patient. Most of the patients I had no trouble with, but it was very difficult for the young male patient.

The nurses were tremendous, particularly at Presbyterian. I was really fond of the girls that trained there. The supervisors were great. I learned a lot of medicine from some of the supervisors who had been around a long time. I talked to them a little bit about how they felt about women doctors, and one of them told me once, "Look, doctor, I want to call somebody that knows what they're doing. I don't care whether they wear a skirt or trousers." They never hesitated to call me, even at times when I was not on call.

I had a couple of experiences that I still remember as very upsetting experiences, when it was brought home to me that I did not know as much as I thought I did. I also had the feeling of increasing my experience and being better able to make decisions and developing clinical judgment; I could actually feel the growth of the power of being able to cope more effectively and being surer of myself. But it was a hard path to reach that point.

Residency

Dr. Ed McCluskey, who was Chairman of Pediatrics and the man who had become my mentor, talked to me then about residency, and he asked if I would not apply for a pediatrics residency. I did not know what I wanted to do really. I thought probably internal medicine, but I also thought anaesthesiology was a nice specialty for a woman, and the subject matter interested me. At any rate, I really felt that I was not cut out to be a pediatrician. I liked children, but I felt I related to adults better than children. One of the reasons I felt I did not relate so well to children was that I was overly sympathetic with their problems—it really got to me that I could not do more for them, whereas with the adult I could relate in a much more comfortable way on that score. I told McCluskey this. As I say, I admired this man tremendously, so it took a great deal of courage for me to say no.

What he said to me was, "If you will come here for a year, I'll support you to go to any other medical center in the country to get your training in pediatrics, if you will then come back and go on the staff at Children's Hospital full time." I said, "I don't want to open an office. I don't want to be in private practice." He said, "I'm not talking about private practice, I'm talking about you being on the Faculty here and on the staff of a hospital." What he was describing to me was a full-time academic position, but I did not recognize it. He must have really been frustrated with me. What he intended to do was build a full-time academic faculty. This was in the late forties, and Pittsburgh had not been developed on this level.

There was one man who was in the Children's Hospital, Ted Danowski, who had just come from Yale. He had brought his whole entourage with him and was called Research Professor of Medicine. He had laboratories there, a metabolic clinic, and a metabolic ward. He was the only full-time person. So I told McCluskey that I would go to Children's Hospital for a year if I could have an appointment in Danowski's department. I spent my first year of residency there.

There was an interesting attitude on the part of my classmates, who said, "What happened to you that you have to take that residency? You ought to be able to get any residency that you want!" They did not value that kind of appointment. They said, "Do you have to take that for a year before you can get a regular pediatrics residency?" I just said, "No, I don't think so" and laughed because I had already been offered a regular pediatrics residency and turned it down. I went to Children's because they provided this special opportunity for me. I realized that I was drawn to that kind of career. I was interested in the science, in the investigation, and in the complicated diseases that we were working with. But I did not understand McCluskey's concept of the full-time academic physician. That was not the model that existed in Pittsburgh in my day.

Marriage and Family

My husband is an engineer. He's a graduate of Carnegie Tech and a Pittsburgher. What I've been able to do with my career has been influenced by the type of career he's had, which has been quite unusual. He was a bomb disposal officer in the navy in the Pacific theatre. He enjoyed that experience in spite of the fact that it was hazardous work. I think this probably says something about his personality. He's, in a sense, a loner; he's not an organization man.

I met him at Christmastime of my freshman year in medical school. I was very attracted to him immediately. I probably would have married him in a minute if he'd asked me, but he wasn't about to ask me—and didn't until six years later. I'm not sure he ever asked me! But over the course of the rest of my medical school and my internship, Lynn would reappear on the scene in Pittsburgh. Then, he would go off somewhere else, and just when I would think I would never see him again, he would turn up again. Needless to say, every time he turned up, I fell madly in love with him all over again.

When we finally did get married, he said he had wanted to make sure that I finished medical school. I suspect he had a feeling that he could probably persuade me to quit school and get married, but he knew that that would be a bad thing to do from the standpoint of the marriage, that I would always regret it, and I would have.

It has never bothered him that I had a career. In fact, he's always liked the idea that I was a physician. He found it interesting. He's liked to hear about medicine. He said it was the one thing he did not know anything about, and he's the sort of man who does know a great deal about many things.

Five years ago, I would have said that the division of roles in our household was not traditional. I really thought that my husband had carried a larger share of running the household and raising the children than the average husband. I finally came to the conclusion recently that that's not the case. It was a funny experience recently to come to the realization that really I've maintained the kind of home and I do the kinds of things for the children that I think any mother does, or any person who runs a household. He does more repair of things around the house, which is traditionally male anyway, and he does it really because he wants to do it. If I did not show up for dinner, he would make a peanut butter sandwich and tell me that that was all right with him—"I like peanut butter." But it would bother the daylights out of me that my husband had a peanut butter sandwich for dinner. In other words, I felt a tremendous compulsion to have the kind of home life and family life that my mother provided for my father!

We were married for eleven years before we had children—not because we could not have children but because we did not want to have children before then. Part of it was that we really enjoyed being together. This was a very romantic marriage for me—to have really been in love with someone for six years and then to have married this person! We really did not want to share our lives and each other with anyone else. We just had a great deal together, even though we never did terribly exciting things.

I was thirty-seven when my first child was born. We had begun to talk about having children more and more and finally decided we did really want to have a family. We both were only children, and we both felt that we did not want to have an only child. Our feeling was that it's a lonely life, and we did not want our child to experience the loneliness. So we had another child when we felt it was time. I was forty when the second child was born. My son is fifteen; my daughter is twelve. That was in the right order. I'd always wanted a brother three years older than I, and that's exactly what my daughter has.

I took six months' maternity leave when each of my children was born. I felt that it would be important for me to spend the early weeks and months of my children's lives with them. I wanted very much that experience. I wanted to nurse the children. I thought it was better for them, that it gave them a better start. I also thought it would give me more of a feeling of being a mother, that that was something that I could really do to be close to my infants. I did, and I was glad. I felt I got more out of that than I did the actual birth experience because it was a very good experience to hold them and look at them and see them respond. That was really fun from day to day.

I have some feelings about when mothers should leave their children, incidentally. I think if you're going to continue your career after you have children, that either you ought to come back right away or you ought to wait until they're well established in school—maybe six or so. A lot of people recommend, and a lot of women return, at about two years. I think that's a bad time because the children are very dependent. At that point, they're consciously aware of life-style, a way of living for them, and it's a terrible wrench at that age. I came back when my children were still very young infants, so they were always used to our way of living at home.

I felt much more torn by the conflicting demands of career and family when it came to the children than I did when there were just my husband and myself. I really feel that this is an important issue for all women in careers, whether they're in medicine or any other career. These days, with the kind of appliances we have in the home and the ease with which you can run a fairly large household, I do not think you really have many conflicts until you have the children. It's a matter of time and the *quality* of the time.

Today is a significant day in our family because the woman I have had for fifteen years is taking another job today, for the principal reason that she is a practical nurse, and she needs to return to nursing before we both get too near retirement age. I hired her originally as a nurse for the children, and her job was exclusively to take care of the children. I had other help for cooking and cleaning. I tried two or three other people first, and they left, or I fired them for one reason or another. Finally, I identified Mary Frances Allen. She came to us right before Lynn was a year old and has been with us ever since, until today. She was literally like a third parent—so that when I have to travel extensively, as I have in this position here at the association, they felt perfectly comfortable as long as Nana was going to be there.

My children asked me when they were younger why I did not keep house like everybody else's mom. I usually told them it was because I did not like to do housework. The fact is, I don't mind doing housework. I rather enjoy having a beautiful house and having it the way I want it. I do not mind doing what has to be done to do that, if I have the time. The problem is that I could wear myself to a frazzle if I did all those things. I realize that my children have, if push comes to shove, a fairly traditional view of the classical woman's role in the home. I do not know where it comes from, because I have not lived that kind of life ever.

I feel that being an older mother was an advantage. I realize that it was a risk from the standpoint of birth defects, and I was physically very tired as a result of my age. I'm sure I would have had more vigor following the pregnancies if I had been younger, although I felt very well during my pregnancies. I had some complications but nothing serious. But I felt that I was better able to cope with the career and with running the home. I knew how to interview people and to hire and fire them. I was more affluent; I was able to pay a practical nurse's salary for fifteen years. It's been terribly expensive, but if I had not been in the salary bracket I'd been in, I could not have afforded the household help I *had* to afford. I knew how to manage insurance and health care and dealing with physicians to take care of their health. I just knew better how to cope.

I realize how fortunate I am that my children have been healthy and normal and handsome and charming altogether. They really are a delight, and I am very proud of them. But I have had the thought that if things hadn't turned out so well that I might have had a different feeling and had regrets. My only regret about having children is that I wonder about their future in the long range. I realize that because I am older, I may be doing well if I live until they're out of college, so they'll be pretty much on their own.

Career

Lynn was not particularly enamored of my being a resident and never showing up when we had dates before we were married. When we came down here, I started talking about being a resident at Georgetown; I went over to Children's Hospital; I went to GW [George Washington] and all around, and I talked about internal medicine here, pediatrics there, pathology at Georgetown. So he said, "Do you really want to be a resident?" I said, well, I wasn't sure that I did. I honestly didn't know what I wanted to do. He said, "Well, why don't you just talk and explore." It had never occurred to me that I might not follow a traditional medical career. I talked to about thirty people here in Washington. I had been referred by Danowski to someone at the NIH whom I subsequently met and know very well and thought I could get a job with him right away in the research laboratory—and he turned me down. I was just crushed. This was the first experience I'd had in going after something that I did not get. So I went from one person to another. One of the interesting things that happens in this city—and I've advised many young people coming here to do exactly what I did—is that if you talk to a couple of people, they give you two or three other names, and you talk to them, and it expands. So I ended up learning a great deal about the city, the government, and the hospitals, and I was offered all sorts of jobs from running a Red Cross bloodmobile to a residency in pediatrics at Children's Hospital.

What I ended up doing was taking an administrative job at the Veterans Administration. I really did not know what that was, but the proposition was something like this: "When you come to work, we will pay you twenty-five dollars a day any day you come to work. We have a project we want you to do, and no hard feelings if you decide in a couple of weeks that you don't want to do this job. But we desperately need somebody who has a medical background to help us. You don't have to make a long-term commitment, we just want you to come and try this." I did not know what the word administration meant. They had maybe two or three hundred research contracts that they had put out at the close of World War II all over the country. They were reviewed and evaluated by the National Research Council from a technical standpoint—and they did not so much as have a list of those contracts. They did not know what they had accomplished, what ones ought to be terminated, what ones were good or bad. I decided I had nothing to lose. I could do something useful while I made up my mind what next.

The first thing I did was to familiarize myself with the projects and learn who was doing what, when, where, and why. It introduced me to the prominent investigators in about twenty fields, so that I got to know what was going on in peripheral nerve injuries, peripheral vascular disease, prosthetics development, cardiovascular disease, endocrinology, all sorts of things. The men I met through the evaluation process and through the advisory committees were some of the giants in medicine in those days.

I stayed there eighteen months to two years, working at getting all the research contracts organized, making a report about them, and making a projection as to how to phase out the program—because it was at this time that the VA was beginning to phase in their own research program within the VA hospitals. So they were moving from the contract kind of project research on the outside to getting the work they needed for veterans' care done through an intramural program.

I really did not miss clinical medicine at all during this time. I was newly married, and I was enjoying life. I was interested in the city of Washington. I moved away from Pittsburgh; it was really the first time, other than college, that I had been away from the family. And I was interested in the project I was doing. I felt it was useful work, and it did require some organizational skills and writing ability; and I learned a lot about government.

When Lynn got out of the navy, we did not think we wanted to live here. We did not know where we wanted to live. So we put our possessions that we needed to exist day-to-day in our car and took off to tour the United States. We went across the northern part of the United States, down California and into Mexico, and back the southern route and ended up in Florida because we thought we wanted to live on a coast and in a warm climate. I really loved the west coast of Florida, although we went to Miami because we thought that that would probably be the best place to try first to get jobs.

I did not know what I was going to do. I remember driving across the United States and looking at physicians' offices and thinking to myself, "I miss being a physician, practicing medicine, being clinically involved." I kept going from one extreme to another: "Do I want to do that, or do I want to give it up entirely and just be a vagabond?" I've often thought that if the Peace Corps had existed, that's what I would have done at that age.

After we arrived in Florida, we were there a month or so just finding an apartment and getting our furniture, etc. My husband became very ill with something which was never diagnosed. We thought he might die. He had a prolonged convalescence after that. So I just took care of him, and we stayed at home. Then, I began getting anxious about what I was going to do. I realized that I wanted to get back into the mainstream again. I also realized that just talking with people casually could not be my life. So I began exploring what I could do in Miami. It was very limited. The medical school was really only getting started. I talked to a couple of people whose names I had, and I soon realized that there was not much doing there except to become a resident. The only department that was established was the Department of Pathology. I was not terribly interested in pathologic anatomy, but I was interested in clinical pathology because it was about as much like what I had done with Ted Danowski as existed in Miami, the biochemistry, for example. The new Professor of Clinical Pathology had just arrived on the scene. He was a hematologist, John Miale. So he gave me a residency slot, and I spent the next two years with him. I enjoyed it. I got back into medicine again. It was not completely clinical medicine, but we did have patients.

We were out of money at that point, and my husband was offered a job back in Washington with Chrysler Corporation; they were doing some defense work. So we decided to come back. We came back here, and I again began to look for a job. I had written to some people I knew at NIH. I did not, at first, tell the Veterans Administration I was coming back because I had gone back to clinical medicine and I did not want to leave it again. I said, "Never again will I get into an administrative job." So I came back and talked to various people. Actually, Ray Shulman [a researcher at the Naval Medical Center specializing in coagulation work] offered me a job with him, and I guess that's really the only regret I ever had—that I ought to have taken that job and stayed in hematology.

But the Veterans Administration heard that I was back in the city, and they asked me to come back to work with them. They offered me a very good job, and they asked what terms would I accept? I said, well, really, they were not offering me what I was interested in. They said, "What are you interested in?" and I responded, "Medical education. I do not want to do research administration. Furthermore, I want to continue to do my hematology and do my research." So they offered me a laboratory to continue to do my work in hematology, and they offered me a job in medical education administration, working with their residency and internship programs and with their allied health training programs. The combination of that and the laboratory and a higher grade salary was very attractive.

I continued to go over to the lab for a period of about two years. Then, I began to realize that I had heavy responsibilities in my administrative job; my personal life was becoming a little more complicated—more responsibilities, more contacts with my husband's friends, more entertaining—and I got to the point that I had to make a decision about whether I would become an administrator or I would go back to clinical medicine or laboratory or what. The final decision was something that I probably just drifted into. I was highly successful in my administrative work. I started a new program for the Veterans Administration, which still exists today and is one of, I think, their better programs; at least they tell me it is. This was the VA Clinical Investigator Program. It was one of the first full-time research jobs that was established in the Veterans Administration.

I have wondered if I could have made a greater contribution if I had been in clinical practice taking care of patients, or have I made a greater contribution through the kind of work that I have done? I have had the opportunity to start many new programs over the years, and in each position I've had, I have started new programs—even in the government I had the opportunity to do that—which have reached many people and, I think, influenced institutions. Perhaps that's just a rationalization for having sold my birthright, so to speak, which was to practice clinical medicine.

A friend of mine recently asked if I was ever aware of discrimination. I said, "Not really, until I got to certain levels in my career. Then, I began to realize that if I had not been a woman, I think I might have been offered certain jobs that a man was selected for." I think a man who accomplished as much as I had accomplished, if he had been the same age as I and had the same education, would have probably been given the opportunity. Even though it was a bigger step, he would have had the opportunity to prove himself. I do not think the tendency has been to let women prove themselves; they are selected for their past accomplishment and not potential.

That's why I left the VA in 1960. My supervisor, the division head, left the immediate division and was promoted to Assistant Chief Medical Director, and a man was brought into his place who would be over me, who was not as well trained as I, who did not have the experience, and whom I would have found it impossible to respect, much less to work for. I simply resigned. It was easy. The minute it was announced, I simply picked up the telephone and called a friend at NIH and said, "You've been trying to get me to come to NIH for a long time. I'm ready." It was that simple. Incidentally, the man that they gave that job to lasted about a year and a half, they had to send him out to the boonies.

Dr. William Middleton, who was the Chief Medical Director of the Veterans

Administration, stopped by my office after he had heard that I was leaving the VA and asked me to come and see him. He said, "I'm going to ask you just one question. Are you leaving because of the man who was appointed as head of the division?" I said, "Yes." And he replied, "I was afraid of that. Thank you for being so candid." We remained friends and corresponded until he died. Dr. Middleton's picture is on the wall there.

I went to four or five institutes at NIH. A significant event from the standpoint of women and discrimination was that when I was interviewed at the Heart Institute, the man asked what grade I was applying for; when I told him, he said, "Well, I'm offering a grade lower than that, but that wouldn't make any difference to you because you're married, so you don't have to worry about income." The grade I requested was at the same level as I had in the VA, a GS15. I had "Chief" grade in the VA by 1960—that's twenty years ago now. He always said he couldn't understand why I didn't come to the Heart Institute! I never bothered to enlighten him. But I simply did not want any further discussion with anyone with that mentality.

I went to work for Ralph Knutte, who was then Associate Director of Extramural Programs at the Arthritis Institute. And I will say this—I think it's a significant thing from the standpoint of career development: Ralph Knutte's wife was a physician, and Jim Shannon's wife was a physician, and those two men were really excellent people for me to work for. Jim Shannon was the Director of NIH, and the fact that both of them had an accepting view toward women physicians, probably because they were married to women physicians, was a piece of good luck that I had.

Then the opportunity came along for me to go to the National Library of Medicine with Dr. Martin Cummings, who had been Director of the International Program at the National Institutes of Health and then moved over to be Director of the National Library of Medicine. He asked me to go with him and offered me a super grade so that I was early on one of the few women who had the federal super grade; he gave me a GS 16 when I went there in 1964. As Associate Director, my job was to develop an extramural program to build libraries, to train people in the information sciences, to equip libraries, to do some special research projects around information handling. That had to be designed; we had to come up with the concept of what that program was going to be. Then, we had to develop legislation; we had to get the legislation through the Congress; we had to get the money for it, the appropriations; then, we had to implement the program. There was no staff, no anything. He asked if I would come and do that program, and I did. We did it all within three years.

Then, I went back to the NIH and took a job in the Office of Program Planning. One thing I had wanted to do was take a year off to write a book about the impact of federal funding on medical education, but I really felt I could not ask the National Library of Medicine for the time. So I went back to Jim Shannon of the NIH and said, "Look, the Library is a small organization and really cannot afford to let an Associate Director go off and do this. Besides that, I've already had maternity leave; I've got a loyal staff who have put up with this nonsense [maternity leave] twice now, and if I'm going to do this—it's a very selfish kind of thing—I'd better get out of there into a bigger organization.'' He said that he really wished that I'd come back and work in his office instead. I knew that he was going to retire in another year, so I did that. When he left, he said something interesting to me. He said, ''Don't ever take a job as some super-administrator's special assistant. Only take a job that provides you an opportunity to run your own programs.'' That was good advice.

Subsequently, I brought up the question of the book again, and the NIH agreed to give me six months' leave. That was to start in September 1970. Along about February or March, John Cooper, President of the Association of American Medical Colleges, began talking with me about the possibility of coming to the AAMC. I pointed out to John that I was scheduled to have six months starting in September, and what he was offering was that I come to the AAMC in September instead. He said, ''Well, it's all right with me. It would be in the interest of the AAMC for you to go ahead and do that project. I'll have some grants, and I can probably give you some technical support to write your book if you come to AAMC.''

I asked Marty Cummings if I could have an office out at the Library and told him that I would probably be out there one day a week. Marty agreed to that. In fact, I still had my stack pass. That lasted about three months. I found out that I would go to the Library, but I would dictate other reports rather than working on the project. My responsibilities at AAMC were growing by leaps and bounds so I really just gave up on that aspect of it, and John Cooper and I never discuss it very much.

The principal thing I was hired to do was to manage the accreditation process for AAMC. The second thing that John Cooper added to the job, between the time he first talked to me about it and when I come on board in September, was to do the staffing for the Council of Deans. I then became deeply involved with deans, vice-presidents, with many of the programs that I've worked with here. So I abandoned the previous book project on federal impact and began studying the deans and their career patterns. I developed a management program that gives deans training and experience in management and works with institutions in problem-solving. I began this collection of career profiles of deans and looked at the turnover question so that I developed a burgeoning body of data and information about governance and executive roles in academic medicine.

Because I have been deeply concerned about all the propaganda about the stress of the job of Dean, about the turnover, the instability, and so on, I felt that it was rather important that I try to pull all this data together and publish the story of what's been happening in the last ten years about leadership in academic medicine. I realized that I wasn't getting that done in the course of my daily work, so I went back to Cooper and said, ''I'd like to pick up that old ticket''—as it were—"on that time to do the book. I want to do it now about deans. If I can raise the money to support me for a sabbatical period, can I do it?" He said, "Well, I realize that you're going to have to get that out of your system sooner or later, so go ahead. I think you ought to do it." So the Commonwealth Fund provided a book grant, and Dick Ross welcomed me at Johns Hopkins and gave me space in the Dean's office and a nice support system. So I went over there from January to September of last year and was working on that project. I hope that I'll have it completed a year from now.

On Women in Medicine

I think that the principal change that has come about in the status of women in medicine is consciousness about civil rights and affirmative action. People have been looking at medical school admissions on the basis of qualification rather than sex, and most medical schools have stopped having quotas that limited the number of women. Many deans told me as long ago as five years that when they began looking at women candidates simply on the basis of their qualifications and being blind about their sex, the numbers increased appreciably immediately. There were schools such as Stanford, University of California-San Francisco, Harvard, Yale, University of Washington-Seattle—the prestigious institutions. They were the leaders, really, in increasing the numbers of women.

Twenty-five percent of the graduate education population is going to be female. So of necessity, it's going to open up more residency slots for them. More executive positions will be offered to women. Affirmative action: on the one hand, you have to do it. On the other hand, just in terms of sheer numbers, more women are going to be in the pool. They're going to be looked at, and a few of them will get the jobs. Then, they will rise to top positions. Those things will happen. I do not think that we'll ever have 25 percent of the deans women, 25 percent of the department chairmen women. It has not happened in Russia, and it has not happened in other countries where the majority of the physicians are female. The top jobs still go to men.

We're trying to start a network of women physicians. In a sense we have developed an informal one, in that there are a few women physicians in academic medicine that I know—maybe there are a dozen or so of us in one network—and we know that there are two or three of those people interested in becoming Dean or Vice-President. I helped one of the women get a vice-presidency by making sure that she got interviewed, that they paid attention to her, by supporting her while she went through that process. Because she was a woman, it was awful the kind of questions they asked her. I asked her, "Is it worth it to you? If you really want it, put up with it. But it's a price you may not want to pay."

I hope that the women who come into the profession in the future are aware of their relationships to other women—aware of women patients and of the fact that almost 80 percent of the four million people that are employed in what they have come to call the "health industry" are female. I think women physicians need to be concerned about those relationships and see that they are developed to the fullest. I think there is an opportunity there, but I am afraid that women physicians are not particularly conscious of it.

One of the big issues is the relationship of the nursing profession to the medical profession, and I would hope that the women physicians in the future would try to do something about that. The nursing profession is very reluctant to have involvement with physicians or to get into any conjoint or mutual problem-solving around those issues. A lot of physicians have written off the nurses because of that. Many nurses in the nursing associations almost refuse to be receptive to any conversations with medical organizations. Well, I think the way they have been treated by physicians has resulted in the way nurses behave now, and because the nurses behave the way they do, the physicians have become turned off. It is a vicious cycle. I suggest to predominantly male organizations in medicine that they ought to be in a statesmanlike way addressing this problem, but I do not get anywhere. I tried it with some nurses recently, and I did not get anywhere, either. But I believe that it is an important issue for women physicians. If they cannot work toward change by other than example, I hope that they will at least be conscious of the example of interpersonal behavior they exhibit.

On Her Life Today

My friends have been primarily colleagues—not necessarily physicians, but people I have worked with; and frequently people who have worked for me, which is interesting. Two men who worked for me in the Arthritis Institute and went with me to the National Library of Medicine are still very close friends. I do not see them very often, but they are close friends. A woman who roomed with me when I was an intern, who worked with me as a colleague, is one of my friends.

Most of my friends have been men over the years until just recently. I have just developed friendships with more women in the last couple of years than ever before in my life through this emerging network of women in academic medicine. Up until that time, I never had more than one or two women friends at any one time. I have acquired two very close friends that I met only two years ago—one woman I had met about twenty years ago, but we never really knew each other until recently. A young woman who is on my staff is probably my closest personal friend now—Amber Jones, a clinical psychologist who works in the management program.

My social life is practically nil. I attend a number of social events that are involved with my work at the Association, but I do not consider those real social occasions. Frankly, I consider those part of the job. I am a member of several boards, and, while I see their social events as more relaxing and often more interesting than the Association social events, I still see them as work associated even though interesting and enjoyable. I think it may be different for men. I suspect they look forward to the companionship, the drinks, and the jokes. I look forward to getting home. I cherish serenity and privacy, and I rather rigidly separate my private life from my work life. On the other hand, there are a few colleagues from my work environment who have easily crossed that line and whom I enjoy as friends in the private, family, and social environment.

I make my home my "other interests," because it's children and job and husband—and my husband feels somewhat neglected, I might say, in recent years because of the tremendous demands of the job and the growing children. But I am an unquenchable optimist. I'm always sure that it's going to get better next year. I have to say that my drive back and forth to Baltimore this year has been of value from that standpoint. I spent an hour on the road each way. I really couldn't think a whole lot about how I was going to write the next section of the book, but I could muse about my life and what I valued and what I wanted to emphasize and what was happening to me and what disappointments and what good things I had experienced. I think there have been things missing personally that I want to emphasize more in the future, such as personal time for enjoyment for things that I like—the beauty in my personal, daily living, the time to think and contemplate that we so often put off until another time.

I have said several times during this interview that I am usually reluctant to discuss these personal aspects of my life and would prefer to focus our discussion on the work I have done. I do not want to give the impression that I have been concerned only with personal matters and trivia because the fact is that I have worked *exceedingly* hard throughout my career and have exercised considerable self-discipline. It is true I had a very normal childhood and adolescence. I chuckle now at how headstrong and romantic I was when I was a young woman in medical school—I had tremendous energy and strong emotions; I was probably a much more colorful personality then, than I am now. But in the later years, I have put all that energy into doing my job and raising my family. Perhaps I am now ready for still another phase of my life.

Did you read the current popular book *Passages?* Well, I think I experienced a "passage" in the last year, and what it was, was that sense of independence that you reach when you pass through midlife. I think perhaps for physicians it might be a little later chronologically because we mature later professionally. But probably the most important thing from the standpoint of getting me through the next twenty years was realizing that I had reached a point of true independence. I have arrived at that time in life that I can do what I want and do it on my own terms. If something does not go just as I want it to or the way I think people expect it to, I do not need to feel that I am a failure. I do not have to answer to that other authority figure anymore. Me—*I* am that authority figure now.

Washington, D.C.
November 1, 1977

DISCUSSION: PART II

Beryl Michaelson, Marjorie Spurrier Sirridge, and Marjorie Price Wilson came of age in an era of accelerating social change and technological development. Born in the immediate aftermath of World War I, they were too young to be affected deeply by the dizzying but fragile prosperity of the twenties. By the time they were old enough to have achieved a measure of political and social awareness, the nation had plunged into the Depression, which was succeeded during their college and medical school years by a second world war even more cataclysmic than the first. They were welcomed into medical school because of the temporary wartime shortage of physicians, but they began their careers in the postwar atmosphere of "back to normalcy," when thousands of young men unleashed from the military were scurrying to reclaim "their" places in the business and professional worlds.

In some ways, women of Michaelson, Sirridge, and Wilson's generation found themselves in a more problematical position with respect to medicine than those who preceded or followed them. The old conviction that for women true dedication to medicine was incompatible with family commitments was breaking down; but as yet, there was not the theoretical framework, later provided by the revitalization of feminism, to justify and even advocate the attempt to combine the two. The nineteenth-century idea that women had a special, God-given, separate-but-equal mission within medicine had lost its force; it had been reduced to vague sociological platitudes about the maternal instinct. All but one of the medical institutions established for women in the latter half of the nineteenth century had shut their doors, victims of increased specialization and the new emphasis on basic science and crisis intervention. Coeducation contributed to the breakdown of the community of women that had sustained the women physicians of an earlier generation.

Caught in an in-between period, their values and ideals formed in an age that believed woman's place was in the home, buffeted by a series of political, economic, and social dislocations, less likely than their predecessors to be buoyed by a sense of mission, and unprotected by a tradition of mutual support among women, Michaelson, Sirridge, and Wilson nevertheless chose to pursue careers in medicine. While their backgrounds and philosophies differ as widely as the courses their lives have taken, each in her own way did not conform to society's expectations for her behavior. Despite circumstantial evidence to the contrary, it occurred to none of them during early childhood that women couldn't be doctors if they chose to do so. Somehow, each was able to find within herself both the conviction that *she* was different from other girls and a wellspring of energy and determination to act on that conviction. By the time they were exposed to heavy doses of prejudice and discrimination, they had long since passed the point of no turning back.

How these women managed to escape the normal pattern of socialization for girls of their generation is a matter of speculation, but their descriptions of their early experiences are suggestive. In keeping with the pattern observed earlier, two of the three were only children; the third, Michaelson, was the only daughter. All came from families that encouraged their daughters to set high standards for themselves: "You can be at the head of the line," Michaelson's father told his children, "or you can follow along like the old cow's tail." All shared close relationships with fathers who offered respect as well as encouragement and seemed to relate to them not as girl-children per se, although Wilson's father did take an active interest in her personal appearance. Sirridge's father found nothing odd about taking his daughter hunting as other men might take their sons.

Perhaps of even greater significance was the enthusiastic support they received from their mothers to develop whatever potential they had. Wilson's mother, who had been thwarted in her own desire to become a nurse, specifically propelled her daughter toward medicine. Michaelson's mother, while uninterested in academics, urged her to make her own decisions and pursue her own interests. Within the family unit, all three mothers played an important role and projected an air of competence and independence. Michaelson's mother, in the time-honored rural tradition, worked shoulder to shoulder with her husband in the fields. Sirridge's mother was herself a professional woman. Wilson remembers her mother as the stronger and more influential of her parents.

Like the women in the previous section, the decision to go into medicine was made fairly early and clung to tenaciously. With some variations, their school experiences were positive, and all found at least some teachers who strongly encouraged them in their ambitions. All realized quite early that they were capable of outstripping most of their classmates intellectually, which may have contributed to their sense that they were somehow different from other girls. This feeling proved a source of strength rather than alienation. "I think I liked being the kind of girl that I was—a little bit different," says Sirridge. All did well in mathematics and science and seemed oblivious, perhaps because of their innate conviction that it was all right to be different, of the social pressures that often cause bright girls to turn away from these subjects as they reach adolescence. All evinced leadership qualities at an early age; Wilson reflects wryly on her election to the girls' athletic leadership club despite her lack of athletic ability. For this reason, the subordinate position implied by nursing held no appeal for any of them.

It was at the college level that these women first began to encounter active discouragement of, or at least massive indifference to, their goals. Even Wilson, who attended a school that cultivated a strong tradition of achievement for women, remembers with some bitterness the inadequacy of the counseling she received. But the doubts of others, far from deflecting them, seemed to spur them on. "I will make it," Sirridge told her scornful advisor. "If I decide that's what I'm really going to do, I will." Yet, two of the three, Sirridge and Michaelson, hedged their bets by actively preparing for alternative careers. Another revealing aspect of their commitment is their unshakable sense, possibly born of the Depression, that they would have to support themselves. All three women worked in college. Two of them felt the need to complete their education as rapidly as possible; two worked in medical school as well.

Both Wilson and Sirridge were socially successful and oriented toward marriage; both speculate that they might have succumbed in college to pressure to marry and might have resigned their medical aspirations had they met the "right" man. Wilson also credits her mother with helping to keep her attention focused on her goal during this period. Michaelson, harking back to an earlier tradition—perhaps because she was forced to put herself through school— decided fairly early that she could not combine marriage and career and deliberately held herself aloof from close relationships with men. Her continuing closeness to her family may have supplied some of the emotional rewards that other women seek in marriage.

All three women experienced discrimination in varying degrees in medical school, and it started with their admissions interviews. Though all felt that the wartime situation facilitated their admission, they still belonged to a tiny minority within their classes. In some cases, other women students provided a certain degree of encouragement and assistance but only limited personal emotional support. All felt they were on their own; both Sirridge and Wilson speak of seeing themselves in a special category, outside male systems of competition and camaraderie. They were aware then, as later in their careers, of being watched closely because they were women; both had a conscious need to prove themselves. Sirridge and Wilson remember lacking access to quiz files, but they did well anyway (Sirridge graduated first in her class) and seem to have derived satisfaction from succeeding without crutches. Though they met and admired a few women doctors, they struggled along with remarkably little in the way of role models. When it was necessary they sought inspiration from male mentors.

In different ways, each of the three women arranged her personal life to accommodate her career. Sirridge married a doctor, who well understood the demands of medicine. Wilson chose a nontraditional man interested in science and medicine, a man not threatened by his wife's accomplishments, and then postponed childbearing until her career was well established. Michaelson elected not to marry at all, a decision consciously perceived as a sacrifice. Thus, all three neatly sidestepped a certain species of domestic conflict. Yet for Sirridge and Wilson, neither husband carried much of the burden of running the household. In common with most women of their generation, the most they could hope to receive from their husbands was emotional and psychological support. If they were to have help, they had to hire it. Professional women were expected to be good mothers and housekeepers—a need generated from within as well as from without; Sirridge's and Wilson's compulsion to excel evidently carried over into all aspects of their lives.

If their professional lives had an impact on their personal lives, so too did their personal lives affect their work. Because her husband was "not thrilled" with the demands of residency, Wilson allowed herself to be diverted into an administrative position that eventually coalesced into a career. The birth of children exacerbated the sense of being torn between competing responsibilities. Sirridge chose her specialty to accommodate both family and professional considerations and even then took five years off from her career to devote herself completely to them. When she resumed her work, she was only able to juggle her several roles by dint of prodigious organization. Still, her children often found themselves waiting for Mommy in the car or playing in an empty hospital office.

The resurgence of feminism in the mid to late sixties came at a time when Michaelson, Sirridge, and Wilson were well established in their careers and might have been expected to resist or ignore the spirit of change. Yet, for Sirridge and Wilson the movement struck a responsive chord, and both speak of their growing feeling of closeness to other women over the past few years. Both are intensely concerned with the need to reform medical education and to establish professional networks among women. They are eager to see more women in medicine and are convinced that it need not be as hard for others as it has been for them. Michaelson, on the other hand, has never identified herself with feminist ideas, perhaps because her bedrock rural general practice has exposed her to less discrimination than Sirridge and Wilson have experienced in their connections with urban, academic medicine.

What can we conclude about the personal qualities that prompted Michaelson, Sirridge, and Wilson to follow a direction so different from that of most of their contemporaries? First of all, these women all reveal remarkably self-actualizing personalities. They all began at an early age to define for themselves the parameters of their lives and required relatively little outside affirmation of their decisions. None simply accepted the expectations and assumptions she inherited; though none of them can be described as an outright rebel, each woman carefully weighed and tested accepted assumptions to discover what was applicable to herself and what should be discarded.

A related characteristic is the striking persistence they have exhibited throughout their careers and an almost awesome willingness to set aside personal considerations in the interests of medicine. They have applied amazing energy and tenacity to overcoming financial and practical barriers. Though all have experienced periods of depression, they have displayed an ability to come back that indicates a large fund of inner strength. Their response to discouragement is not to retreat but to work harder.

Finally, these women have in common an unusual degree of flexibility. They have been conscious of being on their own and the resulting need to improvise solutions to both professional and personal crises. For Wilson and Sirridge, day care was unheard of; each had to experiment until she achieved a satisfactory child-care arrangement—one of the most demoralizing tasks a professional woman must face. In their careers, these women frequently have had to tap their resourcefulness; "every step of the way," states Sirridge, was "a way in which I'd had to work it out myself." All have made several changes of direction in the course of their careers. Indeed, all three women are still developing and evolving. Wilson speaks poignantly of her current attempts to reassess her life and priorities. Both Sirridge and Michaelson, disillusioned with private practice, recently mustered the courage to make major career shifts—Michaelson to the Indian Health Service, Sirridge to academic medicine.

For these women, persistence has been rewarded with a great deal of career satisfaction, though all are acutely aware of the sacrifices involved. The lot of the woman physician is changing gradually, in part because of the pioneering efforts of women like Michaelson, Sirridge, and Wilson. But as the stories of the younger women in the next section demonstrate, the problems these three women faced are a long way from complete eradication.

PART III
BLOSSOMING

Joni Magee

UNORTHODOX OBSTETRICIAN

Joni Magee's own experiences with the medical world have determined the direction of her career. Two unhappy years at the New York University School of Medicine led her to seek a different kind of education at the Medical College of Pennsylvania, formerly the Woman's Medical College of Pennsylvania. She decided to focus her career on the humanization of obstetrical and gynecological care after her own doctor discouraged her from natural childbirth. She now works closely with nurse-midwives at the Booth Maternity Center, an innovative birthing facility in Philadelphia that stresses family-centered childbirth and minimizes institutional interference with the process. Much of her published work, which draws on personal experience, is aimed at educating physicians to the point of view of the patient, whether in the office, the stirrups, or the delivery room. Now divorced, Magee is the mother of three children.

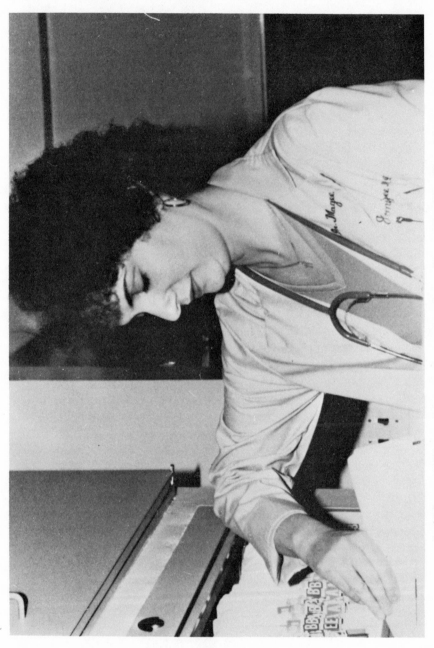

Joni Magee (1981) examining a patient at the private offices of Franklin, Glass, Magee and Nelson, Philadelphia.

Childhood

I was born in Philadelphia in 1941. I was an only child. My father is Jewish, a first-generation American. His father was a cantor in Poland who came to this country and had stage fright, so he never did take up his profession again. He became a buttonhole maker and then had various jobs, not tremendously success-ful. My father never liked school, although he did get a high-school diploma. He did not go to college. He became a professional musician. He played at private parties and occasionally had a steady job in a band in a theater. He contracted his own jobs and organized a band to fill the job. He sometimes sang. We were middle class. My father worried a lot about money, but that was not because we didn't have it. He just worried.

I'm under the illusion that I had an unhappy childhood, but probably it really wasn't that horrible. My father was not a warm person. He was not there. His work took him away a lot at night. He slept during the day. I don't have too many memories. There were a few years where he used to take me out on Saturdays, making a direct effort to develop a father-daughter relationship, and that was nice. I was around nine, ten, or eleven at the time. I think my father rejected me when I was a gawky kid. He liked me when I was cute and little and when I was about seventeen and became half a woman. But in between five and seventeen, he didn't have much use for me.

My father always said that I needed a man. He made me feel that I wasn't fully a woman unless I had a man. Although he always said it, I never realized he was always saying it until about two years ago; and then, he said it one time, and I went back over all the millions of times I had heard it. On the other hand, it never occurred to me that anyone was ever going to take care of me, and I'm sure I got that from my father also. He was not generous; he did not give me the impression that if I grew up and had no occupation, he was going to support me for the rest of my life. It always seemed to me that I was going to have to make my own way, although no one ever came out and said that.

My father always said, ''Don't beat the boys at tennis. Don't be the smartest one in the class. Don't bring home all 'A's.' '' Once I did, and I apologized to him for it. I really believe that he meant it, although he says he was kidding. I used to get mostly ''A's'' and a ''B,'' and this time I got all ''A's.'' I brought home the report card, and I said, ''Gee, Dad, I'm sorry I got all 'A's' because you said I shouldn't.'' He says that what he was really trying to do was make it easy for me; not make me feel like I always had to perform. But I did have the drive. I certainly did try to perform.

I never learned the proper woman's role. I never learned that I was supposed to find a man to support me—how to do that effectively and how to work life that way. For example, I tried to get a job when I was seven. I went to every merchant on the local street and asked them if I could be a delivery girl or something—because I felt then that I needed to find some way of filling my own needs.

My mother is also Jewish; she's also first generation. And both my father and mother, I would expect, were in the lower economic class when they were growing up, but my father got us into the middle class.

My mother had to leave school in sixth grade, or tenth—before she graduated from high school—to go to work. Her brother went to college, but she never even graduated high school. And she worked in a furrier's store as a seamstress—or salesgirl, maybe, not a seamstress—until she got married. Then, she worked until I was born, which was three years after she got married, and then she became a housewife.

My mother was kind of interesting in that she always was supposed to be sort of weak and sick; and although since I became a doctor, I've tried to figure out what my mother had, she never really had anything. But my mother always had a maid, and so I never got the picture of the mother or the woman of the family doing a whole lot of housework. My mother did the cooking, and she made the beds, but as far as scrubbing and so forth and so on, she usually didn't do that. I didn't see much housework getting done. In fact, my father helped out at home. He did more housework than most men.

My mother smoked a lot of cigarettes and drank a lot of coffee. She read mystery novels, did crossword puzzles, and when TV was invented, she watched a lot of television. She had friends mostly on the telephone. She was in the PTA when I was in elementary school. But she sometimes didn't go out of the house for five and six days at a time. She was very much a homebody.

I reacted very negatively to my mother; she was something I absolutely never wanted to be. She was overprotective. She was very, very concerned with my health and tried to treat me as if I were very delicate and was always bundling me up and feeding me and so forth. And very early in life, I became very rebellious, and I was not a dutiful, respectful child. I spoke back to my mother, and she was kind of a martyr. She was always sweet and nice, and I was always screaming at her. I always felt guilty because it wasn't obvious to the outside world why I was screaming at her, but it was because she was trying to bury me in a foam rubber pillow, and I was trying to get out.

My mother and I were not close. She never dated. She didn't go to school. My mother didn't do well in school. My mother could never help me with my homework because she didn't understand it from the time I was in third grade. She didn't wear makeup. Her clothes—she only wore housedresses. So there was really no aspect of my growing up that I could share with her. I do not think she was a happy woman.

From the age of five to twelve, I lived with my father's parents and his brother and my mother and father. It was a very depressed atmosphere. They didn't do anything. None of them did anything. My uncle didn't have a job, and my grandparents were retired or just not working; and everybody just always sort of stayed home. I spent a lot of time with friends away from home. I used to go to a community center two or three nights a week.

I loved school. I was very fond of structured, strict teachers. I usually got along with them. The teachers whom all the kids hated, I usually liked. They were giving me something. I mean, I could go in, I could learn—it was easy. I think my life at home was very unstructured. I very quickly became a match for my mother in that she said, "No," and I said, "Yes," and I did what I wanted. I had no limits. And I appreciated the fact that these women would say, "Okay, now you're going to learn how to do an outline," and then I learned how to do an outline. We could relate in a very understandable way. If I did what I was supposed to do, I got a good grade, and they didn't yell at me. It was very clear-cut, and I like that. Everyone always said that I was very intelligent, and I was able to do things. Teachers gave me great encouragement. I was always at the top of the class, and that was nice.

As I look back on my childhood, I have an image of myself operating on a teddy bear with a shoehorn. That was only one incident. But I did that. I mean, my entire idea of what I was going to do ever in my life always involved: I was going to take care of something; I was going to cure; I was going to heal; I was going to find out what was wrong, and I was going to fix it. There were times when I was going to be a veterinarian or a nurse or a doctor, but I was constantly fantasizing situations like that. I'm sure it had to do with my mother's hypochondria and my father's depression—that they had thrust on me the responsibility of finding out what was wrong with them and fixing it. I never did do that, but I think that probably I went on to try.

I had a few good friends, but I didn't date much in my adolescence. I would say I had a wide circle of acquaintances and just people with whom there were good feelings. I was strange. I was always either smarter than everybody else, or they always thought I was. And so there was a point beyond which there really was no communication, because I was the brain. I think what also hampered my dating was mainly that I didn't know how to act like a girl. I mean, I didn't know the most elementary things about dress, make-up. I didn't know how to let someone open a door. I mean, I went through—"No, you can't open the door for me." I have gotten to the point where now if somebody opens the door because he got there first, I just say, "Thank you," smile, and walk through it—and it works. But it took me all this time to know how to deal with my femininity. And there was very little interaction in my house.

I had one very close friend all through from tenth, eleventh, and twelfth grades. I always had one particular girl friend. It wasn't always the same one. I always wanted a sister. I always thought I was very lonely because I had no siblings. And I always tried to be very dependent on one girl, where I would tell her everything that ever occurred to me and would spend as much time as possible with her. There was one girl in high school that I was really close with. She subsequently got a Ph.D. in physical chemistry and does cancer research.

College

For as long as I can remember I wanted to be a doctor. Then, when I was twelve or thirteen, someone must have told me that it was unfeminine to be a doctor, but I haven't the vaguest idea who or how. But that was what happened, and from then on I decided to become a nurse. I read all the Cherry Ames books, all the Sue Barton books, and I was going to be a nurse. I went through high school in the accelerated curriculum, close to the top of the class, but I was going to be a nurse. In the summertime, I volunteered at Philadelphia General Hospital, which is the city hospital; I became friendly with student nurses and thought this was really super.

My parents weren't thrilled. I got the standard, "Oh you'll never be able to empty a bedpan. You'll never be able to take it. Nice Jewish girls don't become nurses." But of course, they never said, "Why don't you become a doctor?" In the meantime, the counselors were telling my father that I was too smart to be a nurse. My parents thought that the only reason I wanted to be a nurse was because I wanted to get out of the house, and nurses had to live in the nurses' dormitory. So my father refused to allow me to go to nursing school and said I had to get into a degree program, which meant Penn or Villanova. And my father, being a society musician, had a kind of snob idea that his daughter should go to the University of Pennsylvania because lots of the bigwig Philadelphia society people he played for went to the University of Pennsylvania.

So I had applied to Penn; you had to get into the liberal arts college and into the nursing school to be in the degree program. I had done that, and I had been accepted into both. I took a test for a Mayor's Scholarship in senior year in high school, which was a four-year, full-paid scholarship to the University of Pennsylvania, and I won it. So then, I decided to do it—to take liberal arts. It was only maybe a month before I graduated high school that I decided not to go into nursing but to go into liberal arts. But I still wasn't going to be a doctor. So I floundered through four years with no direction at all. It was terrible. And then, right before I graduated, I sort of got a flash of inspiration and said, "You know why you felt you haven't gone anywhere for three years? Because there's really only one place you wanted to go, and you weren't going there."

Then, I got hit by a car my senior year in college, and I had two broken legs and a fractured skull. And that shook my father up so much that he agreed to pay for one year, where I would take my premed courses in the daytime. So after I graduated, I went back, and I took biology, chemistry and physics—on crutches—and I lived in an apartment on Penn's campus. And then I went to medical school.

My father never believed that I would get into medical school. He thought that he was giving me a year to just jolly me along. My mother didn't respond. In fact, the only active discouragement I remember was from my premed counselor at Penn, when I walked into his office on crutches and announced my plan. He was condescending and patronizing. He said, "There, there, dear. Of course we'll get you into medical school." Like it'll never happen. But I assumed that kind of attitude was natural. It did not occur to me that a counselor would behave in another way. In fact, it probably strengthened my resolve. I worked best in adversity. I felt, "I'll show them."

Someone who did encourage me was the doctor who took care of me when I had the accident. He later became the Chief of Surgery at the University of Pennsylvania. And I believe he also had some influence in getting me accepted to NYU because he was very friendly with someone who was influential at NYU. Yet, he only knew me as a patient. But he said, "Oh, yes. I think you'll get into medical school." And I asked him for a letter of recommendation, and he very happily wrote one. And when I told him all the schools I had applied to, he said, "Oh, I think you'll get into NYU." And I did. So that's why I thought he had something to do with it.

I didn't know many doctors when I was growing up and no women doctors at all. This man, I think, served as a model because he gave the kind of medical care I wanted to give. He was a very compassionate southerner, and he was even then a full professor of surgery. And he certainly was very concerned about me. I developed fat emboli, which is a potentially fatal complication of fractures, and he came in to see me at various times of the day or night—sometimes at three o'clock in the morning. I was very impressed with the fact that he didn't leave it all to the residents and the people under him—that he himself actually did come. I heard later on from people that that was his way, that there was at least one big, important physician who could be concerned about one patient. I thought that was really nice.

I didn't do well in college. I think that it had a great deal to do with the fact that I didn't have to study in high school and hadn't formed the kind of work habits that I needed. I wish I had been challenged sooner because in medical school it was a real problem.

I was a political activist. I marched for integration, and I was a member of various politically active organizations; and I was a beatnik in those days, I think we called ourselves. I traveled mostly in a group of mixed—men and women, girls and boys, whatever we were. I had to help the underdog; I was immersed in guilt. I picked the Negroes because it was the civil rights movement and because I went to a high school which was half black. I got along well with blacks—I know everyone says, "Some of my best friends are black," but I find that I'm very comfortable with black people and only recently have discovered that a lot of people aren't. I mean, that half of it never came through to me until I was with some people and just felt them kind of stiffen up when they saw black people on the street. That doesn't happen to me, and I never thought it was unusual. But maybe that's why I had a great many black friends. I dated a black guy for a while. I suppose if it had been the Vietnam War in those days, I would have been marching against the Vietnam War. But it wasn't.

Occasionally I paired off with somebody for a while. My relationships were always very serious. I was always in love. I didn't have terribly much fun. I didn't laugh a lot. I didn't go to movies. I did not conventionally date.

I also wanted to get married and have children—that was always a big thing in my mind. I wanted to have six. I think one of the reasons I went to medical school is because there wasn't anyone around to marry. I think if someone respectable had asked me to marry him, I probably would have and given up the idea of becoming a doctor, at least temporarily. People say, "Why did you ever become a doctor?" And I say, "Well, I couldn't catch a Jewish doctor, so I had to be one." But there's more than a kernel of truth in that.

Another indirect influence, I think, was a relationship with a guy when I was a sophomore. He was a Cornell student, and he was premed. My dating habits were as rebellious as the rest of my life; I never dated anyone that was socially acceptable—except him. And I really liked him, and for awhile, he really liked me. However, the relationship ended, and he did go to medical school. And there was an element of, "Well, if you can do it, I can do it"—in going to med school because one of his objections to me was that I was too leechlike; I wanted not to live my own life; I wanted to be too dependent. And so I think part of my ambition was to make myself acceptable to him, although I never saw him again.

But I was mainly attracted to medicine because I liked being able to fix things; I liked finding what's wrong and fixing it, and there was the added thing of just being able to make people feel better. . . . That kind of fixing was more attractive to me than carpentry. .

I was certainly not interested in going into medicine to help other women. I hated other women. I thought the same thing about women that every man thought and wrote in a book—that I couldn't be friendly with them nor ever have anything to do with them as patients. I didn't ever get involved formally in women's liberation. My consciousness got raised on the delivery table and in medical school and with various things along the way. In the beginning, I thought the last thing in the world that I would go into was obstetrics and gynecology.

I thought I was weird—that I was a physiological female and an intellectual male. I never remember wishing I were a boy, but I always remember thinking of myself as male in my head. I never found myself physically attracted to women; I was always emotionally and physically attracted to men, but I also felt more comfortable talking to men and describing myself as masculine in my thinking. I always said that: "I think I'm not feminine." I think this feeling came from the impression that my mother was just a worthless individual, and I didn't want to be like her. I think I defined women in terms of my mother.

Medical School

I went to NYU because it was the only medical school I was accepted at. I applied to ten schools, including the Woman's Medical College of Pennsylvania.

Penn refused to accept my application even. They were very nice; they gave me back my application fee and said, "You just haven't done enough, and we just can't consider your application this year, dear. Go away." MCP interviewed me, but it was a flop.

I had an interview with one woman who said—it was ten o'clock in the morning—and she said, "Are you tired?" And I said, "No." And she said, "Well, you look tired." And I said, "Well, I'm not tired." And she said, "Are you always tired at this time of the morning?" I suppose I was nervous, and when I'm nervous, I go sort of blank; I remove myself from the situation. That may have been what she was perceiving as fatigue. But anyway, it was a very weird interview. That was one. I don't remember what the other was. And I will not quote who told me this because he's still on the Faculty of MCP, but at my senior dance—this is another really conceited remark—but at my senior dance, I danced with this guy, and he said, "They didn't accept you because you were too pretty." Because in those days they thought that anybody who looked like a woman would not really pursue her medical career and wouldn't be a good bet. So they didn't accept you.

So I started NYU in 1963—the class of 1967. I lived in the dorms. My years at NYU were the worst two years of my life, partly, I think, because they were in New York and partly because I was a woman. And I think that the antifeminine stuff at NYU—it was very covert, but it was extremely strong. But I didn't realize it until three years later. I thought I was crazy. For instance, on my first biochemistry test, I was taken in by Dr. Spier to get my results. They never gave you your grades. You had an interview. They didn't give you report cards; they talked to you. So I got a C+, which, as I talked to other people in the class, was actually very good. Well, that was the first; it was the only exam I passed that year. Then, Dr. Spier took me in, and he said, "My dear, are you sure you want to be here? Do you really want to be a doctor? Are you sure you want to be in medical school?" The impression I got from that was, "Boy, I really must have done crappy. I mean, something must be wrong with me." The whole thing there was the same. Everybody sort of shit on you—covertly.

My whole remembrance of the two years was that it was not pleasant. It wasn't pleasant for anyone, but I think it was less pleasant for the women. There were 10 of us out of a class of 120, and it was just very difficult. For me, it was especially difficult because I was one of maybe 10 Philadelphians out of 120, and the other 110 were from New York, so they were home. I had one year of premed, and most of those kids had been premed from age six. And so very quickly we passed anything that I was familiar with, where lots of them had had the medical school courses already once in college. They were very well prepared, and I once again felt quite at sea; and I really don't know how I managed to pass the first year. Plus the fact that when Kennedy got assassinated in November, I, being a very political being, was knocked for a loop for a whole month and just didn't do anything for a month. So I lost a whole month of what studying I could do in my freshman year.

We women did not stick together much as a group. Only one was a very good friend of mine. We were both kind of—I don't know what we were—we were the oddballs, I suppose. I think without Emily I probably wouldn't have gotten through those years.

I had a couple of friends among the male medical students, but mostly it wasn't terribly cordial. I always thought that they were more interested in money than we women were. I think to a large part, they still treated us as freaks. The women who were sexually available, they went after for sex. Then, the ones that they fell in love with, they fell in love with. Then, there was me, and I sort of wasn't quite in either category. I was engaged—quote, unquote—to my husband who was in Philadelphia. As a matter of fact, he wasn't in Philadelphia; he was in six months reserve training; he was away—I forget—Georgia or someplace like that. So I did go out but not terribly much. I don't recall much support. I don't recall much friendliness. You know, it was difficult.

Another thing that was difficult for me was that I don't function well in undefined situations; I function well in defined situations. And there was tremendous competition at NYU, and everyone kept saying it was a noncompetitive school, and I was confused, and I found it very difficult. I mean, I just didn't know what I was supposed to do, because it wasn't competitive and everyone was cutting everyone's throats—sort of under the table, though, you couldn't see them doing it. It was wild, terrible.

There were very few women role models at NYU. The second year, in physical diagnosis, there was a female resident who taught us, and who, I was thrilled to find, seemed to be a competent physician. That was a delight—to find out that there was a woman who actually was doing that. I think it may be the first time that I came in contact with any woman doctor. So that was a really great thing.

After my second year at NYU I transferred to MCP. I was married my second year, but he was in Philadelphia, and I was in New York. I got pregnant in January and finished in June, and I told NYU that I wasn't coming back. I needed to transfer to Philadelphia. My husband and I were going to live in Germantown. My husband was not a medical person, and I wanted to make our marriage succeed. I read all the women's magazines about what you were supposed to do, and one of the things you're not supposed to do is threaten your husband. I felt that if I had gone to a coeducational medical school, I would have friends that were men, possibly affairs with my fellow students; but more important than that, if I wanted to socialize with my fellow students, their other halves would all be wives, whereas if I wanted to socialize with my fellow students at Woman's Med, their other halves would all be men, and so my husband wouldn't be such a weirdo.

I was accepted when I applied again to Philadelphia. I applied to Penn, Jefferson, and Woman's Med, and I was not accepted at Penn, but I was accepted at Jefferson and Woman's Med. I chose to go to Woman's for those two reasons: one was we lived close by, and the other was the social thing. That was overriding—that there were, not no men, but there were people who would have boyfriends and husbands.

The atmosphere at Woman's Medical was very different than NYU. It was much more low pressure. It was much friendlier. And I had a better experience than other people. My class was unique. My class started at sixty and ended at thirty-six. There used to be mass transfers out of MCP for various reasons. I transferred in. I was older; I was married, and I had a child. And I was one of two in the class that had a child, and one of three that were married.

The attending physicians and instructors seemed to treat me more as an equal than as a student, and I did well. I mean, I have certain capacities. I unfortunately can't express them all the time; I would like to be strong enough to always be me and always produce, but I found NYU almost got me. They didn't get me, but they almost did. At Woman's Med I did just much better—besides the contrast between the preclinical and the clinical years, which also was there.

But I was much happier with myself. I think having had a child was very good for my ego, knowing that I had a home to come home to with a child in it. My husband and I never got along real well, but I had a husband, and that was something which was good for my feeling of self-esteem. And I was amazed at Woman's Med. I had—and probably still have—the same prejudices, and I expected to come in to a place of not quite very good people and was always amazed that people seemed to know what they were doing, that the women doctors were competent physicians. I feel I proved something because in the National Boards, where I competed against all the medical students in the country—my second-year boards—out of high-falutin' NYU, I was in the forty-third percentile nationally, and in my senior boards at Woman's Med, I was over the eightieth percentile and got honors in two boards. Now, I was still me, and the rest of the people in the country were still the rest of the people in the country, so Woman's Med—supposedly pooh-pooh little Woman's Med—was teaching me more than NYU had.

The irony, of course, was that when I came to Woman's Med, I felt that it was a second-rate institution because it was all women. But I don't think so anymore. And by the time I was a medical resident there, I didn't want them to take men, where, when I came as a junior student I always kept saying, "Why don't you take men? I was 1 of 10 with 120, I did fine. I got into a man's medical school. Woman's Med rejected me. What do you mean you need a school for all women?" And I changed my opinions quite a bit.

Marriage

I met my husband at the University of Pennsylvania in my senior year. On my third date with him, I got hit by a car; as we were walking across the street, and I was on my way to a date with someone else after dinner, I got hit by this car. He came to visit me every day in the hospital after that. Everyone disappeared. It was senior year, and everyone I knew was scattered to the four winds, and he was around. Then, I was home in bed for two months with two casts on up to my hips, and he came to see me every day. There was never any great romantic love for him on my part, and I never really did figure out what he saw in me. But he was there. I tried to tell him what marriage to a doctor would mean. You know, I said, "I'm going to medical school." He said, "Fine. Do whatever you want."

So I went to medical school, and actually, our relationship was very much my doing. The main thing he didn't do was run away. I was going to transfer to Philadelphia after my first year. But I had done everything but get a letter of transfer from NYU, and it was like July or August, and Richard had not said anything about getting married. So I said, "Listen, I'm not coming to Philly to live with my parents. So I think I'll go back to NYU." So I went back to NYU. Then, I got pregnant, so we got married—and I stayed at NYU, and he stayed in Philadelphia until the end of the year. So obviously I didn't put marriage before career because I did finish out the year. It never occurred to me not to. And then, I came to Philly, and we began to live together. And Richard had a job, a low-paying job, with the Redevelopment Authority.

He did go to night law school for awhile, but he never finished. He had parents who had some money and gave us too much money, so that we never had to live on his income. He never paid for my medical education. I went on a quiz show after my year at home and won almost $4,000 and used that. The Medical College gave me a scholarship for tuition, and I used the $4,000 to pay the baby-sitter and buy my books. And so I actually paid my own way through the second two years of medical school. I had borrowed for the first. So he didn't contribute to my education.

So anyway, the marriage was never very good. Richard never really got past the idea of a traditional wife. His mother scrubbed a lot, and his father yelled at her a lot; his father drank a lot and traveled a lot and didn't come home much. My idea of a marriage was sharing. I was out of the house as much as he was, so he should do as much in the house as I did. It seemed to me to be quite fair. And when my first was a baby, he really was quite taken with her, and he spent a great deal of time with her. He was a pretty supportive father, anyway, when I was in med school and she was little. But it was also difficult for him to be supportive of me.

He would go out and get drunk and not come home the night before an exam. Now, that really is not terrible, except that I was beside myself wondering where he was. I was a newlywed at the time, and this was a great threat to my ego that my husband wasn't home. So what I did was, I learned to arrange to be on call the night before every exam. I volunteered, and everyone was very happy about that. So that way he came home because he had to take care of the baby, and I stayed and worked; and I didn't have to deal with my anxiety about studying because if I was busy I didn't have to study anyway. I had a good excuse.

Our difficulties went on for several years, and then, finally, I got the courage to leave. I have been separated for eight months.

Internship and Residency

My decision to go into OB-GYN had to do with the terrible experience I had having my first child. I had decided—I'm a very, I think, rigid person. I try not to be. I always want to do things the right way. I always want the best; I read what's the best; and I buy the best. It seemed to me the right way to have a baby was to do it by yourself, not to have medication, and that breast-feeding was important. It seemed to me that I always knew that. And another thing I can't tell.... I'm sure I learned it somewhere; I'm sure I had influences, but I don't know where they came from. And when I came to Philadelphia, I was five months pregnant, and I asked for a doctor reference. And I got one at the University of Pennsylvania, which I went to because I had been there when I had my accident—that was my only hospital experience. And this guy was supposedly up on natural childbirth and liked it.

But with all the physical problems I had had not too long before—I wasn't really nervous about being pregnant, I was just sure that I was going to die; I was going to die on the delivery table or something. Plus, I had just moved from New York to Philadelphia, and I had just taken my National Boards, and I was not sure that I passed them. And I walked into this doctor's office on my first visit, and I broke into tears. I told him that I was going to die and just was very out of control. He probably got the impression that I was certainly not a candidate for natural childbirth and probably wrote that down. And we decided on—first we talked about a caudal, and then I changed my mind about a caudal after I learned a little more about it; said I didn't want it.

I took childbirth courses. My husband did not come with me to most of them. He came to about two. He was not supportive, and the thrust of the childbirth course was, "This is a family thing, and if you don't have...." They didn't say it, but they said, "Support is important," intimating if you don't have support, you can't do it.

So anyway, here I was, and I was really nervous about labor until I went into labor. I went into labor, and I suddenly became manic. I thought, "Oh, my God. Here's this wonderful thing—I'm going to have a baby!" I can't recapture the feeling. I've only felt that way three times in my life—and it's all three times I've been in labor—that nothing could hurt me. I knew everything was going to be terrific, although I would never have believed it five minutes before my first labor pain.

I ate a steak sandwich, and I felt great. And I called the doctor, and I said, "I'm having pains every seven minutes, and I don't want to go to the hospital yet unless you think I should because they tell me they're going to shave me and give me an enema—maybe I should go while I'm not having any discomfort and get all this crap over with." And he said, "Go to the hospital. They'll give you something for your discomfort." And I said, "No, I'm not uncomf..."—you know, we went back and forth. And finally, he said "Go to the hospital."

And I went to the hospital—and I still had pains every seven minutes—with a portable radio, lollipops, knitting, a book to read. I was perfectly happy. I carried my own suitcase in while my husband went to park the car, and laughed hysterically when—when they discovered I was in labor, automatically a wheelchair appeared, where two seconds before I had been walking around with a suitcase, and suddenly, everything changed.

And then, I went upstairs. A little, fat resident huffed into the room and said, "You're having a caudal." I said, "No, I'm not." He said, "Well, you'd better, you know. It doesn't get better, it gets worse. As a matter of fact, it hurts like hell." I said, "But I don't want anything." He said, "Wait a minute," and he went away. Oh—he examined me. He came back with two syringes and said, "You're going to be in labor for fifteen hours. Now, I'm going to put you to sleep for ten hours, and then you can wake up and go on for five hours and have your natural childbirth." I said, "Look. I'm perfectly happy, and I'm comfortable, and I don't want any medicine." He said, "Take it," and I said, "No," and he said, "Take it," and I said, "No." My husband said, "You take it. You're not a doctor, and he is, and if you don't listen to him, I'm going home." I said, "Well, they said I couldn't do this alone, so all right, give me your needles."

So he gave me his needles. And I must add here that I love dope. Anytime I have severe pain—which, I would also like to add, is about once a year—I take codeine; I take a lot of it. The two or three times in my life I've had Demerol, I've loved it. It's terrific. I'm sure—I think I was doped and had Demorol. So they put me to sleep for not very long. I woke up; I looked around. I said, "I'm not floating anymore. Give me some more." They gave me some more; I went back to sleep. Then, I woke up just about to deliver, but I didn't know it. I begged for a caudal, which was a spinal, which I got. I could barely breathe. I had a forceps delivery, a depressed baby, a sphincter tear, a great deal of blood loss.

I wanted to room-in, and they wouldn't let me because I didn't have a private room and my husband wouldn't pay for it. Every time they took my baby away, I felt like they were kidnapping her. One nurse came in and said, "You'll never nurse with those nipples." Another one came in—the baby was not hungry when she came to me.

It was a horrible experience, and I decided to go into obstetrics. I was going into pediatrics before that. When I went into medical school, I said, "I don't know what I want to be, but the only thing I'd never want to be is an obstetrician-gynecologist, because I can't deal with women; I don't like them; I don't think the same way they do." And I would have said that up until the day I went into labor. And the next day, I said to myself, "My God, someone has—

there's got to be a doctor for people like me. Granted not everybody wants to do what I want to do. But there's got to be somebody who will treat people the way I wanted to be treated, so I think I'll go into OB-GYN.''

And I nursed my baby; and I shot my mouth off for six-and-a-half years until I had another one, wondering in the back of my mind whether I was lying or not. You know, wondering, ''Gee, maybe you're crazy. Maybe you really couldn't do or wouldn't like this kind of treatment or this kind of delivery.'' I had my second one without medication and was very happy about it.

But the first delivery was a really negative experience. My daughter is eleven and a half, and every time she trips, I am certain it's because of her Apgar five [poor health rating for a newborn] and that there's three brain cells that she lost. I know there must be millions of women in this country with the same kind of feelings. I felt betrayed; I felt very angry—very angry. That's what did it. I mean, that was really the peak—if you talk about peak experiences, that was it.

I interned at Presbyterian Hospital in Philadelphia. I had no problem getting accepted because it wasn't a really high-powered, popular internship. I chose it because the head of their Obstetrics Department was a name on the Advisory Committee to the Childbirth Education Association, and I thought their obstetrics would be congenial to my feelings; the obstetrics at Woman's Medical College was not the kind of obstetrics I wanted to practice. As it turned out, they did very little private obstetrics. They did almost no natural childbirth. But it was a nice hospital, and it was a nice internship.

My internship year was fine. I had gotten a lot of clinical experience my last two years at Woman's Medical, so it was a very easy transition.

I got into a good thing. I play bridge, and one of the other interns—male—who also was interested in OB-GYN, also played bridge, as did some of the operating room nurses and one of the OB residents. So that was my group, my friendship group, and that was part of the fact that it was a nice year. We all switched our night schedules so that we'd be on the same nights, and when we weren't busy we played bridge. That was fun.

Being married also helped me psychologically. I think that my own personality needed to be married—that I felt, ''I have arrived. I have a ring on my finger and that makes me a person. Therefore, I'm allowed to be an intern also.'' I never could do one thing. I had to do two. I had to be a wife; I had to be a mother; and I had to be a doctor, too.

I had a marvelous baby-sitter, and that I think is the secret, in case anybody wants to know. I was really lucky. I put an ad in the paper, and this terrific lady came, and she stayed with me for ten years. You know, she was two years younger than me. She was black. She still is—she's still two years younger than me, she's still black. And I feel some of it had to do with my ideals. I was quite realistic, I felt. I was interested in someone young because I thought my child was missing a mother and needed a substitute mother, not a grandmother, so I didn't have an older woman. I also felt that my child was the most important thing, so although Bernice did my housework, she didn't do it very well, and I didn't care. She did the laundry, and she kept us clothed. After the first couple years, she also cooked dinner, and so I didn't have to come home and wait an hour and a half to eat until I cooked it, which used to drive me crazy.

I mean, things weren't all rosy, and I had my differences with her. But she was very supportive. She was very nice. She happened to be a woman who had no family of her own. She did not want to get married, for some reason—because she has a boyfriend. She loved my daughter, and she said she didn't like boys, but she loved my son when he came, and she loved my third one. If I was on and my husband didn't turn up because he went out and got drunk—which he did with a fair degree of frequency—she stayed. She was a very flexible person.

I felt I treated her fairly; as I always told her, I paid her as much as I could, and every time I got a raise, she got one. I tried not to take advantage of her. She knew I never asked her to baby-sit if I wanted to go out on the town. I only asked her if I was working, and she seemed to understand that. So I had not a terribly difficult time except when she was sick or her car broke down or it snowed and the buses weren't running or something like that. But I always was secure because she was there and I knew I could depend on her.

When I finished my internship, I felt I wanted to have another child. Consequently, I turned down an OB-GYN residency, a really choice one, saying, "Oh, I can't promise you an uninterrupted three years." Now, a man would never do that. A man could know that he was going into the service in two months, and he would do it anyway. I think that was the dumbest thing I ever did.

But I didn't get pregnant. I didn't know what to do with myself. So I called up Woman's Med and said, "Do you want an internal medicine resident, only for a year?" I thought I would benefit from the training. So I did that, but it was pretty bad. I wasn't very interested in internal medicine. I wasn't happy, and what annoyed me, I wasn't very good at it. I feel bad about that.

Still, I didn't get pregnant. So then, I became a house physician for a year at Haverford General Hospital—combined D.O./M.D. [osteopathic and regular medicine] profit-making hospital. I decided that I wasn't making enough money, and I was working too hard to be just wasting time. I only worked days, not nights, and I earned a decent salary. I probably knew more than most of the docs there, so I didn't learn anything. Then, I turned thirty in April of that year, and I finally decided that I didn't owe my life to any head of any OB-GYN Department and that I was going to apply for an OB-GYN residency no matter what I was going to do with the rest of my life. So I applied and was accepted to Jefferson—and got pregnant the next month.

I started in August because I had to cover an extra month. Three months pregnant—and it was okay; I told them I was pregnant. I ran up against just one guy who was, once again, an undercover saboteur. I can't deal with undercover saboteurs, only up-front ones. But aside from that, it wasn't so bad at Jefferson. I was a first-year resident. There were a couple of senior residents who sort of ran interference for me.

Anyway, then I quit after seven months and took off ten months. Then, the fun began. That was all all right. They were rather positive about it. I planned to come back January 1. But January 1—oh, anyway, I thought that I could get away without contraception. That was what happened. I had hostile mucus, and I had to douche with bicarbonate of soda; I got pregnant. I decided I had gotten pregnant the first time because I had a lot of indigestion and I was taking a lot of bicarbonate of soda; so all I had to do was stay away from bicarbonate of soda. Brilliant, right? I'm a doctor, I'm one-third of an obstetrician, and I didn't even know contraception—got pregnant the night of the day that I went back after my leave of absence. Now, this time they were not so thrilled about it at all. As a matter of fact, they were downright nasty. The head of the department did not talk to me again when I informed him I was pregnant.

I had decided that I was not going to have an abortion. I decided that I could not psychologically handle an abortion. There was never any doubt in my mind that I was pro-abortion—I did them—and that I was also pro-free choice. As a matter of fact, as an aside, I worked in an abortion clinic when I was on my leave of absence one day a week and never could get it together with the social workers because I tried to talk people out of abortions who didn't want them—and the social workers thought that I was anti-abortion, or they didn't think that I understood. But I really always believed that women should have a choice and that certainly no man has a right to tell a woman to have a baby. But once abortion became legal and the shoe got on the other foot, it became a social stigma to have a baby. And I also don't believe anyone has a right to tell a woman NOT to have a baby.

But anyhow, I felt that there were good reasons for having a child, although I certainly did not on purpose try to get pregnant. I really do not think I thought I was going to get pregnant. The reasons were the fact that my two kids were so far apart, they weren't really company for each other and the fact that I felt an abortion would be a denial of my two kids. That's how I felt—that I would be telling them, "I don't like you enough to have another one," and I could not deal with that feeling. So I decided to have the child. My husband threatened to kill me, and everybody at Jefferson was very pissed off. And so once again I was forced into a situation where I was alone against the multitude, and I do well in that situation.

So I continued my residency. I left my husband. I told them I was going to leave, and I was going to leave for a year. I said, "Ten months isn't enough. The kid was too young. I shouldn't have come back. I'm going to stay out a full year this time." And they said, "You have to come back in six months because we need somebody in May." I think now that I was stupid, but what I said was, "Listen, my kid will only be zero to a year old once in its life, and I have the rest of my life to worry about my residency. I will not come back in six months. If you don't take me back in a year, I'll worry about it then."

Then, the department chairmanship changed while I was away. I had sixteen months in by now—seven the first time and nine the second time—and the new department chairman said, "You can come back and begin your second year at the beginning and give up your four months." So they got this committee together, and they said, "Would you come back under those circumstances?" And I said, "No," which was another stupid move; however, what happened was that they never said anything else about it. So I came back with my four months, and I discovered another thing about women is that if you stand up like a man, and you have balls, you can get away with a lot.

So then, I went back, and I changed. I had done a lot of thinking. All these leaves had been very good for me. I became much more aggressive. I decided that I was a resident, and I damn well was going to put in my time, and I was going to work, and I was going to read journals like the other people because, although I had it all over them on sensitivity, there was a real lot of knowledge and competence that I had to acquire and that was what it was all about; and that I was going to play the game because that was what the game was. So I went back for twenty-two months—a different person really. But anyway, it was a very chopped-up residency—it was five years long.

Since completing my residency, I have worked full time at Booth Maternity Hospital, where I worked part-time when I was on my leave of absence with my third child. I have a very small private gynecologic practice. The obstetrics end is an unusual practice; there's nothing like it in the country—three doctors and ten midwives or more. I get paid by the chief. He pays me a stated amount, but I'm technically self-employed.

On Her Professional Goals

I would like to do in a group the kind of obstetrics they do at Booth. Booth is kind of a combined clinic and private practice. I would like to work in a hospital, a full-service hospital, but I would like to do the same thing we do at Booth. I think midwives are great, and I would like to work with midwives, but that I would sacrifice. I would not go into practice in OB if I couldn't do family-centered maternity care because I'd be too uncomfortable. If I couldn't offer patients the options that I think are so important to them, I couldn't work. So that's why I'm where I am.

Of course, women have a harder time of it breaking into private practice for a number of reasons. First of all, nowadays, I don't know anybody who goes into practice for themselves. It's a vicious circle. The older guys take in the younger guys. The older guys don't take in the younger girls. You can get a job with the department, full-time teaching; there's not terribly much discrimination against women. But the private male practitioner does not want to take in a woman. One that I know of, that I talked about it with, said, "Well, you've got a husband to take care of you. You're not going to take your job seriously." Despite the fact that he watched me work 100 hours a week when I was a resident, he thought that I wouldn't be a good partner for him because I wouldn't work hard enough. He just saw what he saw, which was his idea—it wasn't the reality. I suspect that may be part of the reason. And I think it's partly true. Women with families are really not interested in the demands of private practice. I mean, I somehow would like to be able to create my ideal situation.

Another thing, it was my experience in medical school that we were not taught any way of relating to patients. No one *told* us to maintain our distance. If they did, it was by example. That's one of my beefs with medical school in general— that we were not taught anything about how to deal with patients—specifics. We were taught lots of theory of what's wrong, like physical diagnosis and how to examine. That's one of the reasons I write some of the stuff I write, because no one really does teach you bit by bit, which is the way you really have to know it because you're just like a kindergarten child when faced with a new toy. Someone should teach you on a kindergarten level and not be afraid of insulting your intelligence.

I have written and published articles which attempt to deal openly with the communication gap between patient and doctor.* My colleagues have responded with indifference or grudging acceptance, but the medical students were thrilled.

I think the giant defect of medicine is its need to be godlike. I think the malpractice suits and everything that's happening in medicine today is our own—not our fault, the fault of our predecessors, who told the people that they were Santa Claus. And when people found out they weren't Santa Claus, they got really mad. Whereas if they had said to the people, "We are not God. We make mistakes. We do this; we do that. This is what's wrong with you; I don't know if this will work, but I'm going to try it," I don't think the people would get as angry, and I don't think they would sue as much. After all, the doctor is just a person. And I suppose that makes some patients feel insecure, but that's their problem.

A doctor musn't be threatened by somebody else's competence. That is, if your patient is smart enough to understand what you're doing for him, that shouldn't threaten you. It doesn't hurt to educate a patient, but I think a lot of us feel that, "Well, if we educate them, then we're not special anymore." But I think they won't get sued so much if they see the patient's health as a joint endeavor between patient and doctor.

On Women Doctors

Women doctors definitely have a harder time being assertive. This means that they generally have a harder time with the decision-making process at first. I would say that I didn't learn to really do it until about two years ago. Because we have to be perfect, because we think we're inferior, and because we think the men are perfect, therefore, if we don't do it right. . . . So women are much more

*"Labor: What the Doctor Learns as a Patient," *The Female Patient,* 1, (December 1976): 27-29.

timid than men. They talk about being aggressive—I didn't understand until recently what that was—in house officer's training. Aggressive means doing something whether you know how or not. A woman is much less likely to do that because she's taught that you're not supposed to do it wrong, and you have to really know how before you do something. Men don't talk about their mistakes. Women are much more likely to say, "Boy, I really goofed that up." It wasn't until I opened my eyes very wide—and it wasn't finding out what I could do, but it was finally becoming aware of the goof-offs made by my superiors—that sort of made me give myself permission to deal in imperfection. That was a great relief. I've been much happier with me since I learned how to do that.

I don't know that women are any different than men as far as some specialties go, but I think in OB-GYN they have to play a special role. Some of them are trying, but there aren't enough, and there aren't enough of the unconventional kinds. Well, I guess I'm a feminist OB-GYN; and I suppose some feminists would argue with me because I'm a feminist OB-GYN, and a lot of the feminists think it's only GYN that's important and that you shouldn't have children—and you know, like that. But I think there should be many more women in obstetrics and gynecology. And there should be women who are also interested in obstetrics and in the total aspect of womanhood. Because just like they tried to keep us from being people by making us be mothers, we should not let them turn around and throw us out of being mothers by being people. We are both. Many of us want to be both.

I also feel that women are still discriminated against. It's just more subtle now. You're allowed to go to medical school, but you're directed towards a suitable specialty. And I think some of the women faculty are right in there with the men, shunting women into "feminine" specialties. For example, I think private practice could accommodate many more women. Just like medical schools could and did, private practice can, if it will. You just need more—maybe you need two women instead of one, so that you don't have to work 140 hours a week to be in private practice.

Residency programs also need to be structured differently. The women who want a family will feel that it's too difficult to combine a surgical specialty with a family. And it is. But it doesn't have to be—I mean, I don't think it's inherent in surgery itself.

I think if there are nine male residents and one female resident, she's got to do what they do. If she's going to get the same training and get the same degree, she's got to do what they do. But this training is inhuman. I mean, I think the whole postgraduate training idea is crazy—internship and residency is crazy—because you can't see people; or just physically—you can't do well when you're asleep on your feet. It's inhuman to the residents and to the patient.

I believe professional organizations are important to me. For example, I would love to see everybody in the American Medical Women's Association also join the AMA and subvert it. I certainly think we need our own organization. But I also think that by itself it will never have any great influence on anything until it can make itself heard in the male medical establishment. For the same reason, I didn't think an all-women's medical college was a good idea when I attended MCP. But I think they should certainly make a place for more women than other places do.

On Her Children

I try to spend time with them. My relationship with infants is terrific. I am a marvelous infant mother. I will take them everywhere I go. I find physiological things very understandable, and as long as I have a nursing baby, I know how to deal with it.

My relationship with my eleven-and-a-half-year-old girl is getting much better, I feel. There was a period between the time when—well, I guess she was four—maybe three—and seven, before my second child was born, where I rejected her a lot, or I felt more committed to my work. And I didn't want to spoil her; I had all kinds of what I consider now horrible ideas about child-rearing—that you shouldn't spoil them, you should make them listen, and so you go away—I didn't hug her and kiss her enough.

Then, I had the new baby, and I was in therapy. And one day I held the baby on my lap, and she came up and went to kiss me, and I drew away from her. And I thought, "My God. You've drawn away from your own child," and I began to try very hard to become more affectionate with her and get through this barrier that I had set up. And its been five years, but we're much closer than we were. And now, she's going to get into adolescence; it's going to be very interesting.

But I like my children. And again, I don't know if I'm weird: I hear mothers complaining about their children, and I hate to hear mothers complain about their children. It makes me feel so bad for the children. I chose to have them all. They didn't choose to come; they didn't ask me. I owe them a lot, and I feel like I've got to give it to them—not just material things; they need a sense of their own worth. I need to tell them they're terrific because they've got nobody else to tell them they're terrific. And I do—I tell them they're terrific, and I try to arrange my schedule so that I get to school when I'm supposed to be there. When there's supposed to be a parent, I try to do it. And I don't do well with them in the home—I'm not a home person—so I try to take them away. I take them swimming. I do very well with them in a swimming pool. I don't like to swim, but I like the water, so I teach them to swim. And people look and say, "Oh, you marvelous, patient person. You can stand there for two hours and do nothing but paddle these little kids around." But I can do that, and so I do it.

On Feminism

I've gotten angry; I've gotten aware. Well, I became aware of discrimination that happened to me in the past, which I was unaware of at the time and which would have helped me to be angry rather than threatened. A lot of things I didn't know. It educated me. I never went to a consciousness-raising session, but I found my consciousness raised. Entering into the divorce proceedings is raising my consciousness much further.

I think the women's movement has influenced me indirectly. I don't know whether I'm too threatened to be influenced directly or not. But as I say, I haven't joined a group. I participated in hearings on women and health that were held in Philadelphia in 1974 on the Steering Committee, and I contributed some. I learned a great deal. I met women who were active in the women's movement, and I have a great respect for them. I felt, after I wrote this article, that it was helpful that I wasn't a member of the women's movement, that I wasn't a raving feminist. I thought that if my role could be to get to the medical community and have them listen to me, that would really be doing much more for women than if I got active in the movement and became identified—because then they could say, "Ahh, she's just another crazy like Betty Friedan, and we don't have to listen to her."

On Her Life

Do it. Don't let anybody stop you or tell you you can't do anything. You can do whatever you want if you're willing to make the commitment and to find a way to do it. And I wish more people would. I just wish more people would have kids and go to medical school, so people wouldn't think I'm such a strange, wonderful person—"Oh, look what you did!" It wasn't really all that difficult. It just took a long time.

As far as going into medicine, I think it was terrific. If I had it to do again, I would have been more aggressive in my fertility work-ups, and I would have had my children earlier and all together and probably have taken off more time each time I had one—or maybe all together. I certainly never found that a leave of absence hurt me professionally. Everybody says you'll forget; every time I came back, I did better than I had done before I left. I got strength, I got time. One of the big things in medical school is if you have personal problems and you're tired, you can't cope with anything. So you take off a year and sleep nights. It gives you strength.

My big feeling as far as women in medicine goes—and women in general, professionally—is that the women's movement and the male establishment have both combined to make us feel that we have to make a choice. I think we all ought to get together and say, "No, we will not make a choice. We want to have it all."

Philadelphia, Pennsylvania
April 1, 1977

8

Susan Benes
OPHTHALMOLOGIST IN TRAINING

Balancing the claims of a demanding residency in ophthalmology at Wills Eye Hospital in Philadelphia, Pennsylvania, with the needs of her husband and two small children has been something of a struggle for Susan Carleton Benes. Various compromises have been made and not without doubts about the wisdom of her choices. Her initial reservations about placing her children in a day-care center have been allayed by the happy adjustment they have made. Her uneasiness about choosing a specialty more from convenience than commitment, however, remains to be completely resolved.

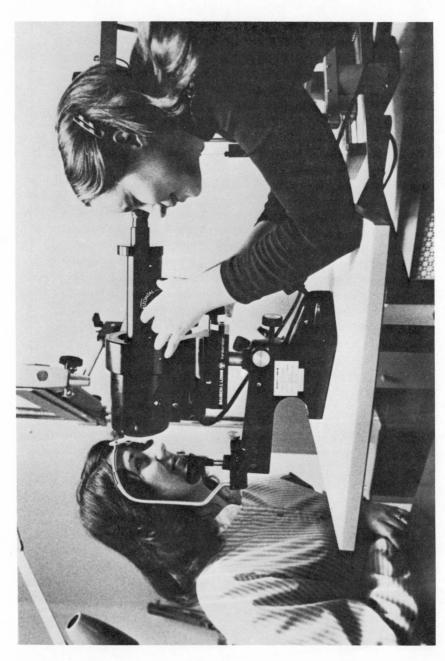

Susan Benes (1980), Staff Physician at Graduate Hospital, Philadelphia, measures a patient's cornea curvature using a Keratometer.

Childhood

I was born in Cleveland Heights, Ohio, in 1948. My father was an engineer. His father was a physician, and all of his ancestors had been medical missionaries on both sides of the family. Their missions were part of the Presbyterian church. As my father grew older, he became more and more religious and was active in the church.

My relationship with my father was very close. I admired him very much and wanted to be just like him. He was very shy and reserved—loved nature and science and thinking about things. He always took me on long walks, teaching me how to identify different forms of trees in the winter by their buds and their bark, different kinds of leaves, different kinds of insects, and all about the flowers that bloom in the spring.

My mother graduated from high school at the top of her class and won a scholarship—which she needed because there wasn't enough money in her family—to go to college. She went to Ohio Wesleyan and graduated with a very high standing. She majored in medical economics and home economics. Before I was born, she worked as a buyer and financial analyst in a department store. Then, she threw herself into mothering with volunteer activities and organizations as her outside interests.

I grew up during the postwar years, and most of the war brides, which my mother was—even those with the amount of education that she had—decided to stay in the home and raise their children. They felt that their education would enrich what they gave their children and didn't feel they had to pursue outside careers. So it was a foregone conclusion with both my mother and my father that this was how it would be done. I don't believe he ever felt that a woman shouldn't have a career because he always wanted to know what I wanted to be when I grew up and was always interested in my answers. He thought that I could do anything that I wanted to do.

In my teenage years my mother and I didn't really get along well together. It's very hard to say whether it was because we were too close to get along or whether we were too much alike. We're both very aggressive overachievers, and despite my straight ''A'' report cards and numerous activities at school, it always seemed she would compare herself to me as a successful student. I felt that I could never please or satisfy her.

However, she *was* pleased that I wanted to be a doctor. I think it was an ego trip for her. She was proud that I had that ideal. When people asked her what I was thinking of doing, she said, ''Well, she says that she's going to go into premed, but we'll see.'' She always had the reservation. She contended that I was a good teacher, that teaching would probably, in the long run, make me happier.

She said, ''Oh, you'd be a perfect teacher. If you went into medicine it would be a waste of your teaching talent. Besides, if you went into medicine, you'd never be able to get married and have kids.'' So she felt that in order for me to have a life that I could be happy with—and she fully expected that I wanted to get married and have kids—that I would have to have a more time-limited career, and teaching would probably be what I should do.

I had a brother and a sister who were very much younger than I was. I was very close to my brother, but he was treated differently partly because he was a boy and partly because he was younger. To be specific, when I was in high school I wasn't allowed to smoke or drink or anything like that; such activities were considered terribly immoral. My brother, on the other hand, both smoked and drank in high school, and rather than simply forbid him, they had to accept that he did it.

Other relatives influenced me, especially my grandparents and my father's sister's husband, who was a physician. One day I was out in the middle of a lake in a rowboat with him—I was maybe a third grader—and he said to me, ''Well, Susan, what are you going to be when you grow up?'' I said I was going to be a nurse, and he told me, ''Oh, no, you're not, because you're too smart to be a nurse. You're going to be a doctor.'' I told him that ladies couldn't be doctors, and he said, ''Well, why not?'' I said, ''Doctors and nurses take care of people, and they call the men doctors and the ladies nurses.'' At that time I thought a nurse was a lady doctor. He told me that it wasn't that way at all and that a woman could be a doctor and could have more responsibility. He told me what courses to take, and I remembered every word he said. Even now, I can remember him saying, ''Take a lot of physics, take a lot of math—because I didn't take enough physics when I was going through—and I really think you can do it.''

Even when I was two and a half, I knew then, for some reason, that I wanted to take care of sick people. I just felt like I wanted to be nurturing. I can't describe it, but I even have a picture of myself dressed up as a nurse playing with kids at that age. I was always the one they picked to be the nurse or the doctor. So there was never a time in my life when it wasn't clear in my mind that that is what I wanted to do. Everyone else agreed, and they always asked my opinion about things. In junior high school, when we were finding out about the facts of life, all my friends would come to me and say, ''Is it true that you have to do *that* to have a baby?'' They always treated me as the last source. I mean, ''If no one else knows, ask Sue.''

As a child I was a Camp Fire Girl and an avid camper. My leaders and counselors all thought I should have been born 200 years ago in pioneering times, since I craved adventure and hard work, including cooking over a campfire, cutting and gathering firewood, and clearing or digging latrines! My desire to return to more primitive society was mingled with religious fervor and idealism. My grandfather's people had been medical missionaries in India for four generations; my grandmother's father was a religious missionary in Japan. So I aspired to follow in their footsteps and become a missionary.

I was a leader and extroverted in high school—even when the family moved during that period, something I was very sad about. Things were fairly easy for me then. I just played, did what was necessary to get straight "A's," and joined every activity that came down the pike: Camp Fire Girls, Girl Scouts, swim team, choir, choral groups, youth fellowship, Red Cross lifesaving and water safety instructor, etc.

I was socially accepted in my group of students, my friends. We were all in the same honors classes together. I *did* care about what the other nine-tenths of the students thought about me. They thought that I was old-fashioned, a stick-in-the-mud, very naive, because I didn't smoke and I didn't drink and I was a prude in that I wouldn't even kiss boys goodnight. That bothered me a lot because I wanted to be socially acceptable.

But by the time we were seniors in high school, they apparently approved of me or admired me, because every year there was a school vote for the homecoming queen and I won. The previous years, the homecoming queen had usually been the fastest, wildest, most gorgeous girl in the school, but I was not fast, wild, or gorgeous. Yet, I *was* voted homecoming queen. It was a very good feeling. I think I cried for about forty-five minutes after they announced it and during the halftime of the football game.

I had a rebellious side, and one thing that I really rebelled about was that I wanted to be a cheerleader. My parents told me that in no way, shape, or form could I possibly be a cheerleader and then go on to be a doctor, because it would impress the admissions officers much more if I did volunteer work at a hospital as a candy striper or something like that in my spare time. I told them that wouldn't be any fun compared to cheerleading, so I tried out for cheerleading anyway, and I was a cheerleader throughout junior and senior high school.

College, Marriage, and Teaching

I chose Michigan because I wanted to stay in the realm of sports, having been a cheerleader in high school, and I wanted to go to a place that was coed. My first choice was Cornell, but it was much more expensive than Michigan, and that would have been hard for my parents even though they made it clear to me that they were willing to make the sacrifice.

The high-school counseling service had wanted me to go to either Radcliffe or Smith, but I was afraid of not being sexually sophisticated enough for eastern schools. I had heard all kinds of stories about women who were in women's colleges all week long, cooped up with each other, getting into a bus on Friday night, and being shipped "like a herd of cattle" to some male school for the evening for a wild party. I realize now that was a naive view of what the social life was there, but it frightened me to think that was the kind of social situation I'd be getting into. I wanted a much more natural relationship.

Socially, I did a lot of growing up in college. I was there during the Vietnam War. It was a time when beer was on the outs and drugs were on the ins. I hadn't even gone through the beer state in high school, so it was really a big jump for me. Even so, my whole upbringing prior to college had been so prudish and so Ladybug-oriented that I remained prudish and Ladybug-oriented, comparatively, to the rest of the crowd at college. I tried oral drugs and decided they "weren't my bag." As far as I wanted to go was drinking. That automatically put me in a different sphere from the more politically active people, the SDS, Weathermen, Black Action Movement, and the anti-Vietnam War people who brought tear gas and National Guardsmen to the University of Michigan campus.

I joined a sorority (Kappa Kappa Gamma), even though in my freshman year I was completely turned off by the whole rush situation. I had been rejected by the house where all my closest friends had pledged. In the freshman year, we were all out-of-staters, very much alike. They had put all of us in one hall, fifty-five out-of-staters, just like a bunch of peas in a pod. We'd all been cheerleaders; we'd all been on student council; we were all either the homecoming queen or some other kind of queen; we were all straight "A" students; we were all career-oriented. We were all exactly alike except for our looks.

I didn't feel my college friendships were very close. Michigan was such a huge school that it wasn't at all like I had envisioned that college life would be. My friends in college were all very interested in one another, but it wasn't an inbred situation. We were all very interested also in separate and divergent ways; we simply lived near each other and were very friendly with each other and had good times together. It was just a friendly time; we passed through college, went on to other things, and now write yearly Christmas cards.

When I got into college I realized, after I'd gone through my rebellious period, that there had been a certain amount of self-doubt that had been ringing a bell with my mother, because I did, in fact, go into teaching before I went to medical school. Halfway through college, I chickened out. I decided, "Oh, I can't stand the competition. These people in the premedical courses are so obnoxious, I can't stand them. They won't help each other; how could they help patients? You can't get any notes from them; if you missed class, it was just too bad." And the students cheated, stole tests, and sabotaged each other's chemistry experiments. I took the path of least resistance and dropped out into teaching.

There were 2 women out of maybe 400 in each classroom, and I couldn't even get along with the other woman. They always wanted the two of us to be lab partners, and I couldn't stand her. It was just altogether negative, and I decided it would be a safe bet to get the teaching degree; at least I'd have that under my belt, and if I ever wanted to try to go into medicine later, I could try. At that time I felt zero self-confidence for some reason, and I doubted that I'd ever be accepted to medical school. If I weren't accepted, at least I'd have something for sure. So in fact, I did go and get my teaching certificate and teach.

I was generally depressed at that time of my life, so the decision to give up my dream of going into medicine was just part of the overall depression. I think I had gone through my rebellion, gone through this big social revolution, was totally knocked off my feet, didn't know which end was up. In addition, during my sophomore year I was the victim of rape combined with assault and battery, which blew my mind. I was the thirtieth victim of a rape and abortion ring but only the fourth to prosecute. The other girls, under twenty-one years of age, would have had to get their parents to countersign charges, and they feared that if their parents were informed of the sad events, they would make them leave college. I went to court. It took about a year and a half to go through all the ten million postponements and red tape and everything else involved with going to court, and then he was found not guilty. About a month and half after my court case, the thirty-second victim had the guts to go to court, and the rapist was convicted for the first time.

The time when I was prosecuting the rape was horrible. The emotional turmoil and just trying to keep up with very, very rigorous courses was just too much for me. So I found it a relief not to have to worry any more about my performance.

The following summer I went to Europe with three girl friends, and I still wasn't really back together; I wasn't my normal self. I had lots of self-doubt; I was very defensive and critical and sharp in the way I spoke. I wasn't at all flirtatious or youthful like I had been prior to the whole experience, and I'm sure I was terrible company for my poor friends.

Taking preteaching courses at Michigan was like falling off a log. If you have half a brain, they are downright boring. I did it the least painful way I could think of. I thought it would be a terrible bore to do it in the United States, so I asked the School of Education if I could take the education courses in Europe. After coming back from Europe, one of my friends and I applied to the University of Keele in England. Michigan said yes, they would accept all our credits, even our student teaching if we did it there. So we went and took all our education courses and student teaching in England.

I think it was probably then, in that removed environment, that I got myself all together again and felt strong about myself. I had limited funds; I was there with few friends; and I was successful. I enjoyed it. I enjoyed teaching the kids, and I enjoyed being the ''American school teacher''—the first one they'd ever had. I enjoyed living in England and traveling. Every weekend I hitchhiked all over the place and just had a wonderful time. The success despite odds and the fresh start made me happy and confident again.

While I was in England, I decided to reestablish my relationship with Jim, my high-school boyfriend. He is now my husband. We were very serious in high school, and during the first year at college, we wrote every night and saved up our quarters and called every single weekend. We even wrote on toilet paper if we ran out of other paper. We sent presents to each other back and forth in the mail. We both dated. I dated a lot more than he did; I went out every weekend. But I still came home and wrote a letter to Jim. It was a week after we had broken up that I had been raped.

Well, during the time I was in England, I started to write Jim once every two weeks. We were still very good friends. In the back of my mind I was thinking that some day I wanted to get married. I was thinking very much that I wanted to have something secure again, and I was hoping I would marry him. Maybe this was a very immature thought and founded on wrong feelings at the time, but prior to all of the rape mess, my times with Jim had been wonderful, and I think what I wanted to do was to go back to that time when I was secure and happy and safe.

Cultural pressures to marry were coming from everywhere. I was living in a sorority house, and many of the girls were in nursing programs and teaching programs and general female-type niches. They had boyfriends and were getting engaged. There were ceremonies around dinner time—candlelight and singing and serenades, pinnings and lavalierings and engagements.

My mother and father had always wanted me to marry Jim, but they wanted me to finish my education first. When I came to them in August, prior to beginning my senior year, and said I wanted to get married at Christmas in the middle of my senior year, they nearly flipped: "Not only are you not going to be a doctor—you're giving that up—*now* you're not even going to graduate from college! You're going to get married!" I said, "Now, wait a minute, wait a minute. I didn't say I wasn't going to graduate; we're going to finish. That's the hitch. If we get married we're going to need help with the tuition until we finish." I told them that if they would approve of our getting married now and if they would support us partially, for tuition only afterwards, then we would try very hard to get jobs and work double and triple shifts to pay living expenses and make it work out. We just wanted to get married. At that time, we had been going together off and on—very off and on—for about four-and-a-half years, and we just decided that there wasn't any point in waiting any longer. We were married during the Christmas of my senior year.

My husband was in a five-year program at Michigan. Because we graduated from high school together, that meant I was done a year before he was, so I had to do something to earn money. I was a night waitress at the Big Boy and smelled like a hot dog for one solid year. On the weekends, Jim and I were the apartment managers for our apartment complex. We painted the insides of the apartments; I was the enamel, and he was the latex. That paid $100 for fifty hours a weekend. During the weekdays, after classes, I reupholstered the furniture in the apartments.

I couldn't get a full-time job teaching at first because they had been spoken for before, and I didn't know how much of the next year I was going to be there at that time. I also had in the back of my mind that maybe I would try this medical school thing after all. So I put my name on a substitute list. The first couple of weeks it was very lean, but then I got called practically every day. I taught in secondary school, mostly math, science, and physical education. Then, I was well enough known in one school that when the physics teacher became seriously ill I ended up with his job for the rest of the year. I liked teaching physics very much; I loved it.

But medicine came back to haunt me. It seemed that all day long people would come up to me and say, "Well, I wasn't here yesterday because I had the flu." I'd say, "Oh, really? What was the matter with you?"—I'd go through all the details of what was wrong with them. They'd come up to me and ask me what was wrong with their regular teacher, and I explained what MS was. I found that I still was fascinated with medicine, and as much as I liked teaching, especially teaching physics, I was a little disgusted with having to fill out a pink slip every time a student had to go to the bathroom. I was only four years older than they were, too, and I looked at least as young as they or younger at the time. If they fell asleep listening to me, I didn't get terribly upset about it—and I figured that I just didn't fit in because the other teachers in the school got upset about things. They accepted their enforcer role—to go in and bust a bunch of kids who were smoking pot in the john; that wasn't my bag. So I just didn't feel like I fit in.

In the middle of that year, I finally decided to apply to medical school. I said, "Jim, I'm thinking of applying, but I don't know if I can make it." He said, "You're never going to know unless you try." So I tried. I don't think either of us had any idea what it was going to mean. He just knew that it was my dream and that I wanted to take a shot at it.

From day one he had known that I wanted to go into medicine. When I moved into the new high school at age fifteen—my last name was Carleton, his was Benes—I sat behind him in the A through D homeroom, and I was introduced the first day by the teacher as "Miss Carleton, who has transferred from Euclid, Ohio, had straight 'A's' there, and is going to be a doctor."

Medical School

I applied to six schools, one in each of the six biggest cities that might hire engineers. We were trying very hard to be in the same city, Jim with a job and me in medical school. So I went through the brand-new AMCAS [American Medical College Application Service] system, which cost $250; that's all we had at the time. It paid for six applications—that was the basic package; you had to pay extra for any beyond that.

I applied to Woman's Medical College in Philadelphia. I figured that if you wanted to be a lady doctor, it would be logical to go to the lady doctor's school. Interestingly, I didn't know that there were other medical schools in Philadelphia. I had no idea. I didn't know a thing about Philadelphia. In fact, I didn't even know where the city was located. When I opened up the map the day we drove there and saw that it touched New Jersey, I nearly croaked.

I did get to the interview stage at other schools. One was a real classic. There were nine men sitting at a table with me, and they grilled me the entire time about what form of contraception I was using. Would I promise not to get pregnant while I was in medical school? How could I possibly hope to be both a doctor and a mother?—because I told them straight out I intended to have kids some day— and on and on. The whole interview was based on my personal aspirations and my personal plans; they never once asked me a professional question. That was in complete contrast to my male friend who was being interviewed the same day—the person after me. We compared notes afterward. They spent the entire time asking him: Had he ever worked in a hospital? What were his favorite subjects? Would he consider doing research? If he did research, what areas would it be in? What did he want to specialize in? I was accepted at that school, much to my surprise, after that maddening interview.

At Woman's Medical, the interview was totally different. Jim got one job offer, and that was here in Philadelphia. They gave him four days to respond, and I hadn't heard anything from the school yet. So I called long distance from the school in which I was teaching, and I asked the Admissions Office if they had received my records yet, and if I was already in the discard pile. I just wanted to know that; if I were out of the running, then I would say to Jim, "There's no chance for me in Philadelphia," and that would help us make the four-day decision. If I had a chance, then we'd hang in and hope it would work out. "Well," the woman in the Admissions Office said, "Just a minute; I'll go see." She looked on the pile, and they hadn't even gotten to my application yet. So I was nowhere; I was in limbo. Then, she said, "just a minute, I'll have the Dean speak with you"—which is unbelievable.

The Dean said, "I'll tell you what; I'll take your portfolio home with me over the weekend"—this was a Friday—"and I'll call you back on Monday if we think you have a chance." I said. "Okay, that's fantastic." She called back Monday morning and said, "Fly down here this afternoon; you're going to be interviewed tomorrow morning."

So I went. I stayed overnight in the nurses' dorm. I met the current freshman medical students who were unmarried and also living in the nurses' dorm, and they showed me around the next morning. They were very nice, and I was *so* excited. It was the first time I saw a woman medical student. I was just thrilled, seeing the cadavers and everything. I loved it. It was what I wanted.

I went back after the interview to Ann Arbor to teach physics, and on Wednesday the Woman's Medical Admissions Committee worked me into their agenda, and on Thursday morning they called me and said, "You're in." Then, also on Thursday morning, Jim called Westinghouse and said, "I'll accept," because that was his fourth and final day to respond. Two weeks later we moved to Philadelphia. As a couple, we were amazingly lucky that things evolved so smoothly and so quickly.

The summer before medical school I held three jobs to earn money for the tuition: lifeguard at the YMHA, bookkeeper for an insurance man, and night interviewer for an MCPER drug and alcohol study.

There were sixty women and six men in my class, and most of us were older. It wasn't a class of people that had gone straight through college and then right into medical school. I'd say that over half of the class had done something else. So we were all very excited to compare notes about what we had been and what we had done. Quite a few of my classmates were married; many had kids, which was a surprise to me; I couldn't believe people who had children were going to go to medical school. I felt that it was a very supportive environment. The Faculty was very supportive.

I was surprised to find out that in Philadelphia Woman's Medical felt that it was judged inferior to the other four medical schools. In the Midwest, the school had an excellent reputation. Any woman who had ever gone back to the Midwest from there was very highly thought of, and they said that they had excellent clinical training—even the physicians said that. It was only the people in Philadelphia that seemed to have some sort of snob thing, and that generated an antifeminist paranoia. It took a long time, maybe half a year, before that idea was communicated to us as a class; we all felt it, and we all believed, after the feeling had been projected onto us. The idea was that we were "just a bunch of women."

I feel negative feedback just because I am a woman; and the fact that I came from Woman's Medical College makes it twice as bad. I think if I were a man from Woman's Medical College or from the Medical College of Pennsylvania,* things might be slightly different.

But when I started my internship, I realized that I came from a really good school. I had had doubts until that time, but then I was with graduates from Penn and Temple and Jefferson, and I knew more about reading an EKG than they did; I knew more about treating cardiac arrest than they did. I knew clinically what to do. Now, they were a little bit better at quoting articles; they could stand in the middle of a hallway and quote articles until they were blue in the face. But the first half of the year, they were not as good at knowing what to do for the patients.

The supportive atmosphere extended to the students. We helped each other. For example, one of my classmates was a Ph.D. in biochemistry. None of us knew what was going on in biochemistry, so she voluntarily gave night seminars to help us; if we felt bad about what our knowledge was, she taught us. A Ph.D. in anatomy helped people bone up on anatomy. We always gave each other notes, and we helped each other catch up. There was a lot of sharing of information; there was not much competition.

At first I was afraid I might flunk out of medical school. I wanted to study hard and to get a lot of work under my belt before I got involved in activities, so I only volunteered to be a member of committees. But then I found out that in much the

---

*The College began admitting men in 1969 just prior to the time Dr. Benes started and changed its name shortly thereafter to Medical College of Pennsylvania.

same way as it had been for me in high school, I was not having as hard a time as I imagined I might. I could get by with a little less studying and still make good enough grades—I didn't have to worry about anything. And I enjoyed being active like I had been before. I was President of my junior and senior classes and an editor of the yearbook.

I became much more aware of feminism in medical school. A few of my classmates were very, very avid feminists—real active, so active that they turned the guys and many of the women in the class off. The school started organizing conferences about different kinds of role models, different ways of living your life. It was a good time.

Internship and Residency

I interned at Lankenau Hospital in Philadelphia from 1975 to 1976. It was a straight internal medicine internship. I loved the independence and increased responsibility. I was also attracted to research—clinical research, not test tube research.

It was a really great year. But I was tired because of the sleepless nights, and I had to spend a lot of time away from my family. Two out of three weeks I had one day off, which is not very much. That was the worst part of internship.

I had two favorite experiences. One was my two months in the intensive care unit. I knew those patients were really ill people, and it was a pleasure to have to work hard for them because you knew you were doing something. There was no question in your mind that you were doing good, and I was never so busy in my life. I loved every minute of it.

The other experience was with dying patients. It was the first time I really had to cope with death—not just catastrophic death, which you could easily live through because it is quick and everybody is up, and you're trying to do everything you can and when it is over, it's over, boom. But it was the cancer patients. That was the real pits; that was hard to deal with.

They tried to prepare us in medical school, but it's never the same as when it is your patient only, not somebody's private patient, it's *your* patient. And pronouncing people dead—gee, I never knew. The first time they made me come and pronounce somebody dead, I was so afraid I'd be wrong. I mean, the patient's heart wasn't beating, and he wasn't breathing, but I kept looking at him and he looked all right. I kept thinking, "I hope I'm not wrong." It's a crazy thing. You just doubt yourself. Then, you have to call the family and tell them, and ugh, that was just terrible. Four o'clock in the morning: "Sorry, I have some bad news for you. . . ."

Well, in September of my senior year, I took a rotation in ENT and ophthalmology. That's the deadline for applying for the surgical subspecialty residencies because they're selected by Christmas of your senior year for a year and a half hence. Anyway, I was fully expecting to go into internal medicine; I had written away to fifteen internal medicine programs.

The problem was that my husband was an engineer and was employed in Philadelphia and was in the type of job that one could not find easily in some other city. He was so reluctant to change and to give up a sure thing and to give up a familiar environment while I was going to go through these years of hell— leaving him and the baby. By the way, I had a baby by then. He just wanted to have all the support he could have during the time I was going through my residency, and that included not having to change jobs, being in an area where we had friends, and being in a setting that was familiar to him. So we felt that we should both stay in Pennsylvania, in Philadelphia.

So if I was going to stay in Philadelphia, where would I get my training? I felt the best internal medicine program in the city was at Penn. I knew I wouldn't be accepted at Penn coming from MCP, so I didn't apply there. The person who was number one in our class applied to Penn and was rejected. I figured that if she couldn't make it, I would be rejected for sure. They were only considering students from other Ivy League schools. So that was a write-off.

Then, I was down into secondary programs in the city. I could either go through a community teaching hospital like Lankenau or go through MCP all the way. But I felt I would be too inbred, and I didn't want that; I wanted to go out; I wanted to change; I felt I would be a stronger physician having trained in another environment. Or, I could switch fields.

During the ENT and ophthalmology rotation, I spent four days at Wills Eye Hospital. It looked interesting, and so I thought, "Hmmmm, this would be a long shot. This Wills place is fantastic; it's world famous, and they have a good program here. The residents are really enthusiastic; there couldn't possibly be a better training institution for this than here." So I figured that maybe it would be a long shot, and I'd give it a try because it would combine well with family life. My husband said, "Yes, do it, do it, do it. Internal medicine is going to be impossible." So I did it as a long shot, fully expecting that it wasn't going to pan out. I still had the other fifteen applications in internal medicine active.

But two weeks after I turned my application in, Wills accepted me. They gave me two weeks to answer, and I spent two solid weeks crying because I didn't know what the heck to do. I didn't have the foggiest notion. I had this dream inside of me—at this time my dream had turned into being in internal medicine and academic medicine. All that was a big ivory tower dream, and I was going to have to give that up and go into a total unknown field that appealed to my husband because I wouldn't have as many emergencies. I wouldn't have a person lying dying in an intensive care unit who I would feel guilty about leaving, and I could have scheduleable hours and not feel guilty, yet it would be both medical and surgical, and I could theoretically be professionally rewarded in it. But ophthalmology was an unknown. After four days of practical experience, I didn't know whether I would love it as much as internal medicine.

I decided to do it. I still have reservations, but I'm warming up to it. I like the diagnosis, and I like and am good at the surgery. But it's the medical part that I really love. I just cannot stand the tediousness of refractions.

I was accepted positively at Lankenau. It was a very pro-woman place. On the other hand, ophthalmology is a very male-oriented subspecialty. There is no way there could be a better place educationally than Wills. It's the social milieu, or whatever you want to call it, that drives me bananas. I was asked in the interviewing procedure whether I was planning to have any children during my residency there. No, I wasn't asked; they said, "Of course, you wouldn't have any children while you're a resident here." This was after they had spent fifteen minutes asking me about how I had a child in my senior year of medical school—where was she going every day? Did I feel satisfied that that was good enough care for her? Would that care continue for the years I was at Wills? Then, they said to me, "Of course, you would never have a child while you are here." Well, I didn't answer; I just smiled. I didn't want to say yes, I didn't want to say no; I certainly didn't want to commit myself.

There had been four women residents at Wills before me. My year there were two in one class. The whole institution went into shock! Two women in one class was just unheard of. The other woman was a graduate of Harvard Medical School and Radcliffe. Her record was flawless. She was also an intern in internal medicine at Penn. But they heard that she was engaged. So when she was interviewed, they asked her to leave the room for a couple of minutes and invited her fiancé in, in his dungarees—cut-offs—and asked him what they were planning on doing about having children and how he felt about delaying having children until 1980, when she would be finished with her residency. He, who is a physician also, said, "Whatever Elizabeth decides to do is fine with me," and that's how he left it. So we were both given the message loud and clear that they didn't approve of our having children while we were at Wills. And we were both pregnant within two months of each other the first year!

That is where the problems began. They didn't have a maternity policy for residents. They had one for nurses, so I went to personnel and I said, "Well, could we have the same thing nurses have?"—which is two weeks off. They said "No." So it turned out that the two of us had to use two years' worth of vacations for our four weeks off—last year's vacation and this year's vacation. I was angry. The male residents were all having kids, too, that year, but not one of them was going through the kind of harassment that we were facing.

Family Life

Jim adjusted very well. He seemed interested in what I was doing. I've always been interested in what he has done, and I know his work friends very well; they're probably our closest friends in the city. Jim came and saw my cadaver. When our families came to visit for Thanksgiving, I took everybody to the college and showed them what I was doing and gave them a tour of the hospital. The whole family was very much involved.

My daughter was planned. She was born during my senior year, which is the easiest year in many ways because it is mostly electives. She started going to a day-care center at nine weeks, but at least I was home at night.

We both felt ambivalent about day care. In our hearts we felt that probably the right thing was for the mother to raise the child full time. Jim felt the most sorry about it. He felt very sad when he saw her go off to ''school'' at that age. But the program we chose was really super, and now both of us are very happy, and we like it very much. The new baby is there as well.

I was real depressed after I had Jennifer, come to think of it. I went through the postpartum blues. I was ready to crawl the walls. I felt like I wasn't an anything anymore, because I hadn't gone back to school. Here I had just spent three years developing a new self-image as a doctor and as a functioning adult in the world, talking to other adults all day long, and I was being cooped up inside four walls with a screaming kid. She was a colicky baby and cried eighteen hours a day. She had rashes all the time—it was summer, and we didn't have air conditioning. Everything was fine once I got back to work.

Sometimes, my daughter says, ''Mommy, mommy, please stay home.'' I tell her I can't and then feel guilty. She's gone through phases. There are times when she's more clinging than others. Right at the moment, she's in one of her clingings, and she just can't part from me easily. She'll say, ''I want a hug and a kiss,'' and I'll start to walk away; ''I want another hug and a kiss,'' and she'll start to get hysterical; ''I want another hug and kiss.'' You go back and forth about six times. She just has a hard time parting right now.

We divide the household chores, so I have never felt unduly burdened. Even before the children and before medical school, it was that way. Jim likes to cook, and I like to cook. Neither of us likes to do dishes, but we've always split it up; and we've always both done the cleaning, and we've both washed floors and all that.

Fellowship and Africa

I did a neuro-ophthalmology fellowship jointly at Wills Eye Hospital and the University of Pennsylvania. That was a fascinating year and really helped me grow academically. In addition to learning, my responsibilities included teaching residents in ophthalmology, neurology, and neurosurgery, organizing teaching conferences, writing papers, writing two chapters for one book and a large chapter for another book, and lecturing. It was great fun to be dealing with sick patients who really needed help again.

The pinnacle, so far, was reached when I went with my four-year-old daughter to Africa for two months to teach nurses, lecture to residents and physicians, build latrines, educate paramedical ''barefoot doctors,'' perform surgery, and ''screen the masses'' in several settings: at Kenyatta University for their first class of ophthalmology residents, at Nyeri Provincial Hospital and the outlying underdeveloped areas with the International Eye Foundation, and at a Presbyterian mission hospital with one-third of the patients in the maternity ward! What a fabulous experience! It was a real privilege to wake up every morning excited about the day to come, invigorated at the thought of doing really significant medical work all day long (no paperwork, finances, or politics), and feeling high because you are genuinely needed.

This experience taught both of us many things about culture, nature, and life. Jenny went to a Christian school and met children from Africa and all around the world (missionary children). She even learned to speak and play in Swahili. We enjoyed meeting the dedicated "lifers" from America, Canada, and Europe in mission work; and I personally felt fulfilled in having touched with the "roots" of my ancestors who served in foreign countries. We would love to go again soon.

I would like to go into academic medicine eventually. It would have to be somewhere near Philadelphia as long as Jim remains at Westinghouse. I would like to stay affiliated with Wills at least part-time. The field is saturated and very competitive in Philadelphia, and there are no full-time paid teaching positions in ophthalmology right now. You have to pay your own way by having a large practice, and the teaching is essentially voluntary.

On Lifestyle

I have always admired Dr. Bartuska [Doris Bartuska, M.D., Chief of the Division of Endocrinology and Metabolism at the Medical College of Pennsylvania]. I think she's really an amazing person. She is able to combine marriage and career very successfully, in my opinion. She's academically oriented, and she does a little research on the side, and she seems to have everything combined the way I'd like to have it all combined in the end—only she's doing it in internal medicine.

One of my pursuits outside medicine has fallen by the wayside since the baby was born; Jim and I used to sing together in a chorale group. We do have a big garden. We can and freeze the vegetables. I also like needlepoint, quilting for people, and I play the piano and teach piano.

On Women in Medicine

I think that women address themselves to what I consider to be the true medical issues and less to economic considerations. In medical school, the men were more interested in financial remuneration and the fact that they were going to have a certain kind of life-style, whereas the women were doing what interested them.

I believe women approach certain therapeutic questions differently from men, particularly in areas that relate to the health of women. I'll give an example. Today, a four-week-old baby came into the emergency room with conjunctivitis.

Of course, the mother was afraid that the child would go blind because he had an eye infection. The child has had an eye infection for three and a half of his four weeks of life. Well, we're taught that at a half week of age, it's most likely to be a chlamydial organism, and if it's chlamydia, you're supposed to treat it with a special medicine: topical medicines for the child and systemic for the mother, who is the carrier.

Well, one of the male physicians in the emergency room decided that to go with the statistics, he should treat both the mother and the child with this certain medication for this particular likely organism and tell the mother to stop breast-feeding. I said, "Well, do you know for sure it's chlamydia?" He said, "No, but statistically it is, and it never hurt anybody to stop breast-feeding." I said, "Well, not physically, maybe." He said, "Well, what do you mean? My wife bottle-fed our babies, and everything was just fine. She wasn't able to breast-feed because she had a medical condition. I don't think there is anything that says that breast-feeding is better than bottle-feeding. If she has to take this medicine, she should just give up breast-feeding, and that's the end of it." I said, "Well, I don't look at it that way."

Personally, I wouldn't have been so flippant about telling the woman she'd have to stop breast-feeding because I breast-fed and I know that it was very important for both my children and for me. I felt I was making an important contribution, not only physically but in every other way, to that whole endeavor. Without any proof of the organism and just going by the numbers, it seemed kind of crazy to make somebody go through a hardship unnecessarily, and the mother did not want to stop.

But in general, I do not think women physicians are going to change the practice of medicine that much. I think society will change it. The women at the Medical College of Pennsylvania have been practicing medicine for a long time, and I don't see it as a considerably different brand of medicine from what I have seen in male-dominated institutions. Specifically, I do not think that more women in medicine will subvert it or allow it to be "overrun" by socialism, a sentiment I have heard expressed by many of my affluent male colleagues.

I believe the situation for women in medicine is improving, but I also think that it's good to have a hard shell for some of the punches you're going to get thrown and not be so vulnerable and so self-doubting that you'd let them throw you too far back—because women are very vulnerable, I think, to criticism of all kinds.

Philadelphia, Pennsylvania
March 10, 1978

9

Vanessa Gamble

TOMORROW'S PHYSICIAN, TOMORROW'S POLICY-MAKER

"I would describe myself as ambitious, proud, but most of all, as a survivor," Vanessa Gamble has written. Raised by her mother and grandmother in the black ghetto of West Philadelphia, she gained admission to an academically oriented public high school and then attended Hampshire College in Amherst, Massachusetts as part of its first freshman class. Now, she is living in West Philadelphia once again—this time as an M.D./Ph.D. candidate at the University of Pennsylvania. She looks forward to a career of teaching and involvement in social policy planning as well as the practice of medicine.

Vanessa Gamble at 21 (1974), a few weeks before graduation from Hampshire College, Amherst, Massachusetts.

Childhood

I was born in West Philadelphia in 1953. My father was a machinist. He's from Philadelphia, too. Other than that, I can't tell you a lot about him. He only lives nine blocks from here. I rarely see him. My mother left him when I was six. I don't have very good memories of them living together. It was a difficult time for all involved.

But I think it wasn't just him, because it was almost par for the course. I thought everyone fought. Not until much later did I find out that not everyone did that. He did go to work and support his family financially at that time, but there was no real support. However, in all fairness, I must say that he is trying to make up for past mistakes.

After my mother left my father, she lived with other men. I put a distance between them and me. I don't think it was because I didn't think they were going to be stable. That was just my personality. In many ways there's a distance between me and my family, me and my neighborhood. It's amazing how people who meet me now, when I tell them where I'm from, don't believe me. They say, "You?" My father and some of the other men in my mother's life made me realize why I had to be independent and be able to support myself and not have to really depend on a man to take care of me and my kids. So that's a negative reason, probably, that led to something very positive in my own life.

I was raised by my mother and my grandmother. My grandmother was born in Philadelphia in 1898. Most of my black friends' grandparents did not come here from the South until after World War I or World War II, so it's interesting that she was born here. Her father was a cop, supposedly, at the turn of the century here in Philadelphia. In 1928, he bought the house in which my grandmother lived. My grandmother was a minister of the Metropolitan Spiritual Churches in Christ, Incorporated. She had a storefront church and used to be a medium. People would come to the door, and we'd say, "Nanny, there's a lady here to see you." She'd do readings. That was something special—which, in many ways, I've just admitted recently. I used to feel ashamed that we weren't AME or Baptists or something like that. She was married, but her marriage broke up really early. The first time my mother met her father, she was nineteen or twenty. She didn't know what to call him, so she called him Mr. Northington.

Right after my mother left my father, we lived with my grandmother for about a year and a half. After that, we went to my grandmother's every weekend. When we didn't have food, Nanny would send us food, or we'd go down there to see Nanny, and we'd stay down there. In many ways I was much closer with my grandmother than my mother. You could go see Nanny and just hug her. I didn't do that a lot with my mother, even though we were very close. My grandmother was just really supportive. A few months ago, I was talking to a friend of my grandmother's, and she said, "When you were a little girl playing in the street, your grandmother would say, 'My baby's going to be a doctor when she grows up.' I didn't believe her, of course. But your grandmother certainly did believe that that was going to happen.''

My mother finished high school, and for the rest of her life, she did odd jobs. She worked as a presser in a cleaner's for a while, and she worked for a caterer for a while. My mother was strict. You had to be well-behaved, no back talk. But the thing about it was, there were these women friends of my mother's who some-times stayed with us at different periods in our life—we'd call them ''aunt,'' even though they weren't relatives—and their kids would stay with us. My mother was the one who was most strict with them, but they all loved her for that. My mother would say things like, ''You may not be smart in school, but you can behave yourself.'' ''You might not have a lot of clothes, but they're going to be clean.'' I knew lots of women in the neighborhood who got involved with the early pregnancy type of pattern, but my mother said, ''You'd better not bring any babies in this house.'' She informed us very early that she wasn't taking care of any kids. As I went further and further in my education, there were parts of my life which my mother could not really relate to or be very supportive of. But there were other parts she was very, very supportive of. I was her child.

My mom died in December. It was really very hard for me to deal with, because I was in the medical profession; I knew there wasn't any hope then. And for her not to be there, for someone who always wanted me to be a doctor, who knew I was going to be a doctor. . . . Cicely Tyson recently said, ''The greatest gift of any black woman is having been born of another.'' I really believe that. Just not having her here is a very, very big void in my life.

My mother and my grandmother were both very strong women. I think my grandmother's religion helped her cope with the realities of ghetto life. With my mother, it was more, ''My kids are going to make it.'' My mother's vivacious-ness and outgoingness was a way she coped with it. She had lots and lots of friends. She also had a lot of common sense. She was very street-wise, and she knew how to use that. After I graduated from sixth grade, for example, I was supposed to be going to a predominantly black junior high school. My mother didn't want me to go there because she knew that it wasn't a great school educationally. There was this white junior high school which was out of our district, and I'd have to get special permission to go. So she went to the principal and said, ''Could Vanessa go?'' He said, ''I'm really sorry.'' My mother knew it was the height of the civil rights movement, so she said, ''That's okay. My lawyer will see about it.'' My mother did not have a lawyer! But the next day the letter came saying that I could go to the predominantly white school. When I look around and see a lot of the kids I grew up with, see what they're doing—for a mother to have two kids go to college from her background says a lot. Most of her friends don't have kids in college.

I have a sister who is three years younger than I am. She has an internship with one of the television stations here in the city. I haven't really talked to her for three months. We're quite different. It was very important for my sister to have boyfriends coming in; it wasn't really important for me. She'd say, "How can you go without having a steady man in your life? I'm going to try it"—and the next thing you know, she has a new boyfriend. After she drops one man, she has to have another one.

I think we were close for awhile. In many ways she was my best friend while we were growing up. We moved around a lot, so there was always the two of us. I also had to take care of my sister and make sure she got to school, which, at times, I used to resent. Everyone said, "Take care of Karen. Make sure Karen's okay." No one asked me who's going to take care of *me*. That's the way a lot of things in my childhood were. I had lots of responsibilities.

I didn't think about religion very much as a child. We went to church on Sundays. You didn't question it; you went to church on Sunday, and sometimes you stayed all day. It was the thing you had to do. After I got older, I got tired of going to church on Sundays, and I stopped going.

I think we moved six or seven times by the time I was seventeen. And since after elementary school, I went to school outside the neighborhood, it was really hard to get friendships within the neighborhood. I kept to myself a lot. I wasn't lonely, but I was very alone, and that made me feel very different. In many ways, books were my friends. I did a lot of reading. When I was in early junior high school or late elementary school, I went through the biographies of first woman so-and-so—Elizabeth Blackwell; Emily Dunning Barringer, first woman ambulance doctor; that type of thing.

I've always wanted to be a doctor, ever since I can remember. I had a family physician who, when I told him I wanted to be a doctor, said, "You're going to be a doctor. Don't let anyone tell you you're going to be a nurse." I can't understand how my idea that I wanted to be a physician came to be. I never saw a black woman physician until I went to high school. But it never dissuaded me that I never saw a black woman physician. It was like, "So I don't see any, that doesn't mean I'm not going to be one." It was the time of Ben Casey and Dr. Kildare, so all my mother's friends were going around saying, "Vanessa's going to be a neurosurgeon like Ben Casey when she grows up." When Christmas came around, I got toy microscopes and chemistry sets. So it was encouraged.

Part of what appealed to me about the idea of being a doctor was caring for people. But I think that if you had to pick something in this society which was the pinnacle of success, you pick being a physician. I'm sure that had something to do with it, too. I was going to go to the top, and no one was going to tell me that I wasn't going to go to the top.

My feeling that I was special was fostered by teachers; it was fostered by my mother and my grandmother. People would say, "You are bright, and you should do something with it." But there was luck involved, too. One of the most painful memories of my childhood is when I was in the sixth grade. A boy named

Bruce and I used to try and compete for getting "A's" and being the smartest person in class—I think he probably was brighter than I was in certain areas—and he's a junkie now. I knew how bright he was, and I knew that he had something. And when I saw him on the corner, when I was in high school . . . just seeing him was very, very painful because it made me realize how lucky I was. Being bright just wasn't enough.

One negative thing about growing up, which a lot of people have a hard time believing, is that I had a speech problem when I was a kid. No one could understand me but my mother. My mother said that one time they were going to send me to a school for mentally retarded kids because of my speech problem. I don't know how or when it corrected itself, but in second grade, the speech teacher came in and asked me to repeat some things, and I repeated them, and she said, "Okay, fine." After that I was always the leader type. When I was in fourth grade, I was the first secretary of the student council at the elementary school and that type thing.

One of my favorite teachers was my third grade teacher. Mrs. James was the type person who was very, very strict. *Very* strict. One day I think I'm going to go see her. She would take me to plays; I remember going down to Penn to see a play with her. She expected a lot. She knew I had a big mouth and would talk back, but she was very strict, and I really liked her a lot. I also remember a teacher I hated and detested—Mrs. Hare. She was strict, too, but she was just so bad. She was the type person that if I went back to see her, I'd say, "Look, I made it despite you."

The junior high I attended was a predominantly Jewish school. There were some blacks there, but most of the blacks weren't in my classes. I was put in the accelerated classes. I didn't have to take reading development; they said, "You can take Spanish." On Jewish holidays, I'd be the only one in some of my classes. I'd come, and the teacher would say, "Look, go to the lunchroom, do something." One Jewish holiday, my mother said, "Okay, Vanessa, get up." "I'm not going to school today. It's a Jewish holiday." She said, "Get out of bed! Your name's Gamble, not Gambleberg." So I explained to her. I can't remember whether she let me stay home, but she probably didn't.

Then, there was the whole thing about being different. I remember my mother saying, "Look, you're not white, you can't do these types of things." Before that, I didn't have much awareness of the difference. There were gradations among black folks that the lighter you are, the better you are. I know that family members made distinctions between my sister and myself because my sister's darker than I am. But that was within the black community. When I went to junior high school and they put me in all advanced classes, they'd say, "Oh, you're different." I remember going to a math class where I got a 39 on an exam. The only other person who failed the exam was the other black kid in class, and he and I had gone to the same elementary school. At first, I felt that he and I were inferior, that we couldn't deal with the math. Then I said, "Well, maybe it's the school we came from. They didn't teach us that math in my elementary school.'' But for a long time I thought it was me.

High school was a totally different experience. I went to Philadelphia High School for Girls, which was a magnet school. I used to call it public-private school. People from all over the city came to the school, so I got to meet different people. It was a trek up there. It took me at least an hour every day to get to school. I got involved in student government. I took five majors all through high school, and I was always in the accelerated or the advanced placement classes.

Even then, there weren't a lot of black kids who were visible in my classes. This was from 1966 to 1970, the era of black power and hippies coming out. The black kids wore black arm bands one time, and the teachers tried to make us take them off. When Martin Luther King was killed, I went to school the next day and kept crying, kept crying that day. I was active in the antiwar movement and some black student union things but not very, very active. I was busy doing my work, I still had to cook for my family, I had responsibilities because I was class president and all this business. In many ways, being in school was a haven for me.

I really liked my Latin teacher because she was just such a warm, open woman. We had fun in her class. I stayed with Latin for four years because of her. She wanted us to read *I, Claudius,* and when I saw it on television, I said, ''Miss Golden wanted us to read *this?* I should have listened to her!'' Then, I was close with the woman who was the class sponsor. She was my chemistry teacher, and she had a lot of insight into me. She said things like, ''You only got a 'B' in this course last semester because you wanted that. If you really wanted an 'A,' you would have gotten an 'A.' But you were so involved with so many other things that you just didn't apply yourself.''

If I had to say who was my best friend in high school, I wouldn't name Evelyn, but she's been the most stable. She grew up in North Philadelphia. We learned to like the same things at the same time. We'd go to the movies together, we'd go to plays together, we'd buy records together. Evelyn is always there. Evelyn's my friend who, when I went to college, she came to visit.

The woman who was my closest friend in high school was someone who, when we first met, we didn't like each other. Marolyn lived in this big house up in Chestnut Hill, and I was from West Philadelphia, so she saw me as a militant from West Philadelphia, and I saw her as a boojy black from Chestnut Hill. But we really got to be very, very close and understand each other, and we did until she went to Yale. Things changed once she went to Yale and I went to Hampshire. But she was probably my closest friend.

College

I had a very, very good college guidance counselor. She would get girls from Girls' High into college in August, and school would start in September. She'd call up, "This is Freda Ehrenreich calling," and everyone would know who she was. When I was applying to college, she said, "What kind of school do you want?" There was a big push for me to go to Yale and to Princeton and places like that, and I didn't want to go. I wanted to go to a nontraditional college. Girls' High was traditional enough for me. I wanted to go to a coed situation which was more coed than male-dominated. I didn't want to be another minority within a minority. And I wanted to be out of Philadelphia. Those were the things that I told her. She said, "Well, there's this new school that's going to start in September of next year"—this was my junior year—"maybe you'll consider that." I went through the summer, didn't think about colleges at all. Then, I said, "What's the name of that school again?" She said, "Hampshire College." I got some literature from Hampshire and fell in love with it. Here was a school that was starting up. I could be in its first class. I thought it would be kind of neat being a pioneer, so I applied early decision and got in.

But I almost didn't go to Hamphire. I almost didn't even go to school. What happened is that in April of my senior year my mother had a nervous breakdown. She had been living with this guy for a number of years, and they broke up. That probably was the precipitating factor. I was supposed to tell Hampshire I was coming May 1. I completely had forgotten because I was concerned about my mother. They called my college guidance counselor, "What's the story? Is she coming?" I said, "Yes, I'm coming. I'll be there." But that was the time when I realized how in many ways I was holding the family together, that my mother really was very dependent on me. What would happen with my going away? I'd go to school and cry and say, "My mother is very sick, and I don't know what to do." Then Mrs. Yager, the class sponsor, told me, "Look, you have got to go to school. You've got to get away, you have to learn to be selfish. Sure, you care about your mother, but you have to be concerned about you." Then, three weeks before I was supposed to go to Hampshire, my mother tried to kill herself. They took my mother to the hospital, and I was in the house by myself. It was one of the most harrowing experiences.

I started Hampshire in September 1970. I had never been further north than New York. When I came to this school, some people didn't have doorknobs, our mattresses were on the floor, there weren't any curtains. There were 268 of us. I wouldn't let my mother leave until I saw another black person there. My sister cried all the way home because it was the first time I was going to be away from home.

But I had a good time at Hampshire. The academic structure is different. They don't have a freshman through senior sequence; they have a divisional sequence. In Division One, you have to take an exam in four schools—natural science, social science, humanities and arts, and language and communications. The exams aren't your run-of-the-mill, sit-down, fill-out-this-multiple-choice type test. You develop your own exams. If you're an artist you might show some of your art work; if you're a scientist you might do an experiment; or you might just want to do an essay. People could get "A's" on papers at some other college in the Pioneer Valley and turn that paper in for a Hampshire exam and not pass because they said, "You didn't say what *you* thought. I want you to analyze this."

After Division One, there's Division Two, the division of school studies, where you do a concentration. Mine was in health and society, and it was in natural science and social science. At Hampshire interdisciplinary work was encouraged. That's how come they don't have departments—they wanted to have a lot of interdisciplinary work. My Division Three thesis, which was an independent project, was on a Tuskegee syphilis study. My premise was that it was the use of powerless people in medical research—that they were black, and *that* in that time made them very powerless. It could have been poor whites in Appalachia.

So you have to be able to handle a lot of independent work at Hampshire. When I first went there I partied a lot because I didn't have the self-discipline that was needed to get through Hampshire. I didn't have my mother there saying that I had to be home at a certain time. My grandmother had said, "You know, when you go to this college, you're going to have housemothers, and you can't stay out a lot." When I got there, we had coed dorms and all sorts of things! I had a great time.

After my first year and a half at Hampshire, I took a six month leave of absence because I knew that I wasn't working, that I could work much harder than this. At the time I was thinking about whether I should return to Hampshire or transfer. But after being away for six months—I was on the island of Saint Barthélemy for three months—I came back and worked hard.

In addition to my course work, I had all sorts of jobs while I was at Hampshire. I worked as a reference assistant, I worked in the dining hall, I worked in the personnel office for two weeks giving typing tests—and I could not type at the time!

I did no dating in high school—none at all. I really didn't have any male friends until I went to college. I was very fortunate in college. I became very close friends with a guy who was from North Philadelphia, Jarvis McCarther. We decided that when we got to Hampshire we were going to get through this place together, because both of us were basically survivors and we *had* to survive. We would sit up and talk to each other. We were very supportive of each other, and we still are. When I graduated from Hampshire, they had three student commencement speakers—he was one and I was another. When we finished our speeches, we just grabbed each other and skipped down the aisle. It was like, "We did it!" We had done it.

A big difference in our backgrounds was that I had gone to Girls' High, and Girls' High definitely does prepare you academically. He wasn't prepared academically at the high school he had gone to. He's in law school now, and he has had his problems. He basically failed his first year of law school, and he took a leave and went back. I said, ''I couldn't do that.'' Failure just doesn't come into my book. If I had failed, I would have been just devastated. He said to me a few weeks ago, ''You know, when I failed that first year, you were the hardest person for me to see because I thought I had failed you.'' But when I saw him, I just thought, ''Oh, what am I going to do to help him?'' It didn't diminish him at all in my eyes.

A number of people at Hampshire influenced me strongly. There's my friend Bernice Siegel, who was a secretary at Hampshire. After I left the West Indies, I came and stayed with her one night—and haven't left since. I'm her third kid now. She's a widow who left New York where she had lived with her husband because she didn't always want to be identified as Kenneth's widow. She brought her two teenaged kids to Amherst, and she didn't know a soul in Amherst. She's very motherly, and she still continues to be very motherly.

There was a woman chemist who was my advisor, Nancy Lowry, who wouldn't take any crap from me. I would come to her with all sorts of crap, trying to get over, and Nancy would just say, ''Come on, now.'' She's probably the only person who wouldn't be afraid to say, ''Come on, now''—because some people fell into this liberalism thing, and they let the Third World students get away with anything.

Then, there was Bob von der Lippe, a medical sociologist who really influenced my current ideas towards medicine. That's when I started seeing that there were other ways that you can do medicine and other ways you can do premedical studies—premedical studies didn't have to be just all the premed requirements but could also include courses in medical economics, comparative health systems. Bob, John Foster, who's a biochemist, and myself developed this program. We wrote a grant, and we did get funding for awhile to have a group of core courses in health and society.

Another important person at Hampshire was Miriam Slater, who is a historian. Miriam was someone who was very, very poor when she was a kid. She had gotten a Woodrow Wilson scholarship and had a Ph.D. from Princeton. Just to see Miriam there at Hampshire was enough for me to say, ''Well, I can make it.'' It was very important to have someone like Miriam there.

There were between eighteen and twenty blacks there the first year. The first week we got together in this big audience and said we weren't going to form a black student union at Hampshire because Hampshire was different and we didn't think we needed it. We weren't singing that song by the end of the semester because they were going to cut financial aid. A lot of us were on financial aid, and we thought that by cutting financial aid they would decrease the number of Third World students at Hampshire. Then, we realized that we needed to get together as a political force, and also socially, to be identified as a group, because we were assimilating a lot of the white, WASP, wealthy characteristics of Hampshire, and we realized that we couldn't do that—at least, some of us realized we couldn't do it. So we had to assert our blackness. One year I lived on the Third World women's floor, basically for support and also for identity reasons.

I got along with white and black people. I got along with everyone at Hampshire. Some of the black students felt I wasn't radical enough, though it was never said to my face. My friend Jarvis, the one currently in law school, said, "Don't worry about that. You know where you stand." But the thing is that I could get a lot of things done because the administration did not label me with certain movements. They realized that I was reasonable; I could rationally talk to them; I wasn't going to go sit in the president's office and curse him out.

One of the things I got into was screening for sickle cell anemia. Nineteen seventy to 1972 were the years of sickle cell anemia. It was like—this is *our* disease—we had to do some work in it. Well, I got swept along with the tide and got involved in screening for sickle cell anemia in Holyoke. Then, after awhile, I started thinking about some of the political and social ramifications of screening for genetic diseases, especially in the black population. I started seeing the whole political and social aspects of medicine.

Medical School

The time I hated Hampshire the most was when I was applying to medical school because I thought, "No one is going to take me." I didn't have any grades on my transcript, basically, except for the three courses I had taken off campus. I had these written evaluations. What other types of things did I have on my transcript? The first course listed on my transcript was a course called, "Going with the Dogs." There were these wild dogs in New Hampshire and Vermont and Massachusetts which had not been classified taxonomically, so we were going out there trying to track these dogs. It was a real animal behavior course. But I said, "If someone sees something like this, either they're going to toss it out, or they're just going to say, 'What is this?' and read on." I wanted to go to a program where I could continue to do some sociology, public-health type things, and medical ethics. But coming from a place like Hampshire, I'd go to any place that would accept me, so I applied to seventeen medical schools.

I wanted to come back to Philadelphia because my sister was going away to school and my mother was sick. My mother had a mastectomy in 1973, so I felt an obligation to come back to Philadelphia. I got into Penn Med, and I got into the sociology program here, too. I had to apply to the two separately and getting into one didn't guarantee my getting into the other program. I also received a Medical Scientist Training Program Fellowship from the National Institutes of Health. It's intended for persons pursuing M.D.-Ph.D. degrees and covers tuition in addition to a monthly stipend.

After I got into Penn, I decided that this was the place that I wanted to go, so why stay in the competition at other schools? Harvard was calling all over the place looking for me. They called at Hampshire, and I wasn't at Hampshire.

They called Philadelphia; my mother says, "She's in New York." They called where I was living in New York; they said, "She's at work"—I was at the Hastings Institute at the time. They called me at Hastings, and they said, "You know, you have an interview tomorrow." "No, I don't. I withdrew my application." So there was this joke around Hampshire that Vanessa wouldn't go to Harvard. I didn't want to go to Harvard. I really did not want to go to Harvard.

At Penn the first year, basic science is everything. I was freaking. I was sitting there saying, "What am I doing here? I don't know anything." I became friends with my pathology professor. He basically feels that his role the first year is to hold hands, to get people through. I went to see him about a month ago, and he said, "You know, the only difference between you and everyone else the first year, Vanessa, was that you were willing to tell people you were going crazy. Everyone else feels the same way, but they don't want to talk about it." The first semester was the worst. Second semester was not as bad as first semester. It didn't have anything to do with Hampshire. I think my science preparation was much better than a lot of my classmates'. It had to do with being a first-year medical student. It had to do with coming back to Philadelphia and getting involved with my family again after being away.

My first year, I did all medical school. Second year, I did two courses in sociology. Then, the woman I was going to be doing most of my work with, Reneé Fox, went on sabbatical last year, so I decided to do most of my clinical work. This year I'm totally a graduate student in sociology. I haven't missed the clinical work at all, and I think that's saying something to me. Part of it might be because my mother had been really sick, and I don't feel like dealing right now with very sick people. Then, one day I was walking down the street—and it wasn't at a time when I felt really pressured or anything—and it hit me that I don't care if I never take another blood pressure in my entire life! I guess I'm more interested in the more general issues of health care. In many ways I find graduate school harder than medical school.

I'm just starting some of my ideas for my dissertation. It's going to be on sickle cell anemia. I can't decide whether it's going to be on people who have the trait and whether there's a stigma attached to saying that you have a genetic trait or on the kids who have sickle cell anemia and their outlook on life. A lot of them have a very pessimistic attitude on life, and I don't know whether it's because they have a chronic disease or just because they're black kids.

Out of 160 students, there were 40-odd women in the class. It was the largest number of women and the largest number of blacks that Penn had ever had. There really wasn't that much cohesiveness. I remember telling a friend it was the most untogether group of women that I'd ever met. Individually, we could get together, but we weren't recognized as a force. There were times when professors would be hissed. The first week of medical school, the guy who was chairman of the Department of Medicine said, "Medicine is the profession that separates the men from the boys." He got hissed and could not understand why he was being hissed. He said, "I can't keep on lecturing like this," and someone said, "That's right!" But I didn't find that much support from the women as a whole.

There were fifteen black men and seven black women—Penn didn't graduate its first black woman until 1968. The black students did stick together. It's like, when you go into a room, you see how many black people are there. Something very fortunate that happened to me was that in high school I had a friend and both of us wanted to be physicians. We lost contact with each other during college—and she was in my medical school class. I'm sitting there, and I look up and there's Philomena. The first question I asked her was, had she married Charlie? She's a medical student, her husband is a bricklayer. People cannot deal with that, but he is just very, very supportive of her. But having her there, someone who knew me, has been good. I became friends with another black woman who I'm not friends with anymore because she started competing with me. She was very, very special in many ways, and I'm special in many ways. But she thought that we were competing with each other, and I don't compete with my friends.

I don't have that much contact with a lot of the black men in my class. I think part of the reason is that they think I'm rather spacey, that I'm different. My first year of medical school, I'd say, "Goodbye, folks, I'm going on vacation for a week. I just have to get out of here." My motto is, "Sanity before academics." And when exam time came, I did better or just as well as anyone else. So I don't know whether it's me or my attitude, but I just have not found them supportive at all.

Sometimes I think, "There's a conspiracy to get me out of medical school." My first clinical rotation was Introduction to Clinical Medicine, and it was me and four white guys. Then, when I took medicine, I was the only woman and the only black. When I took surgery, I was the only black person out of sixty people. It was the whole fly-in-the-bowl-of-buttermilk story. In surgery, there was a resident who was a real nice guy, but he was also a product of his background. The first day of surgery he said to me, "Well, you know your stitches, don't you, Vanessa?"—just assuming that since I'm a woman I know about sewing. I said, "Got the wrong person. Look, in order to pass home economics in eighth grade my mother had to finish my skirt." But, there are times when I feel uneasy. I can't put a finger on whether it's because I'm black or because I'm a woman. The thing is, I'm not going to go crazy trying to figure out what the reason is. It's not my problem, it's their problem, in many ways.

It's very important for black students to have role models because having role models almost keeps hope open that you *can* do it. One of the people who has been important to me here is this black woman gynecologist, Helen O. Dickens, who is going to be seventy soon. If you want to go talk to her, she's there. I think she went to either the University of Illinois or the University of Michigan Medical School. I had made the assumption, like a lot of people, that she had gone to Meharry or Howard or Woman's, and she didn't. It's important just to have her there and realize how hard it was for her.

I was born at University Hospital here; I used to go to clinic there. And there are ways that black people are treated there. . . . When I was taking my mother to the hospital, I always made sure I had my white coat; I wanted to say, "Look, I am a member of the club." I hated to have to use that. Once an intern gave me my mother's history and physical to read, and this white nurse came and took it and put it in an envelope and sealed it. I said, "You don't have to do that. I understand everything that's going on here—I'm a medical student." "You have to talk to her doctor about that." I was pissed, absolutely pissed. So when the doctor came back, he told the nurse, "Look, she's a medical student here." She said, "How was I supposed to know that she was a medical student?" She didn't take my word. She saw black woman, and it didn't equal medical student.

A lot of patients would say, "Oh, you're the doctor? I thought you were the nurse." Elderly black men had a hard time when I would examine them because they would think of me as their granddaughter. Young black men have problems because they see me as someone they would want to go out with. Then, there was the time where a patient thought I was a maid. He said to me, "How much do aides around here make?" I said, "I don't know. I'm one of the student physicians." Then, I continued the examination. The next thing I knew, the intern, who was a white guy, came running up and said, "Vanessa, you're not going to believe what he just asked me. He wanted to know why that girl didn't clean up while she was in here." You get things like that.

On Current Issues in Medicine

There are certain defects that I see in medical education as it's set up now. You have to memorize this, do this—a lot of times they don't give you a conceptual approach. No one has ever said to me, "This is how you should approach a medical journal article to say whether it's any good or not"—and I'm going to be reading journals for the rest of my life. It's something that you have to come to grips with yourself, but they could give you some pointers. And I think there is a need to incorporate more of the social sciences into medicine, not as the second-class daughter or the stepsister, but as part of it.

A good doctor is someone who is very supportive, who knows medicine, not just the academically oriented medicine, but who understands people. I have a classmate who's going to be a damn good doctor. He knows a lot, but he's just so caring; he is just so good with his patients. He understands human frailties, but he also understands human strengths. There are some people who could recite every article published in the *New England Journal of Medicine*. That doesn't mean they're good doctors.

I know some physicians who get very upset if patients start asking questions because that's losing their control. I encourage my patients to ask questions, I really do, because I feel medicine is a service profession. If it wasn't for these patients, I wouldn't have my job. I'm there to serve them.

I think any physician who right now does not think that the government's going to take more control of medicine is fooling him- or herself. I don't know whether it's going to be better. It might turn out to be a big bureaucratic mess. But I feel that people should have access to health care which they could afford, and right now you don't. The profession hasn't been responsive to that, so the government's going to do it.

Being a woman and a professional woman, I want to be able to be responsible for my reproduction. But I'm very ambivalent about the Pill. I really think it's been rammed down women's throats without thinking about the complications. One of the biggest experiments that's been done on women in this country is the Pill. When I was taking gynecology, they didn't really talk about other forms of birth control. I said, "Well, what about the diaphragm?" I feel that women should have access to various forms of birth control. But with black women, there is the whole question of coercion, where they're being coerced into some of the more permanent forms of birth control. They had hearings here in Philadelphia for the new HEW laws on involuntary sterilization. I went over for one, and some of those women who were sterilized without their permission, and not knowing they were being sterilized, really shook me. So on one hand, I believe women should have access to forms of birth control, but coercion, misinformation—lying, basically—*that* has to be safeguarded against.

I don't think that abortion should be used as a form of birth control, but abortion should be available. It scares me that the whole anti-abortion, pro-life movement has had such an impact—has really become a very potent political force in this country. My belief that women should have access to abortion is not forcing women to have abortions, and I think the other way is forcing me and people who might want to have an abortion not to have one. Then, it's going to be the whole back-street thing, going to the butcher, or rich women who can afford abortion going to Europe.

On Women and Minorities in Medicine

You can read documents saying, "We are dedicated to having more minorities in medicine," and there are certain places that I think are. But they vary, and I don't know that if it weren't for things that happened in the sixties—in many cases they were forced to—that they really would have started doing it.

I feel that the Bakke case is going to have—and I think it has, with some black people—an effect on morale. They are in precarious situations in a lot of institutions, and it doesn't help to hear someone say that it's just grades and scores that make a good physician. Then people like Bakke say, "I was better than the sixteen blacks that got in." That makes people feel, "Well, maybe I'm here on a special permit. Maybe they did lower the standards for me to get in.'' It really used to get on my nerves when people would say, ''Oh, you're going to get into medical school because you're a black woman.'' I said, ''I'm going to get into medical school because I'm Vanessa Gamble who happens to be a black woman, but I have done such-and-such.'' That used to really make me angry—the implication that the only thing I had going for me was I'm a black woman and they're looking for black women these days. That just really pissed me off.

It's not helpful to lower standards for blacks, especially if you're going to start taking people with 1.6's just because they're black. Lowering standards is, in many ways, a very racist thing—you take people who you know aren't going to make it. But what they should say is, ''We're going to look at MCATs, grade point averages, service to community''—so and so, so and so. MCATs and GPAs aren't the only standard that should be taken into account when you look at admissions.

Being black affects the way I look at certain of my patients because they are of the same class that I came from. It makes me see some of the ramifications of the effects of the black community. Sometimes being a woman affects my outlook. When I hear residents in obstetrics saying, when a woman's having labor pains, ''Oh, those are all psychosomatic,'' I say, ''How do you know?'' Or, you see a black woman come in who's fifteen years old and it's her second child, I say, ''Well, that could have been me.'' They say, ''No, you're different.'' But it *could* have been me; it very easily could have been me. That does have an effect on how I look at medicine.

But I really don't know whether the influx of blacks and women will change the medical profession in any fundamental way. The way medical education is, I think that sometimes there's a role that they want you to fill, and the pressures to conform to that role are so strong. There's a whole thing that if you're different, you're ostracized, you feel that you don't know as much. There have been some changes, but I don't know how widespread they're going to be.

I think more and more women are going into fields like internal medicine. But a lot of women in my class are going into pediatrics. Some are going into obstetrics and gynecology. I only know one who's going into surgery. A lot of women do tend to go into things like dermatology because it is easier to balance the family and profession. I was talking to a woman resident in OB-GYN—her husband's a surgeon, and she just had a baby. She said, ''I really like it a lot. But if I had to do it again, I'd *try* to get interested in radiology and dermatology because it would be easier.''

I don't think that the status of women in the profession is changing noticeably. You don't see the women as the deans of medical schools or as chairmen of departments of internal medicine. They're still in the lower ranks of the profession. Until women and blacks get some access to power, I can't see any changes. I remember telling someone, ''One day I'll be head of HEW''—and the person didn't laugh. That's how come one-to-one medicine is not as important to me as it is to some other people. I think I could be a good clinician, but that's not where I want to expend my energies. I want to do the most good for the most amount of people and doing that means being in some position of power.

On Her Life Today and Tomorrow

When I first came to medical school, I said I wanted to be a pediatrician. But I decided that I didn't like pediatrics that much. When I took obstetrics and gynecology, I liked them a lot. But I don't like the life-style of an obstetrician, and that's very important for me. Medicine is very important to me, but it's not my entire life, and I cannot make it my entire life. Right now, I'm thinking of two things: 1) doing an internship and maybe a second year of residency in internal medicine and then teaching or working in a research organization, or 2) doing a residency in psychiatry. Psychiatry seems to be the major influence right now. If I do do psychiatry, what I'm very interested in is black women, especially black professional women—how they deal with their professional roles. Sometimes they feel very shaky about their positions in life and their professions.

Hopefully, I'll be able to find a residency which will, for the first year, let me work on my dissertation and just do part-time. I'll probably go somewhere else for my residency. It's time for me to get out of Philadelphia. For the next couple of years, I'm just going to travel and see where I want to go—New England or the West Coast. Right now there's a part of me that wants to go to the South. I feel the way a lot of black folks feel—that in this country that's basically where a lot of our heritage is. In many ways, the whites and blacks in the South have been forced in many cities to really work together. In the North, they really haven't because everything's supposed to be cool, calm, and copacetic up here. It's almost like certain areas in the South are Meccas for black professionals, and that attracts me.

I'm getting more active again in the women's movement. At Hampshire there was another woman whose name happened to be Vanessa, too; she and I were the only two black women who were really into the women's movement. We knew there were problems with it, but we also found it supportive. I think the problem for black women with the women's movement is that it doesn't realize that black men have also been oppressed in this society—that in some instances they do oppress the women, but they have been so oppressed themselves that there's a very different type of relationship that black women have with black men. I think the women's movement really did not acknowledge that difference.

It's important for me not to become one-sided. I'm taking dance and ceramics. I'm not a good potter, and I am a horrible dancer, but they're important for me to do. Cooking is the thing that I do best. It's where all my creative streaks go through. When I get frustrated, I come home and bake bread, and then I call friends and say, ''Come and get it before I eat it all myself.''

The people who I consider my close friends in medical school are all from working-class backgrounds, they're all from Philadelphia, and we all went to either Girls' High or Central, which is the boys' high school. I think it's more than a coincidence that the four of us are friends. One is a woman from a working-class Italian family, one is a black guy who's from West Philadelphia, too, and another guy is Armenian. So we're all ethnic peoples, and we just enjoy each other. We don't feel like we have to prove anything, that we've overcome a lot of things in our backgrounds.

Then, I have a lot of friends in Amherst. I go up there pretty often. I get four free trips a year up there, because I'm a trustee of Hampshire now. One good thing about going to Amherst is that I can walk at Hampshire College and feel there's a whole college behind me, from the janitor who I used to work with to the Chairman of the Board of Trustees who feels that I'm a special person. It's good to go someplace and feel that you're special.

Then, I have friends in New York who are in the arts. Once I went to see them, and I said, "Just answer one question. Have I become dull in coming to med school?" The thing that I feared most about coming to medical school was I thought people would not have a sense of humor. I think that's one thing that's made me survive—having a sense of humor.

I'd like to be married eventually and especially now. My mother, in many ways, marked the end of my family, and, for the past couple of months, I've been thinking more and more that I really do want to establish my own family. I'd like to get married one day and have children. I think it's important to have someone to share your life, someone to be the most important person in your life.

The only medical school where I was asked about what am I going to do when I get married was Howard. I looked at the man and said, "Look, I'm not going to be a housewife with an M.D." I'm not going to give up my M.D. or my Ph.D. and my aspirations just because someone says, "If you're going to marry me, you have to stay at home and take care of kids." No way am I going to do that. I've come too far for that.

But I still feel the pressure of, "Where are the men? Have you educated yourself out of a certain marriage market?" Most of the men I run into can't deal with my being a combined M.D./Ph.D.-type person. Sometimes I say, "Well, why do I want to do this? It's going to be very lonely." Judge Leon Higginbotham, who is a black judge here in the city—I'm taking a course with him—picked that up. He said, "It's very lonely for you to be a black professional woman. Hang in there—it'll get better."

For a while I was dating a lot of white guys. They were, in many ways, because of the situations I found myself in, available, accessible. They were there. That used to disturb Jarvis, but, for the past year, he's basically said, "I can understand why you do that sometimes. There are a lot of guys who just can't handle you. Vanessa, that's not *your* problem, it's their problem." It's amazing how our friendship has grown, how as I've grown up, he's grown up.

I still have a feeling of insecurity about being a black woman, being in a situation where people say, "You can't do that. Black women aren't supposed to do that"—especially now with my family situation very rocky. And there's some insecurity about where I am going to end up. Bernice, my friend in Amherst, said, "Vanessa, when are you going to learn that you don't have to do anything to show me that you're special, that you're unique? You don't have to do that anymore." But I have to, in many ways, keep doing it for myself.

There are times when I think that where I am now is almost like a dream—if I bat my eyes, I'll be back in West Philadelphia. I *am* in West Philadelphia now, but a totally different situation in West Philadelphia. I was talking a few weeks ago with Judge Higginbotham, and he said, "Look, you had to be a bit maladjusted, I had to be a bit maladjusted, to get from where we came from"—because if I were adjusted I'd have four kids now and have some guy doing a job on me.

Philadelphia, Pennsylvania
March 15, 1978

DISCUSSION: PART III

With Joni Magee, Susan Benes, and Vanessa Gamble, we reach the generation of women most profoundly affected by the social and political dislocations of the sixties, by the new wave of feminism, and by radical changes within the medical profession itself—including a dramatic rise in the number of women seeking medical training. Advances have been made, but with new solutions come new problems. Here are stories of tradition sustained, tradition transmuted, and tradition abandoned. They are stories still in progress.

Clearly these women share many of the characteristics of earlier women physicians. Gamble and Benes are firstborns, Magee an only child. All were attracted to health care early in life. Magee and Benes speak of an urgent need, even as small children, to heal or "repair" people. Like their predecessors, they sense a strong strain of idealism in their commitment to medicine, and they believe that they are far less likely to be motivated by economic considerations than are their male counterparts.

Yet there are striking differences, too. Both Magee and Benes toyed with the idea of becoming nurses because of cultural pressures pushing them in that direction. This pattern was uncommon among the women of earlier generations, who knew almost to a one that they wanted to give the orders, not take them. Such a shift may suggest a growing dissatisfaction with the proposition that only the strong-minded or the eccentric few who were willing to sacrifice everything could aim at such lofty goals. Girls who might easily have chosen nursing as a more flexible and "feminine" alternative a decade or two earlier are beginning to be interested in traditionally male goals, which lead them to an unwillingness to accept a future of professional subordination. With the support of the feminist movement, these women have insisted that they can pursue high-powered careers without forgoing the satisfactions of family life. The mere presence of Gamble in this group points to another difference: the increasing (though still not great) accessibility of professional training to members of ethnic minorities.

The childhoods of these women—even Gamble's, to some extent—predated the increased social activism of the sixties. Like their elders, they suffered from a noticeable lack of role models, although Gamble, a true post-McLuhan child, is the first to cite Dr. Kildare as a source of inspiration. Their fathers present a whole spectrum of attitudes: Benes' was highly supportive, Magee's largely indifferent, Gamble's absent altogether. If anything can be said to differentiate the early experience of these women from that of their predecessors, it is their surprisingly unanimous negative reaction to their mothers' lot and their desire to avoid a similar fate. Benes' mother, a college graduate, gave up a promising career to raise her children. Magee pictures her mother as a bored, depressed, underoccupied woman who sought refuge from her misery in hypochondria. Gamble saw her mother exhausted by the menial jobs she was forced to take and repeatedly victimized by the men in her life.

It is tempting to speculate that their precocious awareness of the destructive aspects of the postwar feminine mystique and of other limitations placed on women left them and their peers receptive to the expanding possibilities offered by the romantic, rebellious, idealistic, democratizing movements of the sixties. There can be little doubt that this general unrest contributed to the increased numbers of women flocking to professional schools. But a better understanding of the role that these movements, particularly feminism, have played in the recent history of American medicine can be gained by looking back a little farther.

The nineteenth century saw the development of a community of women based on their almost complete exclusion from the male medical establishment. Separate medical schools were established, and separate-but-equal spheres of competence were hypothesized. With the advent of coeducation and a limited acceptance of women in the profession, this community of women-as-outsiders started to break down. Whatever the benefits of this development, it left many women stranded and forced to seek both the sources of and the solutions to their problems within themselves. One of the most important contributions of the revitalization of feminism in the late sixties, therefore, was the reestablishment of a community of women, this time on a more democratic basis. Women discovered, often with amazement, that their problems were shared by other women—and not just other women physicians. The personal, as feminist theory holds, became the political.

Although none of the women presented here is involved actively in any organization, all are keenly aware of the ways in which the feminist movement has touched their lives. Magee, the oldest of the three, has completely revised her youthful perception of herself as a "physiological female and an intellectual male." Like many feminists, her early engagement with the civil rights movement sensitized her to the sufferings of the oppressed and prepared her to recognize and resent the injustices she experienced at the hands of male-dominated institutions. Having had her "consciousness . . . raised on the delivery table," she has dedicated her career to addressing the needs of obstetrical patients. Gamble, several years younger, was involved in the black power and feminist movements even in high school. Her enrollment in an M.D./Ph.D. program attests to her thirst not only for the practical knowledge imparted by medical education but also for a theoretical overview of the problems of women and minorities as they relate to medicine.

Despite the increasing numbers of women like Magee and Gamble, it would be a mistake to assume that the ranks of young women physicians are filled with reformers and radicals. The elitism and conservatizing tendencies of medical education still militate against too much deviation from social expectations. But even Benes, by and large the most traditional of the three women presented here, has readily exercised formerly unavailable options in her choice of specialty and child-care arrangements. She has resisted attempts to dissuade her from combining childbearing with a rigorous training program. A sexual assault that in another era might have produced only shame and guilt has led her to a desire to help others in similar situations.

By the choices she makes, each of these women is participating in the collective process of reassessing the nature of woman's work. How challenging this process can be, how painful at times, is evinced in their aggressive determination to have the traditional satisfactions of family life without relinquishing their professional ambitions. The old notion that having a career was a privilege often involving sacrifice has been almost completely supplanted by a conviction that women have the same right to both career and children that men have always enjoyed. Yet, their efforts to put that belief into practice have been fraught with some of the same difficulties that beset their elders. Both Magee and Benes have succeeded to some extent in forcing their institutions to accommodate their needs as women of childbearing age, but not without considerable compromise. Though Benes' positive experiences with day care testify to the growth of service industries catering to the needs of working women, this country has yet to commit itself to the systematic development of support services. Thus, both women are still forced to improvise solutions to many of their problems, and neither is completely free of the guilt and ambivalence that burdened women of earlier generations.

Nor have the men in their lives dealt fully with the challenges presented by their careers. Magee's husband sabotaged her efforts at several stages, often by simply failing to appear at crucial moments. Benes' husband, while much more supportive, discouraged her from pursuing her preferred specialties, obstetrics and, later, internal medicine, because they might conflict with her family obligations. Gamble, at a different stage in life and facing added complications as a black professional woman, has experienced difficulties in finding men who are not threatened by her education and abilities.

Unquestionably the medical profession has become more flexible, more accepting of women. Medical education is not the lonely enterprise it was only a generation ago—nearly a quarter of today's medical students are women. Legal sanctions prohibit many of the discriminatory practices once taken for granted.

Government and private industry are responding, if somewhat falteringly, to the needs of a society in which a majority of women work. Relationships between men and women are undergoing a collective reexamination.

Magee, Benes, and Gamble have been the beneficiaries of these changes. They also know intimately how incomplete the changes are. The overall impression left by their stories is one of optimisim untinged by complacency. To the task of forging a workable way of life, they bring the same tough energy that their predecessors did, as well as a post-sixties awareness that their problems are society's problems. The lot of the woman physician has improved. Still, as Susan Benes remarks, "it's good to have a hard shell for some of the punches you're going to be thrown."

One wonders how the next chapter of this book will read, the one that has yet to be written. Ironically, just as women finally started to approach equitable representation within medicine, the profession itself reached a serious crisis. This crisis remains unresolved. Piecemeal increases in government regulation without a systematic long-range plan have produced a combination of the worst aspects of socialized medicine and the worst aspects of entrepreneurial medicine. Physicians have lost the prestige they once commanded, a fact reflected in their malpractice rates. Medical costs are soaring; doctor shortages in some areas are offset by an overabundance in others; priorities for primary care, specialization, and research have not been definitively established. Clearly new perspectives and fresh ideas will be needed if this country is to maintain high standards of medical care in the coming decades. This is the challenge—and the opportunity—facing the woman physician of tomorrow.

Bibliographical Essay

Early Works on Women Physicians

Until recently virtually the only historical accounts of women's struggle to enter the medical profession were those written by women physicians themselves. These works invariably display both the advantages and disadvantages of "insider's history." Full of much pertinent information for the researcher, they usually lack analytical sophistication. Nevertheless, Rachel Bodley, *The College Story: Valedictory Address to the Twenty-Ninth Graduating Class of the Woman's Medical College of Pennsylvania, March 17, 1881* (Philadelphia: Grant, Faires & Rogers, Printers, 1881); Emily F. Pope, C. Augusta Pope, and Emma L. Call, *The Practice of Medicine by Women in the United States* (Boston: Mass., 1881); and Clara Marshall, *The Woman's Medical College of Pennsylvania: An Historical Outline* (Philadelphia: P. Blakiston, Son, 1897) remain useful. More penetrating and full of subtle insight is Mary Putnam Jacobi's essay, "Woman in Medicine," in Annie Nathan Meyer, ed., *Woman's Work in America* (New York: Holt, 1891).

The biographies, autobiographies and published letters of several important nineteenth-century women physicians still provide much helpful information, especially Elizabeth Blackwell, *Pioneer Work in Opening the Medical Profession to Women* (London: Longmans, Green, 1895); Ruth Putnam, ed., *Life and Letters of Mary Putnam Jacobi* (New York: G. P. Putnam, 1925); Harriot Hunt, *Glances and Glimpses* (Boston: John P. Jewett, 1856); Agnes Vietor, ed., *A Woman's Quest: The Life of Marie E. Zakrzewska, M.D.* (New York: D. Appleton, 1924); Mary Bennett Ritter, *More Than Gold in California* (Berkeley, Calif., 1933); Bethenia Owens-Adair, *Some of Her Life Experiences* (Portland, Ore., 1905); Lillian Welsh, *Reminiscences of Thirty Years in Baltimore* (Baltimore: Norman, Remington, 1925); Elizabeth Putnam Gordon, *The Story and Life and Work of Cordelia A. Greene* (Castile, N.Y., 1925).

Two amateurish but useful general histories, both by ex-presidents of the American Medical Women's Association, Kate Campbell Hurd-Mead, *Medi-

cal Women of America (New York: Froben Press, 1933); and Esther Pohl Lovejoy, *Women Doctors of the World* (New York: Macmillan, 1957), provide selected facts and figures for the twentieth-century. Similarly informative is *The History of the Woman's Medical College of Pennsylvania* (Philadelphia: J. B. Lippincott, 1950) written by an alumna, Gulielma Fell Alsop. The devoted detective work of Frederick C. Waite, Ph.D., for many years the Emeritus Professor of Histology at Western Reserve Medical School, contributed much toward retrieving the little-known past of nineteenth-century women physicians. Waite authored the *History of the New England Female Medical College, 1848-1874* (Boston: Boston University School of Medicine, 1950) and several articles on women doctors, including "Early Medical Service of Woman," *Journal of the American Medical Women's Association* 5 (May 1948): 199-203; "Dr. Lucinda Susannah (Capen) Hall, The First Woman Doctor to Receive a Medical Degree from a New England Institution," *New England Journal of Medicine* 210 (March 1934): 644-47; "Dr. Lydia (Folger) Fowler, The Second Woman to Receive the Degree of Doctor of Medicine in the United States," *Annals of Medical History* 4 (May 1942): 290-97; "Dr. Martha A. (Hayden) Sawin, The First Woman Graduate in Medicine to Practice in Boston," *New England Journal of Medicine* 205 (November 1931): 1053-55; "Dr. Nancy E. (Talbot) Clark, The Second Woman Graduate in Medicine to Practice in Boston," *New England Journal of Medicine* 205 (December 1931): 1195-98; "Medical Education of Women at Penn Medical University," *Medical Review of Reviews* 39 (June 1933): 255-60; "Two Early Letters by Elizabeth Blackwell," *Bulletin of the History of Medicine* 21 (January-February 1947): 110-12; "The Three Myers Sisters—Pioneer Women Physicians," *Medical Review of Reviews* 39 (March 1933): 114-20.

Expanding Interest in the History of Women Physicians

In the decades after 1950, two prominent medical historians renewed public interest in the history of women physicians with the publication of two suggestive articles, Richard Shryock, "Women in American Medicine," *Journal of the American Medical Women's Association* 5 (September 1950): 371-79, and John B. Blake, "Women and Medicine in Ante-Bellum America," *Bulletin of the History of Medicine* 39 (March-April, 1965): 99-123. In addition, appearing as the tangible result of a conference on women physicians sponsored by the Josiah Macy, Jr., Foundation, Carol Lopate published *Women in Medicine* (Baltimore: Johns Hopkins Press, 1968), an intelligent overview of the past, present, and future role of women in American medicine.

The revival of historiographical concern for women doctors, however, received its greatest stimulus from the reemergence of interest in the history of women. Gerda Lerner, for example, was one of the first of the new historians to raise questions about women's declining status in the healing arts in the nineteenth-century in her pioneering article, "The Lady and the Mill Girl: Changes in the Status of Women in the Age of Jackson," *American Studies* 10 (Spring 1969): 5–15. Moreover, from the beginning of the new women's history one area of investigation proved particularly popular: the treatment of women's diseases and the response of nineteenth-century women to a male-dominated medical profession. Indeed, the confluence of medical opinion and cultural attitudes concerning woman's role has proved one of the most intriguing aspects of recent investigations into the social history of nineteenth-century medicine. An important contribution of this new research has been to demonstrate that medical practice does reflect and has in the past mirrored larger cultural and social ideologies.

Consequently, a number of books, articles, and dissertations inspired by the new historiography deal directly or indirectly with the question of women physicians. Jane Donegan, *Women and Men Midwives, Medicine, Morality and Misogyny in Early America* (Westport, Conn: Greenwood Press, 1978); Judith Barrett Litoff, *American Midwives, 1860 to the Present* (Westport, Conn: Greenwood Press, 1978); Richard and Dorothy Wertz, *Lying In—A History of Childbirth in America* (New York: The Free Press, 1977); and Edna Manzer, "Woman's Doctors: The Development of Obstetrics and Gynecology" (Ph.D. thesis, University of Indiana, 1979); all offer innovative and incisive insights into the history of obstetrics and gynecology. The role of women in health reform and the connection between the health reform movement and feminism is pursued by Regina Markell Morantz in "Making Women Modern: Middle Class Women and Health Reform in 19th Century America," *Journal of Social History* 10 (Summer 1977): 490–507; and "Nineteenth-Century Health Reform and Women: A Program of Self-Help," in R. Numbers, J. Leavitt, and G. Risse, eds., *Medicine Without Doctors,* (New York: Science History Publications, 1977) pp. 73–94; and, more recently, by William Leach, in *True Love and Perfect Union: The Feminist Reform of Sex and Society* (New York: Basic Books, 1980). Ann Douglas Wood, " 'The Fashionable Diseases,' Women's Complaints, and Their Treatment in Nineteenth-Century America," *Journal of Interdisciplinary History* 4 (Summer 1973): 25–52; and Virginia Drachman, "Women Doctors and the Women's Medical Movement: Feminism and Medicine, 1850–1895" (Ph.D. diss., SUNY Buffalo, 1976) treat women physicians as a monolithic, self-righteously feminist group, dedicated to throwing off for all women the shackles of oppression in which a hostile male medical establishment had held them bound. Mary Roth Walsh in *Doctors Wanted: No Women Need Apply, Sexual Barriers in the Medical Profession, 1835–1975* (New Haven: Yale University Press, 1977); and Gloria Melnick Moldow, "The Gilded Age, Promise and Disillusionment: Women Doctors and the Emergence of the Professional Middle Class, Washington, D.C., 1870–1900" (Ph.D. diss., University of Maryland, 1980) take a more balanced view of the struggle of women to enter the profession. Yet both concentrate primarily on the feminist response to the crippling effects of institutional discrimination. In contrast, Regina Markell Morantz in "The Lady and Her Physician," Lois Banner and Mary Hartman, eds., *Clio's Consciousness Raised: New Perspectives on the History of Women* (New York: Harper & Row, 1974), pp. 38–53; " 'The Connecting Link': The Case for the Woman Doctor in 19th-Century America," in R. Numbers and J. Leavitt, eds., *Sickness and Health in America: Essays in the History of Health Care* (Madison: University of Wisconsin Press, 1978); and "Professionalism, Feminism and Gender Roles: A Study of the Therapeutics of Nineteenth Century Male and Female Doctors," *Journal of American History* 67 (December 1980): 568–88, has argued that focusing narrowly on the question of institutional discrimination is too confining. Her work suggests that the feminism of women physicians remained highly complex and riddled with tension between separatism and assimilation, femininity and professionalism.

Other aspects of the history of women physicians have been investigated in Martin Kaufman, "The Admission of Women to 19th-Century American Medical Societies," *Bulletin of the History of Medicine* 50 (Summer 1976): 251–60; Cora B. Marrett, "On the Evolution of Women's Medical Societies," *Bulletin of the History of Medicine* 53 (Fall, 1979): 434–49; Constance M. McGovern, "Doctors or Ladies? Women Physicians in Psychiatric Institutions, 1872–1900," *Bulletin of the History of Medicine* 55 (Spring 1981); 88–107; Helena M. Wall, "Feminism and the New England Hospital," *American Quarterly* 32 (Fall 1980): 435–52; Nancy Sahli, "Elizabeth Blackwell, M.D. (1821–1910): A Biography" (Ph.D. diss., University of Pennsylvania, 1974); Mary Roth Walsh, "Images of Women Doctors in Popular Fiction," *Journal of Popular Culture* 1 (Summer 1978): 276–84.

Biography and autobiography continue to be a rich source of information for the nineteenth-century. See especially the fine sketches of women physicians in Edward and Janet James, eds. *Notable American Women, 1607–1950: A Bibliographical Dictionary* (Cambridge, Mass.: Belknap Press, 1971); and Barbara Sicherman and Carol Hurd Green, eds., *Notable American Women, The Modern Period* (Cambridge, Mass.: Belknap Press, 1980). Also revealing are Alice Hamilton M.D., *Exploring the Dangerous Trades* (Boston: Little, Brown, 1943); Bertha Van Hoosen M.D., *Petticoat Surgeon* (Chicago: Pellegrini & Cudahy, 1947); S. Josephine Basker M. D., *Fighting for Life* (New York: The Macmillan Co., 1939); Rosalie Slaughter Morton M.D., *A Woman Surgeon* (New York: Frederick A. Stokes, 1937); Emily Dunning Barringer M.D., *From Bowery to Bellevue, The Story of New York's First Woman Ambulance Surgeon* (New York: W. W. Norton, 1950); Alfreda Withington M.D., *Mine Eyes Have Seen: A Woman Doctor's Saga* (New York: E. P. Dutton, 1941); Janet Travell M.D., *Office Hours: Day and Night. The Autobiography of Janet Travell, M.D.* (New York: World Publishing Co., 1968); Margaret R. Stewart M.D., *From Dugout to Hilltop* (Culver City, Calif.: Murray & Gee, Inc., 1951); Mary Martin Sloop M.D., *Miracle in the Hills* (New York: McGraw Hill, 1953); Anne Walter

Fearn M.D., *My Days of Strength: An American Woman Doctor's Forty Years in China* (New York: Harper & Bros., 1939); Elinor Rice Hays, *Those Extraordinary Blackwells: The Story of a Journey to a Better World* (New York: Harcourt Brace, 1967); Joy Daniels Singer, *My Mother, the Doctor* (New York: E. P. Dutton, 1970); Dorothy Clarke Wilson, *Lone Woman: The Story of Elizabeth Blackwell: The First Woman Doctor* (Boston: Little Brown, 1970); Dorothy Clarke Wilson, *Dr. Ida: The Story of Dr. Ida Scudder of Vellore* (New York: McGraw Hill, 1959); Elinor Bleumel, *Florence Sabin: Colorado Woman of the Century* (Boulder: University of Colorado Press, 1959).

Two interesting overviews of the problems of women professionals in the twentieth century are Barbara Harris, *Beyond Her Sphere, Women and the Professions in American History* (Westport, Ct., Greenwood Press, 1978); and Frank Stricker, "Cookbooks and Lawbooks: The Hidden History of Career Women in Twentieth-Century America," *Journal of Social History* 10 (Fall 1976): 1–19. Finally, an excellent bibliographical resource for the numerous books and articles on the history of women physicians can be found in Sandra Chaff, et al., eds., *Women in Medicine: A Bibliography of the Literature on Women Physicians* (Metuchen, N.J.: Scarecrow Press, 1977).

M. Sanger
Sister Kenny

Index

Coeducation in medicine, 21–22, 25–27
Cohen, A. J., 60, 61, 66
Cohen, Lou, 66
Cohen, Wilbur, 120
College, 197; Benes, 229–32; Gamble,
 249–53; Magee, 208–10; Michael-
 son, 135–37; Morani, 80–81; Sir-
 ridge, 156–57; Stitt, 107–9; Sturgis,
 52–53; Wilson, 177–78
Columbia University, 80
Columbia University College of Physi-
 cians and Surgeons, 180
Commonwealth Fund, 192
Competition in medical school, 139, 181,
 212, 235, 255; in pre-med studies,
 230
Contraception. *See* Birth control
Cook County Hospital (Chicago), 160
Cooper Art Institute (New York City), 76
Cooper, David, 62, 63, 71
Cooper, Donald, 92
Cooper, John, 191–92
Cornell University, 229
Cornell University Medical College, 26,
 32
Cott, Nancy, 7, 8, 9
Council of Deans (AAMC), 191
Council of the National Institute of En-
 vironmental Health Sciences, 69
*Counsel to Parents on the Moral Educa-
 tion of the Young,* 21
Crippled children program, 116, 118
Cummings, Martin, 190, 191

Dandy, Walter, 176
Danowski, Ted, 183, 186, 188
Deans, of medical school, 191–92
Death, experience with, 77, 105–6, 112,
 236, 246
Decision to become a doctor, 125, 196,
 263; Benes, 228; Gamble, 247;
 Magee, 208; Michaelson, 135; Morani, 78, 79–80; Sirridge, 155; Stitt,
 103, 105; Sturgis, 52; Wilson, 176
deLange, Cornelia, 121
del Mundo, Fé, 121
Department of Labor (U.S.), 117

de Tocqueville, Alexis, 7
Dental assistant, work as a, 79
Depression (economic), 83, 101, 109,
 126, 134, 195, 197
Depression (emotional), 199; Benes,
 230–31, 239; Morani, 90; Sirridge,
 163; Stitt, 106, 109
Dickens, Charles, 117
Dickens, Helen O., 255–56
Discrimination, 125, 127–28, 196, 222,
 223; in appointments, 71, 166–67;
 in early twentieth century, 25, 27,
 32; in government positions, 189,
 190; at Harvard, 118; in internships,
 182; in medical school, 32, 34, 110,
 125, 137–38, 166–67, 179, 181,
 192, 197, 211, 254–55; in medical
 societies, 149; in nineteenth century,
 17–19; in obtaining internships and
 residencies, 32–33, 84–85, 111;
 against pregnant residents, 161; in
 premedical studies, 81; by surgeons,
 92
Divorce, 55, 224
Drinker, Phil, 67–68
Drugs, use of, 229–30
Dubos, René, 68
Duckworth, Dr., 104

Eagleville Sanatorium, 59–60, 66
Ear-Nose-Throat (ENT) specialty,
 236–37
Editorship, 67–68, 69
Ehrenreich, Freda, 250
Eighteenth-century medicine, 5–6
Eisenberg, Carola, 33–34
Eldrich, Dr., 137
Eliot, Martha May, 117–18, 119
Eliot, T. S., 117
Elkton, Md., 53
Emergency Maternal and Infant Care
 (EMIC) Program (Hawaii), 118
Emotion, letting out of, 112, 170
Encouraging influences, 209, 228, 247.
 See also Role models
Engagement, 108–9
England, 231

About the Editors

Regina Markell Morantz received her Ph.D. in American history from Columbia University in 1971. She now teaches women's history, history of the family, and the social history of medicine at the University of Kansas. For several years, she has been working on a historical study of women physicians in America. From 1976 to 1978, she served as Academic Consultant and Principal Interviewer for the Oral History Project on Women in Medicine sponsored by the Medical College of Pennsylvania. Dr. Morantz is the author of several articles on women and health, including " 'The Connecting Link': The Case for the Woman Doctor in 19th-Century America," in *Sickness and Health in America,* ed. J. Leavitt and R. Numbers (University of Wisconsin Press, 1978) and "Professionalism, Feminism and Gender Roles: A Comparative Study of Nineteenth-Century Medical Therapeutics," in the *Journal of American History,* December 1980.

Cynthia Stodola Pomerleau received her Ph.D. in English literature in 1974 from the University of Pennsylvania, where she specialized in the autobiographical writings of women. As a freelance writer and editor, she has published numerous articles and books on a wide variety of topics, including women's health issues. She is a member of the Editorial Board of *Women and Health*. From 1976 to 1978, she served as Director of the Oral History Project on Women in Medicine at the Medical College of Pennsylvania. She currently resides in West Hartford, Connecticut.

Carol Hansen Fenichel is Director of Library Services at Philadelphia College of Pharmacy and Science. She was previously Associate Director of the library at the Medical College of Pennsylvania, where she initiated the oral history project on which this book is based. Dr. Fenichel also helped to organize the college's Archives and Historical Collections on Women in Medicine. She is a co-editor of *Women in Medicine: A Bibliography of the Literature on Women Physicians* (Scarecrow Press, 1977) and numerous technical papers in the field of information science. A graduate of Bryn Mawr College, Dr. Fenichel received her M.S. and Ph.D. from the School of Library and Information Science at Drexel University.